Library of
Davidson College

# Domestic Conflicts
## in
## SOUTH ASIA

# Works on South Asia

**INDIA'S FOREIGN POLICY AND RELATIONS**
  A. Appadorai and M.S. Rajan, 1985

**STRUCTURE OF DECISION**
*the Indian foreign policy bureaucracy*
  Jeffrey Benner, 1984

**BANGLADESH**
*V. 1 history and culture*
*V. 2 domestic politics*
  S.R. Chakravarty and V. Narain, 1986

**BANGLADESH**
*the first decade*
  M. Franda, 1982

**SOVIET POLICY TOWARDS INDIA**
*the formative years*
  S.K. Gupta, in press

**GROUP INTERESTS AND POLITICAL CHANGES**
*studies of Pakistan and Bangladesh*
  Talukder Maniruzzaman, 1982

**PAKISTAN**
*society and politics*
  P. Nayak, 1984

**INDIA, THE SUPERPOWERS AND THE NEIGHBOURS**
*essays in foreign policy*
  A.G. Noorani, 1985

**MALDIVES**
*winds of change in an atoll state*
  U. Phadnis and E.D. Luithui, 1985

**REGIONAL COOPERATION AND DEVELOPMENT IN SOUTH ASIA**
*V. 1 perceptional, military and nuclear arms race problems*
*V. 2 political, social, technology and resource aspects*
  Bhabani Sen Gupta, 1986

**INDIA AND AFGHANISTAN**
*a study of diplomatic relations*
  D.P. Singhal, 1981

# Domestic Conflicts in SOUTH ASIA

## VOLUME 2
## Economic and Ethnic Dimensions

Editors

URMILA PHADNIS    *Jawaharlal Nehru University*
*New Delhi*

S.D. MUNI    *Banaras Hindu University*
*Varanasi*

KALIM BAHADUR    *Jawaharlal Nehru University*
*New Delhi*

South Asian Publishers, New Delhi

Copyright © South Asian Publishers, 1986

All right reserved. No part of this publication be reproduced or transmitted in any form or by any means, without the written permission of the publishers.

SOUTH ASIAN PUBLISHERS PVT. LTD.
36 Netaji Subhash Marg, Daryaganj, New Delhi 110002

ISBN 81-7003-071-4

Published by South Asian Publishers Pvt. Ltd.
36 Netaji SubhashMarg, Daryaganj, New Delhi 110002 and printed at Prabhat Press, 20/1 Nauchandi Grounds Meerut 250002. Printed in India.

# Preface

THE IDEA of holding a seminar on domestic conflicts in South Asia grew out of informal exchange of views in the meetings of the South Asian Studies Division in the School of International Studies. In the process of these informal discussions, we realized that South Asia has had a fair share of domestic turmoil and disturbances since 1947 and not much relevant literature is available to help ns academically cope with the present challenges and future probabilities posed by the phenomenon of domestic crises in the region. From this sprang the idea of organizing a seminar on this theme to bring together, various components of the work that has already been done in the field and on that basis undertake an intellectual exercise to throw new ideas to grasp the dynamics of this phenomenon.

This initial decision was followed by a number of small group discussions amongst the colleagues of the Division to plan the agenda for the seminar. We finally came to the conclusion that the seminar could be split into four sub-themes—(i) related to theoretical knowledge and insight available on the question of domestic turmoil in the Third World countries with particular reference to South Asia and the neighbouring regions; (ii) domestic conflicts as a product of, and challenge for the political systems in the region; (iii) widening economic disparities which are at the root of domestic turmoil in South Asian countries; and (iv) social and ethnic incongruities which contribute to the conflicts.

We were all the time conscious that the seminar must yield some directions as to how would India be affected by the domestic conflicts in its neighbourhood and what could be the possible strategy to help resolve these conflicts and also meet the spill-over effects of them for India.

This was indeed a platefull of issues and we were certainly not naive to expect that a three-day seminar would provide answers to all our questions. However, looking at the papers and the thrust of discussions, we are not disappointed either. The seminar succeeded in identifying major dimensions of South Asian turmoil and made the participants realize that this was an initial exploratory but very essential exercise which needs to be followed seriously and vigorously. The dimensions of domestic conflicts in the South Asian countries have a broad area of regional feature but at the same time, there are significant specificities of each case. The nature of problems being different in the region the tone of papers could also not be uniform.

There is another tendency in any discussion on South Asia—India comes to dominate the discussions. The seminar could not avoid that and why should it have, keeping in mind the size, diversity and magnitude of Indian society and polity. The idea behind publishing the seminar papers is to share our achievements as well as shortcomings with a wider intellectual community.

The seminar could not have achieved even whatever little it did without the help and cooperation of various institutions and individuals. We acknowledge our thanks to UGC, ICSSR and JNU for the financial assistance in organizing the Seminar. To Professor Bimal Prasad, Professor of South Asian Studies and former Dean, School of International Studies, Jawaharlal Nehru University, for his inspiration and guidance at all stages of the preparation of the Seminar and publication of these volumes. We also wish to express our gratitude to our colleagues in the Division of South Asian Studies, Dr. I.N. Mukherji, Dr. Nancy Jetly, Dr. Uma Singh, Dr. K. Labh and Dr. Shyamali Ghosh for their assistance during Seminar and in preparing the papers for the publication. Mr. Jit Singh, meticulously typed the manuscript for the press, and helped us in several other ways

New Delhi  
April 1986

URMILA PHADNIS  
S.D. MUNI  
KALIM BAHADUR

# Contents

|  | | |
|---|---|---|
| PREFACE | | v |
| CONTRIBUTORS | | ix |
| INTRODUCTION | | xi |
| 1. | I.N. MUKHERJI<br>Economic Growth and Social Justice in South Asia: Growing Potential for Domestic Conflict | 1 |
| 2. | KAMTA PRASAD<br>Poverty in India: Trends and Prospects | 26 |
| 3. | GIRIJESH PANT<br>'New' Economic Policy of Sri Lanka: Conflict and Contradictions | 41 |
| 4. | B.M. BHATIA<br>Economic Disparities in Pakistan | 61 |
| 5. | B.S. DAS<br>Economic Development and Social Change in Bhutan | 82 |
| 6. | URMILA PHADNIS<br>Ethnic Conflicts in South Asian States | 100 |
| 7. | V. SURYANARAYAN<br>Ethnic Conflict in Sri Lanka | 120 |
| 8. | UMA SINGH<br>Ethnic Conflicts in Pakistan: Sind as A Factor in Pakistani Politics | 149 |
| 9. | RAMAKANT AND B.C. UPRETI<br>Regionalism in Nepal | 165 |

10. **KAPILESHWAR LABH**
 Monarchical System of Bhutan: Challenges of
 Modernization 182
 Index 196

# Contributors

B.M. BHATIA, Formerly Principal, Hindu College, University of Delhi, Delhi

B.S. DAS, An Administrator

KAPILESHWAR LABH, Documentation Officer, South Asian Studies, School of International Studies, Jawaharlal Nehru University, New Delhi

INDRANATH MUKHERJI, Associate Professor, South Asian Studies, School of International Studies, Jawaharlal Nehru University, New Delhi

GIRIJESH PANT, Assistant Professor, West Asian Studies, School of International Studies, Jawaharlal Nehru University, New Delhi

URMILA PHADNIS, Professor of South Asian Studies, School of International Studies, Jawaharlal Nehru University, New Delhi

KAMTA PRASAD, Professor of Economics and Rural Development, Indian Institute of Public Administration, New Delhi

RAMAKANT, Director, South Asian Studies Centre, Rajasthan University, Jaipur

UMA SINGH, Assistant Professor, South Asian Studies, School of International Studies, Jawaharlal Nehru University, New Delhi

V. SURYANARAYAN, Professor, Centre for South and Southeast Asian Studies, Madras University, Madras

B.C. UPRETI, Lecturer in Political Science, Government P.G. College, Kotputli

# Introduction

WHILE discussing political dimensions of domestic conflicts in South Asia in the first volume, we were conscious of their socio-economic roots and manifestations. Political forces and their dynamics have their own autonomy. Politics is a product of socio-economic transformations. Politics emerges from and acts on society and various areas of activity, particularly economic, cultural and ethnic. As such, at the root of political conflicts are the tensions generated by economic imbalances, ethnic and cultural diversities and the incompatibilities of groups of people associated with these social cleavages in society. We had hinted at this nexus between political conflicts and society in the first volume. No attempt to understand domestic conflicts in South Asia can be reasonably satisfactory unless this nexus is looked at closely.

## II

PROTEST movements and political agitations for economic demands of linguistic, ethnic and regional groups are a common feature of South Asian scene. These movements and agitations arise because of the real or perceived sense of socio-economic inequalities, deprivation and discrimination. This is a manifestation of the distortions in the patterns and processes of development. The question of economic underdevelopment and mal-development have not only been compounded by lack of resources, as is usually argued, but also by improper and unbalanced distribution of economic goods, services and opportunities that are generated through the process of development. There is also the important factor of production capabilities and consumption patterns, among different strata of population in these countries. The phenomena of growing economic disparities and massive poverty in South Asian countries have tended to spark off and aggravate ethnic conflicts and as a consequence produce conditions of political instability.

Though all the South Asian societies are multi-ethnic, the nature, intensity and extent of ethnic conflicts vary from one country to another and from one time to another. Owing to the fact of overlapping ethnic and cultural identities cross national boundaries in South Asia, there is a strong tendency of ethnic issues to reinforce each other from one country to another. In this situation, India occupies a unique place because its socio-cultural diversity encompasses in itself the dominant and minority cultural and ethnic identities of its respective neighbours. As a result, no ethnic conflict in any of its neighbours can leave India completely unaffected. Similarly, any ethnic conflict in India is bound to affect one of its neighbours. The crisis of East-Pakistan (Bengali Nationalism) in 1971, and those of Punjab in India and ethnic conflict in Sri Lanka during the 1980s, are obvious examples in this respect.

The gamut of domestic conflicts involving ethnic dimension in South Asian States, thus, has some significant aspects which call for a cool and close look. The experiences of various South Asian countries in dealing with ethnic conflict and their consequent implications and resulting challenges for political system are relevant to each other. Further, ethnic conflicts in one country have a tendency to cause spill-over effects not in the overall context of domestic political crisis and economic tensions but also in intra-regional relations and regional peace and stability.

It has been mentioned above that ethnic conflicts draw their sustenance and strength from economic disparities and distortions. But then there are many questions that arise here. Do self-reliant economies facilitate integration and social harmony better than the economies which are outward looking and dependent? How does one discern the reconciliation of possibly incompatible objectives of economic growth and distributive justice? Is it really feasible within the administrative and political capabilities as well as economic means to evolve on the one hand a secular polity and on the other, a self-sustained economy? If so, what should be the best strategy(ies) to be pursued in South Asia to achieve that? Some of these questions and their pertinent corollaries were debated and discussed during the Seminar.

## III

As has been mentioned earlier, alongside the quest for a participatory framework is the quest or struggle for distributive justice in South Asia. It can be hypothesized at this juncture that growth without equity creates objective conditions for conflict. How have the South Asian states fared in this respect? Whether objective economic conditions prevailing in South Asian states have conflict potential? In order to deal with this question one has to take into account the levels of development and rates of economic growth as indicated through relative income, consumption inequalities, distribution of assets, extent of poverty, unemployment and regional disparities (I.N. Mukherji). It can be said on the basis of empirical evidence on these indicators of growth and equity, that the multiple facets of social justice have lagged behind by whatever little growth there has been in the South Asian region. Country-wise studies reinforce the same contention, the same trend whether this be in the context of poverty in India (Prasad), intra-regional and inter-regional disparities in Pakistan (Bhatia), or the socio-political tensions consequent to a structure of 'dependent capitalism' in Sri Lanka (Pant).

However, despite such objective conditions, the 'explosion' in South Asian States has been localized in most cases whether this be in the form of peasant struggle, workshop strikes, industrial and service sectors, or youth students' movements. It is of interest to note in this respect that the youth movements of one type or another have proved to be a very effective instrument of protest and social change. They have aimed not only at bringing about incremental and limited adjustments in the polity and economic system but also at total transformation of system and society. The youth movements in Sri Lanka, (JVP insurgency, 1971), Bangladesh, Nepal and Pakistan have displayed robust radical characteristics. India too (Naxalites) has not been free from the phenomenon of radical youth movements. The youths, whether of radical or liberal types, will continue to prove to be a source of strength and even a frontline force in the processes of social change in South Asia. This is not surprising if one views the demographic structure in these countries in which more than half the population is below 25 years of age!

A pertinent manifestation of political and economic inequities has been in the ethnic realm. However, inequalities in power terms amongst two ethnic groups need not *per se* invoke conflict. The preconditions of such conflicts are: a socially mobilized population; the existence of symbols defining its distinctiveness; the selection, standardization and transmission of such symbols to the community by the leadership and presence of a group with which an adversary relationship is perceived in terms of a sense of relative deprivation (Phadnis). To this needs to be added the role of state in the evolution and resolution of ethnic conflicts. Ethnic self-identification, however, has not followed a *'hierarchical'* pattern in South Asia and the role of the State in handling ethnic movements has been both managerial and manipulative.

The ethnic conflicts, whether they be in Pakistan, India, Sri Lanka or Bangladesh, cannot, however, be properly understood without a critical scrutiny of the role played by the State in these conflicts. To illustrate, the State policies in Pakistan had in the main exacerbated ethnic conflicts leading to the restructuring of Pakistan's State boundaries in 1971. The continuing tensions in Sind, NWFP and Baluchistan carry similar potential (Singh). In Sri Lanka, the 'assimilationist' policies of the various regimes has led to the conversion of the demand for autonomy into one for a separate state of Eelam (Suryanarayan). India's "Khalistan" headache in Punjab also has similar elements inherent in it.

In contrast to these cases, the slow pace of development in Nepal has kept the ethnic movements under leash. The controlled political system and regulated participatory process backed by State repression is keeping the lid on over the ethnic unrest. As such, the problem of regionalism and ethnic assertion on the issues of disparity in economic, political and administrative fields has remained managable despite occasional cries from Terai dwellers (Ramakant and Upreti). More or less similar has been the case in Bhutan in which ethnic issues are latent but not absent (Das). Much would depend upon the tact and skill on the part of traditional regimes in Nepal and Bhutan, to evolve a managable balance between forces of change and compulsions of persistence, if social stability is to be preserved and potential for ethnic, regional and sectarian conflicts is to be kept diffused and at low level.

These are all tall tasks. More so because often the preservation of internal balance and stability in South Asian countries and the region is not entirely a function of domestic and regional forces and factors. There are powerful and more resourceful extra-regional factors and forces too which, in pursuance of their specific economic and strategic interests do not hesitate to vitiate regional harmony and national stability. We do not seem to be properly equipped to provide an intellectual answer to the challange posed by extra-regional forces to domestic and regional quest for peace and stability.

CHAPTER ONE

# Economic Growth and Social Justice in South Asia
## Growing Potential for Domestic Conflict

I.N. Mukherji

THIS PAPER proceeds on the hypothesis that economic growth which bypasses considerations of equity, creates the necessary objective conditions for conflict. The subjective conditions are governed by growing awareness of poverty and deprivation generated by spread of literacy, impact of mass media, increasing politicization, emergence of representative organizations to articulate the grievances of the deprived, etc. Conflict, which may be latent initially, could become manifest given the interplay of these two forces. This paper is not concerned with conflict as such, but endeavours to examine whether the objective conditions have created the potential for conflict. The paper first examines the level of development and the rate of economic growth in South Asian countries. Subsequently it seeks to assess whether economic growth has been accompanied by social justice. Social justice is sought to be evaluated in terms of relative income/consumption distribution, distribution of assets, percentage of population below poverty line, real wages of agricultural labourers, and regional disparties. Having consolidated the existing literature on the subject, a search for their consistency is attempted and interpretations offered. Finally, the relationship between economic growth and equity is examined and some policy guidelines suggested.

### 1. Levels of Development and Rate of Economic Growth

THE WORLD Bank in its World Development Report 1984

classified low income countries as those having per capita income below $400. Judged by this criterion, all South Asian countries may be classified as belonging to this category. This should not obscure the fact that some countries in South Asia such as Nepal, Bhutan and Bangladesh are among the lowest rung of low income countries.

As may be observed in Table 1, the period covering the fifties was one of generally low growth rates in GDP for all South Asian countries. The sixties was characterized by some acceleration in growth rates, particularly in Pakistan and Sri Lanka. In Sri Lanka and India the growth rates had accelerated particularly during the second half of the sixties. The seventies was characterized by deceleration in growth rates in most of these countries. The main factors which contributed to this was civil strife that characterized Pakistan and Sri Lanka in 1971, as also erratic weather conditions during the first half of the seventies that led to a series of crop failures with its adverse effect on industrial growth. In most of these countries the dynamism generated by the new agricultural strategy witnessed since the mid-sixties, had started petering out since the seventies. There was corresponding slackening in the pace of industrial growth as well. There is some evidence to indicate that economic growth has again accelerated in Sri Lanka and Pakistan since the second half of the seventies. In Nepal and Bhutan the growth rates, modest as they are, show no sign of either acceleration or deceleration over the different periods examined.

The United Nations had set a target growth rate of 6 per cent per annum in real GDP for developing countries during the First Development Decade. It will be seen, in none of the South Asian countries (with the exception of Pakistan during the sixties) this target was realized. Assuming a growth rate in population of around 2.5-3 per cent per annum in these countries, in only three countries, viz., India, Pakistan and Sri Lanka, the growth in real GDP exceeded population growth. However, in other three countries, viz., Bhutan, Bangladesh and Nepal, the long-term growth rate in GNP per capita has been quite stagnant. While the growth rate in GDP in Sri Lanka has been lower than that of Pakistan, both the countries have achieved similar improvement in GDP per capita. This has been due to Sri Lanka's greater success in controlling its population growth.

It will also be noticed that most South Asian countries are characterized by substantial fluctuations in their growth rates. This has been mainly due to fluctuations in agricultural output caused by vagaries of monsoons.

We can also observe that the rate of growth among the relatively developed South Asian countries has been better as compared to the least developed among them pointing to growing polarization between these countries.

## II. Relative Income and Consumption Inequalities

WHILE ECONOMIC growth may be a necessary condition for an improvement in social welfare, it is not a sufficient condition. It is equally important to see how the benefits of growth has been shared by the society at large. One way of doing this is to stratify the population by deciles and to examine what proportion of the income is accruing to each decile. In the absence of income data the same can be done in case of household consumer expenditures. By stratifying cumulatively the proportion of income or consumption and the corresponding proportion of population or households, it is possible to estimate the Gini coefficient of concentration or concentration ratio (CR).[1]

In Table 2 the CR of incomes/consumer expenditures have been presented using different sources over different reference periods for each country. Wherever available, rural-urban CRs have been indicated separately. It may be seen that in all cases (with the exception of Nepal) inequality in the urban sector is more pronounced than in the rural sector reflecting thereby that increasing urbanization is likely to accentuate income inequalities. Among South Asian countries inequality in income distribution is the highest in Nepal followed by Sri Lanka. It is the least in Bangladesh, while India and Pakistan constitute the intermediate range.

Regarding the trend in income inequality, it will be seen that in erstwhile East Pakistan the CR declined between 1963-64 to 1968-69.[2] A similar trend is to be observed for West Pakistan during the sixties. However, it appears that since 1970-71 income inequalities in Pakistan have started increasing. This is confirmed both by estimates presented by Zafar Mahmood[3] and those presented by the Government of Pakistan.[4] Inequalities in consumption expenditure, however, appears to have declined since 1970-71.[5] No recent studies indicating the trend in income inequality in Bangladesh is available. In case of India it will be noticed that income inequality in the rural sector declined over the decade from mid-sixties whereas inequality in the urban sector got accentuated, thereby, contributing to an increase in overall income inequality.[6] There is some evidence to believe that since the sixties there has been a mildly declining trend in consumption inequality. The estimates presented by Gupta[7] and Ahluwalia[8] also point to this trend. However, in the absence of data on savings distribution, it will be hazardous to draw any definite inference of income inequality. In case of Sri Lanka there appears to be an unambiguous decline in inequality between 1953–73.[9] There is some evidence to believe that income inequality has increased since 1973.[10]

### III. Distribution of Assets

It is from the possession of productive assets that income generating potential is created. Its significance however is wider since assets confer on the owner not only this potential, but also status, security, leisure and access to complimentary resources owing to availability of cheap institutional sources of credit. Since land is the most important scarce asset in the rural sector of South Asian countries, it will be pertinent to examine the distribution of this scarce resource as also the trend over time. This has been presented in Table 3.

An examination of Table 3 reveals that inequality in the distribution of land in all the countries is considerably more pronounced than inequality in the distribution of income. The difference gets further accentuated when zero landholders are included in the distribution of land as in case of India.

As regards the trend in the concentration of landholdings, a disquieting feature is the increasing concentration of landholdings in all the countries in South Asia with the possible exception of India. In case of India the various rounds of National Sample Surveys on landholdings point to a steady decline in concentration. While this may, in fact, have occurred, two surveys of the Reserve Bank of India, All India Rural Debt Survey 1961–62 and All India Debt and Investment Survey 1971–72, point to an increase in the concentration of asset holdings in India. The CR in respect of asset holdings increased from 0.68 to 0.70 during this period.[11]

## IV. Percentage of Population below the Poverty Line

WHILE OVERALL income inequality measures are useful, they fail to identify the target group–that is, those who constitute the poor. This alternative approach seeks to identify that proportion of the population whose purchasing power falls below the minimum necessary to buy a bundle of commodities required to meet the minimum calorie requirements based on some well-defined nutrition norm. It should be noted that in growing economies the overall income inequality and the proportion of population below poverty line need not be positively associated.

In Table 4 alternatives estimates of poverty ratios based on specified definitions of poverty have been presented for South Asian countries for different periods. It will be noticed that not all the estimates are consistent. These nonetheless point to the very high incidence of poverty in all these countries. In India, for instance, the incidence of poverty has fluctuated during the sixties from a little over 40 to 50 per cent of the rural population. The first study on poverty in India by Dandekar and Rath estimated the poverty ratio at 40 per cent in rural and 50 per cent in urban areas in 1960-61.[12] Although Bangladesh has less income inequality than India, in view of its lower per capita income, a larger proportion of the population in the country is below the poverty line than in India. Alamgir's[13] estimate reveals higher incidence than that of Khan[14] because of more restrictive assumption of the poverty norm adopted by the former. The poverty ratio in Bangladesh and Nepal are higher in view of their relatively lower per capita incomes. The incidence of poverty in Pakistan as estimated by Naseem[15] appears to be quite high in comparison to India especially when considering that the per capita income in the former is marginally higher than in India. This difference would have been higher but for the less restrictive definition of poverty in Pakistan than in India.

Looking at the trend in poverty ratios, some inconsistencies may be observed. While Minhas's study[16] covering the period during the sixties reveals a decline in the incidence of poverty, Bardhan's study points to an increase in this incidence. Bardhan's finding is corroborated by Ahluwalia's study, a part of which covers this period. Again both Ahluwalia's and Dutta's[17] findings reveal a decline in the incidence of poverty since the end of the sixties. Ahluwalia's most comprehensive study of the subject covering the period 1956–57 to 1973–74 shows no significant time trend in the all-India poverty ratios. At the level of states his analysis reveals that only two states, viz., Assam and West Bengal show a significant trend of an increase in the incidence of poverty while Andhra Pradesh and Tamil Nadu show a significant decline. For all other states no significant trend in the poverty ratios could be observed. It is significant to note that both in Punjab and Haryana no significant decline in the poverty ratio took place when considering that these states spearheaded the "green revolution". Both Alamgir's and Khan's study point to an increase in the incidence of poverty between 1963–64 to 1973–74. In Sri Lanka the incidence of poverty appears to have declined perceptibly between 1969–70 to 1973.[18] In Nepal on the other hand the poverty ratio increased significantly between 1976–80.[19]

## V. REAL WAGES OF AGRICULTURAL LABOURERS

Agricultural labourers may be deemed to constitute among the lowest deciles or quintiles of a frequency distribution of personal income. An assessment of the real income of this poorest strata may be made in order to assess the incidence of poverty.

In Table 5a the variations in money and real wages in different states of India covering the period 1960–61 and 1969–70 has been presented. It will be seen that when adjusted for the cost of living index of agricultural labourers, the wage rates declined in 8 out of 11 states. The absolute decline was much more pronounced in Gujarat, Mysore, Assam, Orissa and Madhya Pradesh. Among the states showing increases in real earnings, Punjab and Kerala stand out at the top. The increases in UP and Bihar were quite marginal.[20]

The experience of two other South Asian countries, notably Bangladesh and Sri Lanka, is similar as may be seen in Table 5b. In Bangladesh real wages declined during the late forties and early fifties; it rose for a decade thereafter, but after 1964 a pronounced downward trend is visible. Also to be seen is that the real wage index in Sri Lanka in estate agriculture declined over the decade 1963–73.[21]

## VI. REGIONAL DISPARITIES

SEVERAL STUDIES have confirmed that the magnitude of interstate disparities in India widened considerably during the period 1960–70.[22] The coefficients of variation in levels of development in 15 states in respect of per capita domestic product at current prices, irrigation coverage, consumption of fertilizers per hectare in agriculture, percentage of villages electrified to total villages and length of roads per thousand sq km of area widened. These widening sectoral disparities have contributed to the overall increase in interstate disparities. On the other hand, the coefficients of variation in the levels of development in respect of percentage share of secondary sector in the state domestic product, percentage or urban population to total population, credit-deposit ratio, percentage of villages electrified to total number of villages and length of road per thousand sq km have been reduced significantly between 1968–69 to 1978–79. These factors have helped in reducing over-all inter-state disparities during this period. However, it is worth noting that there was increase in concentration in respect of proportion of workers to total population, cropping intensity and in proportion of commercial crops to gross cropped area, in irrigation coverage, and consumption of fertilizer per hectare in agriculture.[23] It is possibly due to these factors that the disparity in per capita state domestic products has continued to increase consistently. Evidence available for 16 states indicates that the coefficient of variation in per capita state domestic product at current prices increased from an average of 22.2% in 1959–60 and 1961–61[24] to 32.1% on an average between 1976–79.[25]

In Sri Lanka Survey of Consumer Finances, 1963 and 1973 permit separation of data into four zones which broadly correspond to ecological regions. Taking these zones as proxy for regions, it is found that inter-regional inequality has also narrowed marginally. The range in the mean incomes of the richest and poorest regions declined from 1.62 in 1963 to 1.48 in 1973 while the Kuznets index of inter-regional inequality also declined from 21.5 to 19.1 between these two years.[26]

Nepal has geographical diversity and lacks basic infrastructure to integrate the country economically. The mountain and hilly region and parts of Far Western Terai are lagging behind as compared to other parts of Nepal. Terai has an area of 23.5 of total land, but 64.8% of the cultivated area whereas 67.4% of population are in hills and mountains with 35.2% of cultivated land. Furthermore, most development activities are concentrated in Terai.[27]

Data on regional product of the four provinces of Pakistan is not officially published. An exercise done in the late 1960s by a West Pakistani panel of economists showed that inequalities within West Pakistan were more acute than between (then) East and West Pakistan. Hedbock's[28] computation of districtwise variations in per capita incomes (at 1969 prices) in the four provinces of West Pakistan reveals that Baluchistan is clearly the poorest province with all but two of its 10 districts having per capita income below Rs. 200. Quetta district, where the provincial capital is located, alone has per capita income in the Rs. 500–600 range. NWFP has two prosperous districts, Peshawar and Mardan, and one very poor district, Hazara—the other three which lie in the heart of Barani areas have per capita income in the Rs. 300–500 range. Punjab and Sind have a more even distribution at the district level. Of the 19 Punjab districts none lies below the level of Rs. 300 per capita income, more than half below Rs. 600. Sind also has a majority of the districts lying below Rs. 600 level and one, Thatta, which is in the Rs. 200–300 range. According to Naseem's[29] estimate nearly 100 per cent of the population of Baluchistan would fall below the poverty line compared to 76% in Punjab, 69% in Sind, and 75% in NWFP. In Sind the per capita agricultural output is the highest while that of Baluchistan is the lowest. The range between the two increased from 2.3 in 1960 to 3.0 in 1972. The coefficient of variation in per capita agricultural output between the four provinces increased from 29% to 36% during these two years.[30]

## VII. An Interpretation of Empirical Evidence

It will be seen that some of the estimates arrived at appear to be inconsistent. Here we need to look at the methodologies used in order to arrive at the estimates. The differing estimates of poverty ratios during the sixties by Minhas and Bardhan arise from the different price deflators used by the two to measure real consumption of the poor. Bardhan's use of consumer price index numbers for agricultural labourers[31] appears to be more appropriate than the national income deflator used by Minhas. Ahluwalia and

Dutta using the same deflator arrive at the same result.

The available evidence in respect of Sri Lanka points to a substantial decline in income inequality during the period 1953–73 although this is contested by Lee who observes an increasing concentration in the distribution of consumer expenditure. Isenman has however provided an alternative explanation for the apparent inconsistency between income and consumption distribution in Sri Lanka in 1973. In his view when the Survey was conducted in January-February 1973, foodgrains availability was at its lowest annual level since 1966. In addition, the 1973 Survey was conducted during a seasonal low point of supply, while that of 1963 was roughly at the time of a major festival. When recognizing that Sri Lanka's social indicators have improved considerably over the last two decades, it seems plausible to accept the more general view that income inequality in Sri Lanka as a whole diminished between 1963–73. Given also that Indian Tamils constitute no more than 11% of the total population, an improvement in the poverty ratio could still be consistent with a deterioration in relative as also the absolute standard of living of the Indian Tamils. This points to the limitation of poverty ratio as an indicator of social welfare because it gives equal weightage to all groups below the poverty line. However, the situation since 1973 appears to have changed with inequalities showing a tendency to increase. As Ponnambalam has maintained, since 1973 a new super wealthy class has emerged in Sri Lanka. In his view "the new super incomes generated by the government's policy of establishing export industries enjoying tax holdings and entitled to Convertible Rupee Accounts not only destroyed whatever levelling of income inequalities had been achieved by 1973, but created the widest cleavage in income and wealth the country had ever seen."[32] In case of Pakistan also we have observed consistent decline in income inequality during the sixties. According to Hicks[33] agricultural growth in Pakistan in the sixties was accompanied by a rise in real wages of agricultural workers as well as employment. Such a rise in the real incomes of agricultural labourers tended to reduce poverty and inequalities in income. The improvement in real incomes of agricultural workers are possible due to restrictions placed on mechanization through import control policies.

Given the decline in income inequality accompanied by rapid economic growth in the sixties, one would expect a corresponding decline in the poverty ratio as well. In reality the poverty ratio declined initially, but started increasing since 1968-69. It appears therefore that neither rapid economic growth nor greater income equality had any perceptible impact on the poverty ratio.

The data used by Naseem to estimate the poverty ratio lends itself to greater credibility since he deflates household expenditures by group specific cost of living indices.[34] His study clearly reveals that the high rate of economic growth in Pakistan during the sixties has made no dent on the staggering level of poverty in the country. This combined with the trend towards greater concentration in land holdings casts doubts as to whether inequalities did in fact decline during the sixties.[35] All indicators unambiguously point to an increase in income inequality during the seventies. The deterioration in income distribution in the 1970s has been explained by the sharp acceleration of inflation in the early 1970s, the deterioration in industrial relations and the decline in productivity both in agriculture and manufacturing.[36] Moreover, unlike the sixties the pace of mechanization in Pakistan's agriculture has been stepped up considerably during the seventies. The number of tractors imported annually increased rapidly from mere 3,879 in 1970-71 to 19,313 in 1979-80. In contrast the number of tubewells installed showed no positive trend. It actually declined since the early eighties.[37] Thus the lower growth of agriculture in Pakistan during the seventies coupled with the labour displacing effect of tractorization, may well have contributed to growing inequalities in Pakistan's rural sector.[38]

Alamgir's estimate of CR income distribution for East Pakistan during the period 1963-64 to 1968-69 reveals some decline in inequality. Like Naseem, he uses the Quarterly Survey of Current Economic Conditions 1963-64 as the benchmark household income and expenditure. The deficiency of the study lies in that comparisons in CRs is made again in nominal terms. A.R. Khan estimates poverty ratio in East Pakistan using the same source. However, his methodology is more sound than Alamgir's because he deflates consumer expenditure on the basis of income specific price indices. Accordingly, the rise in the prices of the goods which have a heavier weight in the budget of the low income groups has been given due consideration. Thus given the growing incidence of poverty between 1963-64 and 1968-69, stagnation in real earnings of agricultural labourers since the mid-sixties, and the growing concentration of land holdings since the sixties, one would have some hesitation in accepting Alamgir's finding of a decline in inequality East Pakistan during the sixties.

It thus appears that in South Asian countries economic growth has not generally been associated with an improvement in the well being of the poor. This appears to have greater validity for the seventies as compared to the sixties. A possible exception to this may be in case of India for period since 1968-69. However, the improvement has been very modest over a considerable length of time. This is particularly disquieting given the fact that even the rate of growth in per capita real product has been almost stagnant in several least developed South Asian countries.

### VIII. Determinants of Inequality and Policy Options for Resolving Conflict Potential

The historical experience of presently developed capitalist countries reveals growing inequality in the initial phase of development followed by some levelling up of incomes at a later phase.[39] Cross sectional studies also tend to confirm an inverted U-shaped relationship with inequalities widening from low income group of countries to middle income group and finally flattening out with high income group of countries.[40] Drawing from the aforementioned analysis, conventional theorists well versed in neo-classical analysis tended to give primacy to economic growth asserting that its efforts are bound to "trickle down" and percolate to the masses.

The data base on which the Kuznet's hypothesis is based is itself questionable because the Gini coefficients are based on nominal values. There is fairly reliable evidence to suggest that relative prices of agricultural products have increased more than the wholesale price index.[41] It is also worth noting that the level of per capita incomes of the presently developed countries was significantly higher than that of the presently developing countries. Further the rich in the low income countries are well known for their conspicuous consumption. On the other hand the poor in these countries are abysmally poor such that a further reduction in their consumption cannot but adversely affect their capacity to work. What is, in fact, necessary in these countries is a reduction in the consumption of the rich and an *increase* for the poor. In the practical context in which productive potential is more broadly conceived, the dichotomy between consumption, like investment, can also be productive. Thus the blind application of "stage theories" of economic growth and income distribution to the developing countries is likely to be inappropriate, misleading and, in fact, dangerous.

As to the determinants of inequality, reference may be made to a cross section study by Ahluwalia.[42] Using regression analysis, the study reveals that the level of primary school enrolment has a positive bearing on the income share of the lowest 40 per cent. Again, a high rate of population growth bears a significant inverse relationship with the share of the lowest 40 per cent. The study also reveals that the share of the lowest 40 per cent is significantly higher in the socialist countries. Thus, the spread of primary and secondary education, control over population as also socialization of the means of production is expected to promote greater equality in income distribution.

Another study by K.N. Raj[43] on inter-state variations in levels of development in India shows that per capita consumption of food does not depend on per capita income alone; it is positively related to per capita output of foodgrains within each state and negatively related to inequality in the distribution of landholdings. Hence it follows that raising levels of food intake requires not only increasing the output of food in each state and region, but also reducing inequalities in the distribution of land.

Ahluwalia's study of poverty and agricultural performance in India points to a close inverse association between growth in agricultural output per head and the poverty ratio at the all-India level. At the level of states a similar relationship is found in respect of 7 of the 19 states. These states account for 56 per cent of the rural population in India and about three-fourths of the rural population in poverty. However the nature of the data reveals that in many of these states other factors are also at work which tends to increase the incidence of poverty. These factors may relate to land tenure system of tenant displacement—factors which may not be independent of agricultural growth. Looking at the trend at the all-India level and after examining the trend in 14 states he claims that his "findings provide substantial confirmation at the state level of the hypothesis... that improved agricultural performance, even within the existing institutional constraints, will tend to reduce the incidence of poverty."[44]

Griffin has questioned the validity of Ahluwalia's hypothesis and findings. In his view two observations in 1957–58 and 1959–60 tend to obscure the rising incidence of poverty that occurred in many states in India from about 1960. Taking two reference periods, the average of the years 1960–64 to the average for 1970–74, he finds that excluding Andhra Pradesh, in all other states there was a tendency for rural poverty to increase. Nor does his estimate reveal any statistically significant negative relationship between agricultural growth per capita and rural poverty. Hence he disagrees with the view that poverty can be reduced without altering the existing inequitable institutional structures.[45]

An interesting finding at the all-India level indicates that in periods when the growth rate in the non-agricultural sector significantly accelerated, the consumption distribution of the household in the urban sector became more skewed. As a contrast the Lorenz ratio in the agriculture sector seems to have a negative correlation with changes in the rate of growth of agricultural income. This suggests that whereas there is some trade-off between equity and accelerated growth in non-agriculture sector, this has not been the case in the agriculture sector. It has, hence, been suggested that in setting targets for accelerated GDP growth in the Plans, a target for faster growth for the rural sector with lower capital intensity will help in achieving the goal of equity.[46]

It may be said in conclusion that if poverty is to be reduced or eliminated, it is vital that food output per head should increase more rapidly than at present. While several South Asian countries have witnessed significant growth rates, food output per capita has either stagnated or increased only marginally. Unless significant increase in food production per capita is attained preceded by appropriate structural and institutional changes, poverty alleviation could remain, at the most, a transient phenomenon; any external shock could easily reverse the status quo ante.

This paper has attempted a synthesis of the various empirical studies on inequality and poverty. The data reveal that the dimensions of social justice have lagged behind whatever little growth that has been registered in South Asian States. As such the objective conditions in the region in the economic realm have significant potential for conflict.

The translation of the conflict potential into actual conflictual situations would depend upon: (i) perception and awareness of deprivation or inequality; (ii) mobilization and articulation of this perception in an organized manner; (iii) the presence or otherwise of an institutional mechanism which can accommodate the demands; and (iv) finally the power of the present day state to deal with conflict whether by accommodation or suppression. It is because of the presence of these factors that we fail to observe any direct correlation between the extent of poverty or inequality in South Asian states with the actual manifestation of conflict.

It is also worth noting that quite often economic factors do not operate in isolation, but in conjuction with ethnic, communal or regional pulls and pressures. But generally it may be said that when levels of poverty are high and the population illiterate the poor are usually too weak to organize protest or assume militancy. However, it is with the spread of education and economic development that the perceptions of deprivation become more marked and so does the capacity to organize protest or assume militancy. It is in this context that economic growth need to be integrated with social justice so that conflictual situations are managed rather than crushed.

There is no inherent contradiction between economic growth and social justice. It is when economic growth helps to improve the purchasing power of the masses that the growth process assumes a momentum of its own. Economic growth which is truncated or fragmented, cannot be sustained for long without creating the potential for conflict. Conflict management thus necessitates: (i) the redistribution of productive assets as also institutional finance in favour of the poor; (ii) shifting of priorities in our plans in favour of more labour intensive employment generating schemes in the rural sector; (iii) expansion of food production particularly in food deficit regions; and, finally, (iv) spread of education with special focus on improvement in female literacy.

### Acknowledgements

The author expresses his thanks to Mr Zafar Mahmood, Research Economist, Pakistan Institute of Development Economics and Mr Godfrey Gunatilleke, Director, Marga Institute, Colombo who were kind enough to send him not only valuable reprints of their papers, but also other relevant literature pertaining to the subject.

Table 1. Per capita income and average annual growth rates of gross domestic product at constant market prices in South Asian countries, 1950–82.

|  | Bangladesh | Bhutan | India | Pakistan | Nepal | Sri Lanka |
|---|---|---|---|---|---|---|
| 1. Per Capita Income US $ 1982 | 140 | 80[a] | 260 | 380 | 170 | 320 |
| Average annual growth rates | | | | | | |
| 2. 1950–60 | NA | NA | 3.5 | 2.5 | NA | 3.0 |
| 3. 1960–70 | NA | NA | 3.8 | 5.4 | 2.6 | 4.5 |
| 4. 1960–65 | 4.6 | 2.0 | 3.7 | 7.4 | 2.5 | 3.8 |
| 5. 1965–70 | 3.3 | NA | 4.7 | 7.2 | 2.6 | 5.7 |
| 6. 1971–82 | 5.7[c] | NA | 2.7 | 4.1 | 2.7 | 5.5[e] |
| 7. 1971–75 | 7.8[d] | NA | 3.0 | 3.4 | 2.2 | 5.6 |
| 8. 1976–80 | 5.7 | NA | 3.6 | 5.7 | 2.4 | 5.5 |
| 9. GNP per capita 1960–82 | 0.3 | 0.1[f] | 1.3 | 2.8 | −0.1 | 2.6 |

[a] 1981
[b] Includes both East and West Pakistan up to 1970.
[c] 1974–82
[d] 1974–75
[e] 1971–81
[f] 1960–81

SOURCE: Sl. No. 1: World Development Report, 1984
Sl. No. 2–5: ESCAP, Economic and Social Survey of Asia and the Pacific 1974, 1977, 1978
Sl. No. 6–8: Key Indicators, Asian Development Bank, April 1983
Sl. No. 9: World Development Report, 1984.

Table 2. Gini concentration ratios of income and consumption distribution in South Asian countries.

| Country | Source/Reference | Year | Concentration ratios Rural | Urban | Total |
|---|---|---|---|---|---|
| 1 | 2 | 3 | 4 | 5 | 6 |
| Bangladesh (E. Pakistan) | Alamgir (2) | 1963–64 | .330 | .410 | .360 |
|  |  | 1966–67 | .310 | .380 | .300 |
|  |  | 1968–69 | .270 | .370 | .300 |
| India | Ojha and Bhatt (6) | 1953–55 | .343 | .401 | .376 |
|  |  | 1961–64 | .319 | .474 | .385 |
|  |  | 1964–65 | .370 |  |  |
|  | Gupta (7) | Average 1960–61 1966–67[b] | .305[a] | .355[a] |  |
|  |  | Average 1967–68 1977–78[c] | .293[a] | .329[a] |  |
| Nepal |  | 1978 | .600 | .550 | .580 |
| Pakistan (W. Pakistan) | Mahmood (3) | 1963–64 | .350 | .381 | .356 |
|  |  | 1966–67 | .318 | .380 | .349 |
|  |  | 1968–69 | .300 | .374 | .355 |
|  |  | 1969–70 | .303 | .357 | .331 |
|  |  | 1970–71 | .295 | .360 | .321 |
|  |  | 1971–72 | .307 | .363 | .340 |
|  |  | 1979 | .324 | .414 | .360 |

|   1 | 2 | 3 | 4 | 5 | 6 |
|---|---|---|---|---|---|
| | Finance | 1971–72 | .308 | .381 | .345 |
| | Division, | | .271[a] | .352[a] | .326[a] |
| | GOP (4) | 1979 | .325 | .399 | .373 |
| | | | .268[a] | .340[a] | .316[a] |
| Sri Lanka | ECAFE (9) | 1953 | .450 | .520 | .500 |
| | | 1963 | — | — | .490 |
| | | 1969–70 | — | — | .416 |
| | | 1973 | — | — | .345 |
| | Central Bank | 1978–79 | — | — | .483 |
| | of Ceylon (10) | 1980–81 | — | — | .401 |

[a] Pertains to household consumer expenditure based on sample surveys
[b] Observations in all years excluding 1962-63 (6 observations)
[c] Observations in all years excluding 1971-72, 1974-75, 1975-76 & 1976-77 (7 observations).

Table 3. Gini concentration ratios of landholdings in South Asia.

| Country | Source (reference) | Year | Gini concentration ratio |
|---|---|---|---|
| 1 | 2 | 3 | 4 |
| Bangladesh | (1) | 1960 | .47 |
| | | 1974 | .57 |
| | (2) | 1977 | .88 |
| | | 1977 | .89[a] |
| India | (1) | 1961 | .59 |
| | | 1970–71 | .63 |

| 1 | 2 | 3 | 4 |
|---|---|---|---|
|  | (3) | 1953–54 | .78[a] |
|  |  | 1959–60 | .73[a] |
|  |  | 1961 | .72[a] |
|  |  | 1971 | .71[a] |
| Nepal | (4) | 1972 | .88 |
| Pakistan | (1) | 1960 | .60 |
|  | (5) | 1972 | .66 |
|  | (6) | 1980 | .79 |
| Sri Lanka | (7) | 1962 | .35 |
|  |  | 1970 | .41 |

[a] Including zero landholders.
[b] Paddy holdings only.

SOURCES: (1) ESCAP, Economic and Social Survey for Asia and the Pacific, 1976.
(2) Estimated from Summary Report, Land Occupancy Survey of Rural Bangladesh, Bangladesh Bureau of Statistics, Bangladesh 1977 as presented in Statistical Yearbook of Bangladesh, 1979, Bangladesh Bureau of Statistics.
(3) Dandekar and Rath (12).
(4) Estimated from data on land distribution presented in Agricultural Statistics of Nepal, HMG, 1972.
(5) Based on 1972 Census of Agriculture and estimated by S.M. Naseem (24).
(6) Based on Census of Pakistan Agriculture 1980, estimated from data presented in Pakistan Economic Survey 1983–84, Annexure II, Table 3.13.
(7) E.L.H. Lee (22).

Table 4. Percentage of population below poverty line in South Asian countries.

| Country | Source (reference) | Year | Percent of population Rural | Urban | Definition of poverty |
|---|---|---|---|---|---|
| 1 | 2 | 3 | 4 | 5 | 6 |
| Bangladesh | Alamgir (13) | 1963–64 | 88 | 82 | Taka 252 and 298 per annum at 1966 prices for rural and urban areas respectively to purchase minimum consumption bundle of 2100 calories and 45 gram protein per day |
|  |  | 1966–67 | 62 | 72 |  |
|  |  | 1968–69 | 79 | 70 |  |
|  |  | 1973–74 | 94 | — |  |
|  | Khan (14) | 1963–64 | 40 | — | Taka 23.61 per capita per month at 1963–64 prices to meet 1935 calories per day or 90 per cent of the recommended intake |
|  |  | 1968–69 | 76 | — |  |
|  |  | 1973–74 | 74 | — |  |
|  |  | 1975 (I Qr.) | 62 |  |  |
| India | Minhas (16) | 1956–57 | 65 |  |  |
|  |  | 1960–61 | 59 |  |  |
|  |  | 1964–65 | 52 |  |  |
|  |  | 1967–68 | 51 |  |  |
|  | Bardhan (31) | 1960–61 | 38 |  |  |
|  |  | 1964–65 | 45 |  | Rupees 15 per capita per month at 1960–61 prices (weighted average of states) to meet norm of 2250 calories per day |
|  | Dandekar and Rath (12) | 1960–61 | 40 | 50 |  |

| 1 | 2 | 3 | 4 | 5 | 6 |
|---|---|---|---|---|---|
| | Dutta (17) | 1968–69 | 50 | | |
| | | 1969–70 | 49 | | |
| | | 1970–71 | 45 | | |
| | | 1973–74 | 44 | | |
| | Ahluwalia (8) | 1957–58 | 42 | | |
| | | 1959–60 | 49 | | |
| | | 1960–61 | 53 | | |
| | | 1964–65 | 50 | | |
| | | 1966–67 | 57 | | |
| | | 1968–69 | 53 | | |
| | | 1970–71 | 49 | | |
| | | 1973–74 | 48 | | |
| Nepal | Tiwari (19) | 1976 | 41 | 22 | Minimum Subsistence income Rs. 2 per day at current prices |
| | | 1980 | 80 | 60 | Minimum subsistence income of Rs. 3 per day at current prices. |
| Pakistan | Naseem (15) | 1963–64 | 72 | | Rupees 27.53 per capita per month at 1959–60 prices to ensure 1995 calories, or 95 per cent of the recommended intake |
| | | 1968–69 | 64 | | |
| | | 1969–70 | 68 | | |
| | | 1970–71 | 71 | | |
| | | 1971–72 | 74 | | |
| Sri Lanka | ESCAP (10) | 1969–70 | 72 | | Rupees 200 per household per month |
| | | 1973 | 40 | | |

Table 5a. Variation in money and real wage rates in states of India, 1960–61 to 1969–70.

| State | Money wages 1960–61 | Money wages 1969–70 | Real wages 1969–70 | Change in real wages over 1961 |
|---|---|---|---|---|
| Andhra Pradesh | 1.46 | 2.46 | 1.40 | −0.06 |
| Assam | 2.29 | 3.80 | 2.04 | −0.25 |
| Bihar | 1.30 | 2.70 | 1.34 | +0.04 |
| Gujarat | 1.97 | 2.94 | 1.73 | −0.24 |
| Kerala | 2.10 | 4.67 | 2.31 | +0.21 |
| Madhya Pradesh | 1.32 | 2.11 | 1.02 | −0.30 |
| Mysore | 1.67 | 2.35 | 1.34 | −0.33 |
| Orissa | 1.26 | 2.15 | 1.01 | −0.25 |
| Punjab | 2.81 | 6.34 | 3.24 | +0.43 |
| Tamil Nadu | 1.43 | 2.65 | 1.39 | −0.04 |
| Uttar Pradesh | 1.31 | 2.61 | 1.32 | +0.01 |

SOURCE: S.M. Pandey (20).

Table 5b. Real agricultural wages in Bangladesh and real wage index in agriculture[a] in Sri Lanka.

| Year | Bangladesh (Takas) | Sri Lanka (1952=100) |
|---|---|---|
| 1949 | 2.36 | |
| 1950 | 2.13 | |
| 1951 | 2.00 | |
| 1952 | 1.97 | |
| 1953 | 1.71 | |
| 1954 | n.a | |
| 1955 | 1.92 | |
| 1956 | n.a | |
| 1957 | 1.99 | |
| 1958 | 1.93 | |
| 1959 | 1.94 | |
| 1960 | 2.06 | |
| 1961 | 2.27 | |
| 1962 | 2.21 | |
| 1963 | 2.36 | 104.2 |
| 1964 | 2.66 | 103.5 |
| 1965 | 2.22 | 103.4 |
| 1966 | 1.90 | 103.5 |
| 1967 | 1.92 | 104.9 |
| 1968 | 2.04 | 114.3 |
| 1969 | 2.22 | 106.3 |
| 1970 | 2.24 | 101.3 |
| 1971 | n.a | 99.8 |
| 1972 | 1.60 | 98.4 |
| 1973 | 1.59 | 101.5 |
| 1974 | 1.42 | |
| 1975 (first half) | 1.29 | |

[a] Refers to estate agriculture.

SOURCE: A.R. Khan (14); E.L.H. Lee (26).

## NOTES

1. Concentration ratio is measured by using the following formula:
$$1 - (f_i - f_{i-1})(Y_i + Y_{i-1})$$
Where $f_i$ is comulative of households or population and $Y_i$ is comulative of income shares.
2. Mohiuddin Alamgir, "Some Analysis of Distribution of Income, Consumption, Saving and Poverty in Bangladesh," The Bangladesh Development Studies, October 1974, p. 775.
3. Estimated by Zafar Mahmood from Household Income and Expenditure Survey, in a paper entitled "Income Inequality in Pakistan: An Analysis of Existing Evidence," presented at Annual General Meeting, Pakistan Society of Development Economists, Islamabad, March 1984.
4. *Pakistan Economic Survey*, 1983–84, Economic Affairs Wing, Finance Division, Government of Pakistan, Islamabad, Table 7, p. 41.
5. Ibid.
6. Ojha and Bhatt, "Pattern of Income Distribution in India, 1953–54 to 1961-64," Paper presented at a seminar on Inocme Distribution, organized by Indian Statistical Institute, New Delhi, Feb. 1971.
7. S.P. Gupta, "Growth, Equity and Self Reliance: A Macro Analysis," *Mainstream*, New Delhi, June 9, 1984.
8. Montek Ahluwalia, "Rural Poverty and Agricultural Performance in India," *Journal of Development Studies*, 1977; World Bank Reprint Series: No. 60, Table 8, p. 317.
9. ECAFE, Economic Bulletin for Asia and the Far East "Intra-regional Trade Projections, Effective Protection and Income Distribution," Vol. III, Bangkok, 1972, Table 2.
10. Estimated from data presented in Statistical Pocket-book of Democratic Socialist Republic of Sri Lanka, 1983, Department of Census and Statistics, Ministry of Plan Implementation. Original data for 1969-70 and 1980-81 is Socio-Economic Survey; for 1973 data Consumer Finance Survey (Central Bank of Ceylon); for 1978-79 data Consumer Finance and Socio- Economic Survey (Central Bank of Ceylon).
11. A.C. Minocha, "Some Aspects of Income Distribution in India," The Indian Economic Journal, Oct-Dec. 1973, p. 5.
12. V.M. Dandekar and N. Rath, "Poverty in India—I: Dimensions and Trends," *Economic and Political Weekly*, January 2, 1971.
13. Mohiuddin Alamgir, *Poverty, Inequality and Social Welfare: Measurement, Evidence and Policies*, The Bangladesh Development Studies, April 1975, p. 171.
14. A.R. Khan, "Poverty and Inequality in Rural Bangladesh," in ILO, *Poverty and Landlessness in Rural Asia*, Geneva, 1977.
15. S.M. Naseem, "Poverty and Landlessness in Pakistan," in ILO, n. 14.
16. B.S. Minhas, "Rural Poverty, Land Distribution and Development," *Indian Economic Review*, April 1970.
17. Bhaskar Dutta, "On the Measurement of Poverty in Rural India", *Indian Economic Review*, April 1978.

18. Estimate presented in ESCAP, Economic and Social Survey of Asia and the Pacific, 1978, Table 76.
19. Padma Nath Tiwari, "National Development Strategies and Complementarities: Nepal," Centre for Economic Development and Administration, Kathmandu, pp.75–76.
20. S.M. Pandey, "Pattern of Wages," Income and Consumer Expenditure of Agricultural Labourer in India: Problems and Policy Perspectives in Rural Labour in India," Shri Ram Centre for Industrial Relations and Human Resources, 1976, p. 63.
21. A.R. Khan, n. 14, Tables 50 and 63.
22. O.P. Mathur, "The Problems of Inter-Regional Disparities: The Indian Background," *Indian Journal of Regional Science*, Vol. V, No. 1, 1973, p. 90, and R.T. Tiwari, "Inter-Regional Disparities in Levels of Development—Indian Experience," *Man and Development*, Vol. VI, No. 1, March 1984.
23. R.T. Tiwari, n. 22, p. 25.
24. Estimated from Distribution of National Income by States, 1960–61, National Council of Applied Economic Research, New Delhi, 1960.
25. Estimated from CSO data, Government of India, presented in Report of the Eighth Finance Commission 1984, Appendix VI, p. 158.
26. E.L.H. Lee, "Rural Poverty in Sri Lanka", in ILO, n. 14, p. 163.
27. P.N. Tiwari, n. 19, p. 53.
28. R.W. Helbock, Districtwise Variations of Income in Pakistan, P.I.D.E., 1975.
29. S.M. Naseem, n. 15.
30. Estimated from data presented in Naseem, Ibid., Table XA. 3, p. 239.
31. P.K. Bardhan, "On the incidence of poverty in Rural India of the Sixties," *Economic and Political Weekly*, Annual Number, February 1973.
32. S. Pennambalam, *Dependent Capitalism in Crisis*, Zed Press, London, 1980, p. 132.
33. N.L. Hicks, "Long Term Trends in Income Distribution in Pakistan," *World Development*, Vol. 6, 1978.
34. ECAFE, n. 9, pp. 108–9.
35. S.M. Naseem, n. 15, p. 45.
36. *Pakistan Economic Survey*, n. 4, p. 42.
37. Ibid., Appendix Table 3.9.
38. Various studies have pointed to the employment displacing effects of tractor mechanization in Pakistan. According to a survey one tractor destroys about 10 permanent jobs, but this is compensated by the creation of jobs for casual workers equivalent in income terms to 5 permanent jobs.
39. Simon Kuznets, *Modern Economic Growth*, Oxford University Press, 1972, p. 218.
40. M. Ahluwalia, "Income Inequality: Some Dimensions of the Problem" in *Redistribution with Growth*, eds. Chenery et al., Oxford University Press, 1974, p. 15.

41. W. Beckerman, "Some Reflections on Redistribution with Growth," *World Development*, Vol. 5, 1977.
42. Ahluwalia, n. 40.
43. K.N. Raj, *Poverty Unemployment and Development Policy: A Case Study of Selected Issues with Reference to Kerala*, Orient Longman, New Delhi, 1977, p. 1.
44. Ahluwalia, n. 8, pp. 308-16.
45. Keith Griffin, "Growth and Impoverishment in Rural Areas of Asia," in *World Development*, Vol. 7, 1979.
46. S.P. Gupta, n. 7, p. 18.

CHAPTER TWO

# Poverty in India
## Trends and Prospects

### Kamta Prasad

DOMESTIC conflicts are often caused or accentuated by economic factors related to the sharing of wealth and income among regions, classes or individuals. For example, many of the inter-State disputes in India arise out of the sharing of costs and benefits of river valley projects or location of industrial units, or division of national revenue. Conflicts between groups of landless labourers and landowners take place on account of disputes related to possession or dispossession of land, tenancy rights, wage rates, etc. Disputes over the wage rates, employment and other service conditions are responsible for most of the conflicts between workers and owners in industrial undertakings. The occurrence of conflict is also influenced by economy-wide trends related to disparities in income, wealth and employment. Rising unemployment or disparities in income tend to accentuate conflicts. A study of domestic conflicts is never complete without a full understanding of the overall trends with respect to the inter-related phenomena of poverty, unemployment and inequality. In the present paper, I would like to confine myself to these very aspect. Apart from indicating past and current trends, the paper throws some light on future prospects also.

### I. Poverty Concept

ANY ESTIMATE of the magnitude of poverty in a country depends upon how this term is defined. In India, the term poverty has been used mostly in the sense of absolute poverty. The extent of poverty is measured by estimating the number of persons whose overall per capita consumption expenditure lies below the poverty line which is defined as the minimum level of per capita consumer expenditure needed to ensure a normative caloric intake. The Seventh Finance Commission 1978 gave a somewhat modified version of this by taking into account not only private consumption expenditure but also per capita monthly public expenditure on (i) health and family planning, (ii) water supply and sanitation, (iii) education, (iv) administration of police, justice and courts, (v) roads and (vi) social welfare. But the estimates suffer from many deficiencies because of which these have not gained much acceptance.

Poverty is closely related to unemployment and inequality, though conceptually as well as empirically there are differences between them. In general, there is a considerable degree of overlap between them. For example, most of the unemployed or underemployed persons belong to the category of the poor. Policies designed to remove or mitigate unemployment and/or inequality would tend to reduce poverty also. Hence, in this paper, while discussing poverty, we would be touching upon trends related to inequality and unemployment also.

## II. Trend of Poverty

DATA ON poverty line and incidence of poverty in India are far from satisfactory despite the fact that poverty is an age old phenomenon and that several attempts have been made in recent years to measure it. A pioneering attempt in this direction was made in 1962 by a distinguished study group comprising of D.R. Gadgil, V.K.R.V. Rao, P.S. Lokanathan, B.N. Ganguli, M.R. Masani, Asoka Mehta, Sriman Narayan, Pitambar Pant and Anna Saheb Sahastrabudhe. By taking into account the recommendations for balanced diet made by the Nutritional Advisory Committee of the Indian Council of Medical Research (ICMR) in 1958, this group fixed Rs. 20 per month per capita expenditure at 1960-61 prices as the minimum below which people should be considered as poor. Since then a bewildering variety of estimates based on varying norms have been given by different scholars. According to some of them the incidence of poverty might have increased during the period considered by them, while according to others it might have decreased. It is not necessary for our purpose to give the details of these estimates. A summary table based on them is provided in Annexure-I. According to some of these studies the percentage of people below the poverty line has increased, while according to others it has decreased. One may be more justified in assuming this percentage to be more or less the same.

In due course, the Planning Commission started giving its own estimates of the poverty line. In an exercise made before the formulation of the Draft Five Year Plan 1978–83, the Planning Commission defined the poverty line at the nutritional requirement of 2,435 and 2,095 calories per person per day for rural and urban areas respectively. These were rounded of to 2,400 and 2,100 respectively. Since then they have provided the base for measuring poverty in the country. Poverty line in money terms is defined as the mid-point of the monthly per capita expenditure class having a daily caloric intake of 2,400 per person in rural areas and 2,100 in urban areas. In this way expenditure on non-food items made by the household is also taken into account. The Commission used the distribution of consumer expenditure for 1973–74 as obtained from the data of the 28th round of the National Sample Survey and worked out the poverty line in money terms as Rs. 61.8 and Rs. 71.3 per capita per month for rural and urban areas respectively at 1976-77 prices. On this basis 47.85 per cent of rural, 40.71 per cent of urban and 46.33 per cent of total population were estimated below poverty line in 1977–78. The total number of the poor so defined was estimated to be about 290 million. About 160 million of these were estimated to be so poor as to be below 75 per cent of the poverty line.[1]

The Sixth Plan (1980–85) followed the same base but recalculated the poverty line at 1979–80 prices, taking per capita monthly expenditure of Rs. 76 in rural areas and Rs. 88 in urban areas. On this basis 302.76 million persons were estimated to be living below the poverty line of which 251.66 million were in rural areas and 51.10 million in urban areas in the year 1977–78. These constituted 50.82 per cent of the rural population, 38.19 per cent of the urban population and 48.13 per cent of the total population. The number in 1979–80 was estimated at 316.8 million (48.4%) of which 259.6 million (50.7%) were rural and 57.2 million (40.3%) were urban.[2]

Applying the poverty line norm of the Planning Commission to the NSS data on consumer expenditure from different rounds, it has been found that nearly 50 per cent of our population has been living below the poverty line during 1972-73 to 1979-80. It is also seen that the percentage of people below the poverty line has remained more or less the same. A similar conclusion emerges from an analysis of the data on consumer expenditure from the different rounds of the NSS, given in Table 1. Constancy of the proportion would, however, imply an increase in the number of people below the poverty line over the period because of the growing population.

Table 1. People below the poverty line.

| Area | 1972-73 % | 1976-77 No. (Millions) | % | 1979-80 No. (Million) | % |
|---|---|---|---|---|---|
| Rural | 54.09 | 251.66 | 50.82 | 259.56 | 50.70 |
| Urban | 41.22 | 51.10 | 38.19 | 57.28 | 40.31 |
| All India | 51.49 | 302.76 | 48.13 | 316.84 | 48.44 |

SOURCE: Sixth Plan: Tables 3.33 and 3.35.

The 1981 census revealed a higher rate of growth of population than had been assumed earlier. Accordingly, the Planning Commission in its Mid-term Appraisal of the Sixth Five Year Plan released in August 1983 revised its estimates of persons below the poverty line from the earlier estimate of 316 million to 339 million in 1979-80. This constituted 51.1 per cent of total population.[3] Separate figures for rural and urban were not given. In the same document, the Planning Commission also claimed that the poverty percentage came down to 41.5 and the total number of persons below the poverty line fell to 282 million in 1981-82.[4] In other words, the poverty percentage was reduced by 9.6 per cent over a period of just two years.

This estimate, if correct, would be regarded as an extremely remarkable achievement. But as has been pointed out by several scholars, this claim is not justified.[5] The two assumptions on which it is based are highly questionable. It is difficult to agree with the assumption that the "increase in real income is uniform in all the expenditure classes." Past experience provides no basis for this. Equally untenable is the assumption that "the number of families brought above the poverty line is relatable directly to the corresponding expenditure in IRDP and NRDP." The evaluation studies conducted so far do not provide any justification for such a bold statement. The two programmes, constituted as they are, are incapable of lifting every beneficiary above the poverty line. Some may not be lifted up, but those who are far below the poverty line may be.

Private consumption expenditure does not include the improvements in living standards brought about by public expenditure on social services like education and health which raise the quality of life. Enrolment in elementary education (class I–VIII) has gone up from 32 percent in 1950-51 to 68 percent in 1979-80. But we are still far off from the goal of universal primary education which the Constitution had hoped we would achieve within 10 years. Education has not much relevance for poor people and this is reflected in the high number of drop outs at the school stage. Much of the benefits from infrastructure have accrued largely to the relatively affluent. As regards control of major diseases like small pox, malaria, etc. the situation is much better now; this is also reflected in a significant improvement in the expectation of life at birth from 32 in 1951 to 54 for males and 53 for females in 1981. But the accessibility of several medical facilities for the poor, specially in rural areas, is still very inadequate.

### III. INCOME DISPARITIES

THE SAME problem of non-availability of suitable data arises with respect to distribution of income. It was for this reason that even a powerful committee appointed by the Government of India in 1960 could not reach any definite conclusion on changes in income distribution, though it suggested that inequality during the first decade of planning might have increased somewhat in urban areas and decreased slightly in rural areas.[6] A few researchers have estimated this for particular years. But being based on varying methods, the different estimates are not strictly comparable over time. Mention may, however, be made of the National Council of Applied Economic Reserach's studies for several periods since 1960 using a more or less similar methodology.[7] The NCAER surveys also provide the only source of direct data on household income. The findings, given in Annexures II and III, indicate a slight fall in income disparities in both rural and urban areas. A comparison of the shares of the bottom and the top decile as well as the Lorenz coefficient of concentration indicates that the decline is more marked and continuous in urban than in rural areas. However, it may be said that the urban data do not take account of the phenomenon of black money, widely rampant in the urban areas, which mostly accrues to those in higher income brackets. Further, there is the problem of the differential impact of the price rise which is not captured by these estimates.

In the absence of direct data on income, there have been attempts to get some idea of inter-group income distribution by using data on distribution of private consumption expenditure. Though the NSSO has been undertaking household consumer expenditure surveys since its inception, some differences between reference periods, duration and timing of earlier rounds, etc. stand in the way of a direct comparison of the results over all the rounds. Taking account of such factors the results have been presented for the period 1953-54 to 1977-78 in Annexure IV.

The results suggest a marginal reduction in disparity in the form of increase in the share of bottom 10 and 30 per cent of the population with a corresponding fall in the share of the top 10 and 30 per cent. But the improvement is not large enough to indicate any visible impact. So far as the middle expenditure groups are concerned, their share remains more or less the same. The above conclusions are also borne out by a slight fall in Lorenz concentration ratio during the period 1953-54 to 1973-74 for both urban and rural areas. For the rural areas, the ratio after having increased from 0.334 in 1953-54 to 0.35 in 1954-55 gradually declined to 0.272 in 1973-74. And for the urban area, the ratio after having increased from 0.371 in 1953-54 to 0.402 in 1958-59 declined to 0.304 in 1973-74.[8] "However, because of the highly aggregative nature of higher expenditure groups in the NSS data and possible differential movement of prices of different consumer goods and services constituting the cosumer baskets of individuals falling under different expenditure groups, it is necessary to undertake a more extensive analysis of the price effect before any definite conclusion regarding the trend in distribution can be drawn on the basis of NSS data on household consumer expenditure."[9]

## IV. Employment

THE LIMITED success in redistributing assets might not have mattered as much for poverty reduction had employment increased incomes. However, the pace of generation of employment opportunities seems to have lagged behind the growth in labour force. Precise estimates of unemployment/under-employment over a period of time are not available. But whatever evidence is available points unmistakably to a gradual worsening of the unemployment situation.

The earlier plans used to present data on labour force, employment created during the plan, and the backlog of unemployment at the beginning and end of a plan period. These data are presented in Table 2. It will be seen that the backlog of unemployment went on increasing with every five year plan not only absolutely but also as a percentage of the labour force.

Table 2. Estimates of unemployment 1951–66.

| Plan | Backlog at the beginning of the Plan (Millions) | Backlog at the end of the Plan (Millions) | Unemployed at the end of the Plan as a percentage of labour force |
| --- | --- | --- | --- |
| 1st Plan (1951–56) | 3.3 | 5.3 | 2.7 |
| 2nd Plan (1956–61) | 5.3 | 7.1 | 3.3 |
| 3rd Plan (1961–66) | 7.1 | 9.6 | 4.4 |

SOURCE: Different Five Year Plans.

The calculations contained in the Second, Third and Fourth Plans relating to creation of jobs in the unorganized sector were found to be subject to serious limitations. Hence no specific figures were mentioned about the backlog in the Fifth Plan. However, according to the data given by the Committee Experts on Unemployment (Bhagwati Committee), the number of unemployed in 1971 was 18.7 million which was 10.4 per cent of the labour force. In the assessment of the Fifth Plan also, employment generation during the preceding Fourth Plan (1969–74) did not keep pace with the growth of labour force.[10] Unemployment in March 1978 was estimated by the Planning Commission at 20.6 million of which 16.5 million was rural and 4.1 million urban.[11] It is, therefore, evident that unemployment over the years has been increasing and not decreasing. Further, the Rural Labour Enquiry has shown that between 1964-65 and 1974-75 the number of days for which employment was available for rural labourers declined by 10 per cent for men, 7.5 per cent for women and 5 per cent for children. The data on average earnings from these enquiries when corrected for inflation also show a decline.[12]

A comparison of unemployment rates in 1972-73 and 1977-78 based on data from NSS 27th Round and 32nd Round is difficult because of the change in the coverage of the labour force particularly in the case of the rural females category. The data for categories other than rural females also indicate a deterioration in the overall unemployment situation as seen below. In addition, there has been an increase in the proportion of casual labour and a reduction in self-employment in agriculture during the same period.

Table 3. Daily status and weekly status unemployment rates during 1972-73 and 1977-78 based on NSS 27th and 32nd Rounds.

|  | Unemployment rates* | | | |
|---|---|---|---|---|
|  | Daily status | | Weekly status | |
|  | 1972-73 | 1977-78 | 1972-73 | 1977-78 |
| Rural male | 6.84 | 7.12 | 3.03 | 3.57 |
| Urban male | 8.02 | 9.41 | 5.97 | 7.12 |
| Urban female | 13.63 | 14.55 | 9.18 | 10.92 |

*Unemployment rate is defined as percentage of unemployed (Principal Status) to the corresponding labour force.

SOURCE: *Sixth Plan*, p. 217.

Evidence from other sources based on data from different parts of the economy indicates the same trend towards deterioration. In urban areas, the figures for the number of persons on the live register provide some indication of the trend. These show an increase from 1.6 million in 1960 to 12.7 million in 1978, an increase that is attributable partly to changes in coverage but which, nevertheless, reflects a substantial deterioration in the availability of employment. Registrations per year with employment exchanges have been continuously rising from 32 lakhs in 1961 to 51 lakhs in 1971 to 63 lakhs in 1981 but the proportion of placements has been falling from 14.4% in 1965 to 8% in 1981. A similar trend is revealed for the most disadvantaged group in the country, namely, the scheduled castes and tribes for whom certain posts have been reserved. The number from the scheduled castes and tribes registered with employment exchanges has been steadily going up and totalled 6.37 and 1.61 lakhs respectively during the year 1977. The number of placements effected, however, was only 69 and 26 thousands respectively. With regard to even reserved vacancies, only 55 and 33 per cent respectively were filled despite the fact that a large number of them were waiting for their turn on the live register of employment exchanges.[13]

## V. FUTURE PROSPECTS

THE OVERALL conclusion that emerges from the preceding pages is that the incidence of poverty has remained more or less unchanged. This, in turn, suggests that the absolute magnitude of the poverty problem has been increasing. The number of poor that we are having today is more than what it was at the beginning of the first five year plan in 1951. The implications of this for domestic conflicts are too obvious to require much elaboration.

As regards future prospects, much would depend upon the nature and quantum of efforts to alleviate poverty. Some measures have been taken in the past also. These included creation of additional employment opportunities, distribution of land to rural poor, education and training, and specific schemes for the target group such as the SFDA, the IRDP, and NREP, Programmes for Scheduled Castes and Tribes, etc. But the magnitude of efforts fell far short of requirements as a result of which there was little impact on reduction of poverty. For example, only 26 lakh families in rural areas have benefitted so far from distribution of ceiling surplus land, each beneficiary getting an average of 0.63 hectare of land.[14] This is like a drop in the ocean. It has also been shown that the combined share of plan outlay on all the schemes for the development of the rural poor to total plan outlay has been around 3 to 5 per cent from first to fifth five year plan whereas the rural poor constitute about 40 per cent of the total national population.[15] Further, this deficiency has in no way been mitigated by the flow of funds from other sources such as financial institutions. For example, the cooperative banks which constitute the most important source of institutional finance in rural areas provided only 3 per cent of their credit to the rural poor in the year 1976-77. The share of agricultural labourers was even less than 1 per cent.[16]

As regards future trends, it may be noted that further scope for land transfers to the rural poor is limited. Out of 28.8 lakh hectares of land declared surplus in accordance with the existing legislation, 22.8 lakh hectares have already been taken over by the State.[17] Of the remaining 6 lakh hectares, 4.87 lakh hectares is held up in litigation giving a balance of 1.13 lakh hectares which can be taken possession of immediately.[18] In addition 3.82 lakh hectares already taken possession by the State remain to be distributed. On the past basis of 0.63 hectare per family, 7.86 lakh families can thus be rehabilitated through land transfers and no more. It is possible to acquire more land by lowering the ceiling limit still further. But such a course is not likely to be politically feasible even if it does not have any adverse effect on farm productivity.

Hence the prospect for reduction of poverty in the near future depends upon the extent to which the Government is in a position to take up schemes for providing gainful employment to the poor. This would require a marked step up in the quantum of resources for poverty alleviation programmes. Some beginning, though a very modest one, was made in the Sixth Plan and further advance is expected in the Seventh Plan. However, even then only a fringe of the problem would be touched. Hence more substantial stepping-up is needed if poverty is to be removed in near future, say the next ten years. Given the overall shortage of resources, this would require a diversion of funds from other fields and sectors—an exercise which would raise the question of relative priorities of different objectives. It is only by giving the highest priority to the objective of poverty alleviation that it could be possible to reduce or eliminate the incidence of poverty in the next ten to fifteen years. That may also contribute to a lessening of domestic conflicts.

## ANNEXURE I

### Estimate of Poverty in India

|  | Definition of poverty (Rs. per annum) 1960-61 = 100 | Period | Percentage of population below poverty line Urban | Rural |
|---|---|---|---|---|
| Ahluwalia | 180 | 1956–57 |  | 53.5 |
|  |  | 1960–61 |  | 38.4 |
|  |  | 1965–66 |  | 54.7 |
|  |  | 1967–68 |  | 56.5 |
|  |  | 1970–71 |  | 47.5 |
|  |  | 1973–74 |  | 46.1 |
| Bardhan, P.K. | 180 | 1960–61 |  | 38.0 |
|  |  | 1964–65 |  | 45.0 |
|  |  | 1967–68 |  | 53.0 |
|  |  | 1968–69 |  | 54.0 |
| Dandekar, V.M. and Rath, N. | 180 (Rural) 270 (Urban) | 1961–62 | 50.0 | 40.0 |
| Spru Minhas | 200 | 1960–61 |  | 46 0 |
|  |  | 1964–65 |  | 39.3 |
|  |  | 1967–68 |  | 37.1 |
| Ojha, P.D. | 2250 calories per day | 1960–61 |  | 52.0 |
|  |  | 1967–68 |  | 70.0 |
| Ranadive, K.R. | 240 | 1953–54 | 40.0 | 38.0 |
|  |  | 1956–57 | 52.0 | 39.0 |
|  |  | 1961–62 | 53.0 | 37.0 |

| | | | |
|---|---|---|---|
| Vaidyanathan, A. | 240 | 1960–61 | 59.5 |
| | | 1964–65 | 60.4 |
| | | 1967–68 | 67.8 |
| | | 1960–61 | 58.8 |
| | | 1964–65 | 56.9 |
| | | 1967–68 | 57.8 |
| Vyas, V.S. | 180 | 1954–55 | 65.6 |
| | | 1960–61 | 63.2 |
| | 240 | 1954–55 | 45.5 |
| | | 1960–61 | 38.5 |
| Bhatty (NCAER) | 300 (1968-69=100) | 1968–69 | 56.4 |
| | 360 (1968-69=100) | 1968–69 | 67.1 |

SOURCE: S.A.R. Sastry, "A Survey of Literature on Poverty, Income Distribution and Development," *Artha Vijnana*, March 1980, p. 86.

## ANNEXURE II

Share (per cent) of income claimed by different quintiles in different periods—Rural Household Sector

| Quintile group of households when arranged on an ascending order of household income | 1960 | 1962 | 1964-65 | 1967-68 | 1970-71 | 1975-76 |
|---|---|---|---|---|---|---|
| Bottom quintile | 4.0 | 5.8 | 7.4 | 4.9 | 6.4 | 6.3 |
| Next quintile | 10.1 | 10.3 | 11.8 | 8.3 | 10.7 | 10.6 |
| Next quintile | 14.3 | 14.5 | 15.8 | 12.7 | 15.1 | 15.0 |
| Next quintile | 21.6 | 21.2 | 20.4 | 20.7 | 21.2 | 21.4 |
| Top quintile | 50.0 | 48.2 | 44.6 | 53.4 | 46.6 | 46.7 |
| Lorenz Ratio | 0.42 | 0.41 | 0.35 | 0.46 | 0.38 | 0.39 |

## ANNEXURE III

Share (percent) of income claimed by different quintiles in different periods—Urban Household Sector

| Quintile group of households when arranged on an ascending order of household income | 1960 | 1964-65 | 1967-68 | 1975-76 |
|---|---|---|---|---|
| Bottom quintile | 4.1 | 5.5 | 5.2 | 5.8 |
| Next quintile | 8.4 | 9.6 | 9.2 | 9.8 |
| Next quintile | 12.3 | 12.8 | 13.4 | 14.0 |
| Next quintile | 19.0 | 18.8 | 19.7 | 20.9 |
| Top quintile | 56.2 | 53.9 | 52.5 | 49.5 |
| Lorenz Ratio | 0.49 | 0.46 | 0.45 | 0.42 |

SOURCE: for both Annexures II and III. I.R.K. Sarma, "Recent Trends in the Distribution of Personal Income," a paper submitted to the first National Conference on Social Sciences on Social Science Research and the Problem of Poverty, New Delhi, January 1981.

## ANNEXURE IV

Distribution of total private consumer expenditure by deciles (per cent)

| Decile | 1953-54 | 1957-58 | 1961-62 | 1965-66 | 1970-71 | 1973-1974 | 1977-78 |
|---|---|---|---|---|---|---|---|
| (1) | (2) | (3) | (4) | (5) | (6) | (7) | (8) |

Urban

| | | | | | | | |
|---|---|---|---|---|---|---|---|
| 0–10 | 2.82 | 3.04 | 3.02 | 3.46 | 3.39 | 3.84 | 3.36 |
| 10–20 | 4.00 | 4.28 | 4.42 | 4.70 | 4.67 | 5.18 | 4.67 |
| 20–30 | 4.99 | 5.25 | 5.33 | 5.49 | 5.61 | 5.81 | 5.59 |
| 30–40 | 6.09 | 6.21 | 6.33 | 6.41 | 6.39 | 6.85 | 6.50 |
| 40–50 | 7.01 | 7.26 | 7.15 | 7.24 | 7.28 | 7.56 | 7.39 |
| 50–60 | 8.20 | 8.49 | 8.15 | 8.37 | 8.67 | 8.98 | 8.69 |
| 60–70 | 9.65 | 10.03 | 9.82 | 9.87 | 9.50 | 9.16 | 9.77 |
| 70–80 | 11.83 | 11.94 | 11.64 | 11.65 | 12.01 | 12.05 | 12.31 |
| 80–90 | 16.28 | 15.65 | 15.10 | 15.38 | 17.17 | 15.07 | 14.24 |
| 90–100 | 29.13 | 27.85 | 29.04 | 27.43 | 25.31 | 25.50 | 27.48 |

| (1) | (2) | (3) | (4) | (5) | (6) | (7) | (8) |
|---|---|---|---|---|---|---|---|
| | | | | Rural | | | |
| 0–10 | 3.13 | 3.25 | 3.22 | 3.73 | 3.91 | 3.93 | 3.65 |
| 10–20 | 4.68 | 4.67 | 4.84 | 5.26 | 5.27 | 5.36 | 5.12 |
| 20–30 | 5.66 | 5.62 | 5.71 | 6.13 | 6.20 | 6.86 | 6.24 |
| 30–40 | 6.55 | 6.61 | 6.81 | 6.93 | 7.24 | 7.28 | 6.56 |
| 40–50 | 7.51 | 7.66 | 7.94 | 7.93 | 8.31 | 7.96 | 8.03 |
| 50–60 | 8.60 | 8.75 | 9.16 | 9.14 | 8.78 | 8.88 | 8.66 |
| 60–70 | 10.12 | 10.11 | 10.59 | 10.35 | 10.73 | 10.76 | 9.84 |
| 70–80 | 12.00 | 11.98 | 12.53 | 11.76 | 11.84 | 10.92 | 11.77 |
| 80–90 | 15.14 | 14.84 | 15.43 | 14.21 | 14.46 | 14.77 | 14.55 |
| 90–100 | 26.61 | 26.52 | 23.77 | 24.56 | 23.26 | 23.28 | 25.58 |

SOURCES: *Indian Economic Journal*, Vol. 25 No. 2 October–December 1977, p. 161 and *Sixth Five Year Plan*, p. 51.

## NOTES

1. Planning Commission, Government of India, *Draft Five Year Plan 1978–83*, p. 3 and 50.
2. Planning Commission, Government of India, *Sixth Five Year Plan 1980–85*.
3. Planning Commission, Government of India, *Sixth Five Year Plan, Mid-term Appraisal*, August 1983 p. 8.
4. *Sixth Five Year Plan: Mid-term Appraisal*, op. cit. p. 8.
5. V. Gumaste' "Is Poverty Disappearing," *Financial Express*, 21 June 1983; K. Sundaram and S.D. Tendulkar "Poverty in the Mid-term Appraisal," *Economic and Political Weekly*, 5–12 November 1983; Raj Krishna, "Growth, Investment and Poverty in Mid-term Appraisal of Sixth Plan," *Economic and Political Weekly*, 19 November 1983.
6. Government of India, Planning Commission: Distribution of Income and Wealth and Concentration of Economic Power, Part I, Report of the Committee on Distribution of Income and Levels of Living, 1964, p. 23.
7. I.R.K. Sarma, "Recent Trends in the Distribution of Personal Income," a paper submitted to first National Conference on Social Sciences on Social Science Research and the Problem of Poverty, New Delhi, January 1981.
8. Uma Datta Roy Choudhury, "Income Distribution and Economic Development in India since 1950-51," *The Indian Economic Journal*, Vol, 25, No. 2, October–December 1977, p. 160.
9. Ibid., pp. 163-64.
10. *Draft Fifth Five Year Plan*, Vol. II, p. 267.

11. *Draft Five Year Plan*, 1978–83, p. 81.
12. *Sixth Five Year Plan*, p. 9.
13. Report of the Commissioner for the Scheduled Castes and Scheduled Tribes 1977-78 Part I, p. 38.
14. Government of India, Ministry of Rural Development, *Annual Report* 1983–84, p. 46.
15. Kamta Prasad, "Inadequate and Inequitable Allocation of Resources for the Upliftment of the Rural Poor" in *Social Science Research and the Problem of Poverty*, Indian Association of Social Science Institutions, New Delhi, forthcoming.
16. Reserve Bank of India, Statistical Statement Relating to the Cooperative Movement in India, Part I, Table 32.
17. Government of India, Ministry of Rural Development, *Annual Report* 1983–84, p. 46.
18. *The Sixth Five Year Plan: Mid-term Appraisal*, August 1983, pp. 53–54.

CHAPTER THREE

# 'New' Economic Policy of Sri Lanka
## Coflicts and Contradictions

## Girijesh Pant

THE ECONOMICS of conflicts and crisis that Sri Lanka is experiencing today can be explained in terms of the structure of the economy and its ideological orientation. Like many developing countries, the economy of Sri Lanka also faces structural limitation in initiating a self-generating process of growth. Evolved around the plantation sector, the economy suffers from structural dualism, ethnic pluralism, weak social cohesion and consumption orientation based on metropolitan standards.[1] It lacks adequate surplus to be ploughed back to sustain a growth rate which could transform the economy into an organic whole. Hence it is understandable it has been trying to import critical inputs to accelerate the pace of growth and development. Though there can hardly be any dispute in Sri Lankan efforts to interact with the global system what needs scrutiny is the premise on which the effort is based. The new economic regime which came into being in 1977, seems to believe in an open door policy. It assumes a relationship between local and external economy based on the market ideology. It also assumes free flow of capital and technology and freedom for its deployment. Though apparently it believes in non-interventionist state, though quite often the State has been asked to play a critical role for creating a conducive climate for the growth of market forces. However, the performance of the open door economic regime during the last seven years does not indicate that the economy has been able to overcome its structural constraints. On the contrary, it appears that during this regime the structural limitation has become more pronounced, sharpening its contradiction, thereby creating grounds for a crisis that has acquired a dimension threateting the very foundation of the economy and society. The central thesis of this paper is that externally oriented economic policy is more likely to sharpen the structural contradiction causing greater stability threat to the system for the developing countries particularly.

## I

THE BEGINNING of export-led era in Sri Lankan economy in 1977 needs to be understood in terms of the socio-economic forces operating in the society. The regime that came into power after independence was dominated by a coalition of merchant capital and petty burgeoisie with incipient industrial capital. Since merchant capital is not concerned with the development of production process, and thrives on exchange economy, it was natural that the UNP Government promoted a policy soft towards foreign capital and heavily based on exports. "Deriving its power base from the urban commercial and propertied class, it did not wish to adopt a policy of import substitution in regard to manufactured goods since this would have caused dislocation of trade of the former and discomfort to the consumption of the latter."[2] However, the merchant class in Sri Lanka is not ethnically homogeneous. It is argued that during the colonial days, Sinhala merchant capital was discriminated against the Tamil merchant,[3] hence all the policies of the governments since independence have been directed to mitigate these disadvantages. "The general thrust of policies pursued by the UNP as well as the SLF government was in the same direction. State intervention or use of political process to reallocate economic resources and opportunities to the advantage of the politically strategic group vis-a-vis the traditional upper class and the ethnic religious minorities. The policies were aimed at helping the small entrepreneurs, traders, farmers, etc."[4] Consequently, a new class of businessmen came into existence which has been able to acquire wealth much more than those who have been having control over plantation for over hundred years.[5]

However, the success of these policies in an export-dominated economy lies with the external market. In the period when external market has been buoyant, like during the Korean war, the ruling government did not find it difficult to promote the interest of Sinhala merchant capital without hurting other interest, but whenever there has been crash, the brunt has fallen either on minority or on poor stratum of the society. The 1977 regime came against the backdrop of a stagnating economy, affecting both to the mercantile class as well as to the people. It was projected that all the problems of the economy were due to state domination and the return of market forces would provide all cure. Thus, a free market-oriented, export-led regime came in 1977 with growth as the major item on its agenda. Some of the important steps taken by the government to obtain its objective are summarized below:[6]

(i) devalued the currency, thus making inputs more expensive and export cheaper in rupee terms;

(ii) removed administrative controls and liberalized imports and payments, opened the economy to liberal imports and ended the state monopoly in imports except in a restricted number of basic food stuffs;

(iii) lifted price controls and placed greater reliance on the market mechanism, effected a shift from quantitative restriction on imports to tariffs as a means of protecting domestic industry;

(iv) moved towards a free market economy by directing state corporations to establish 'realistic' price level, most products manufactured by the state sector have increased prices, services like electricity, post, public transport have raised their tariffs and fares;

(v) created a favourable climate for foreign investment and foreign aid; established the necessary machinery to set up the Free Trade Zones; subsidized investment for tourism, the Free Trade Zone, house building and industry, generous tax reductions have been given to encourage savings and investment on both local and foreign development projects;

(vi) in order to encourage greater savings, increased the rate of interest on bank deposit over 20 per cent. Invited new foreign banks to open branches;

(vii) ended a number of subsidies, e.g. the free rice ration has been withdrawn from families with an income of over 300 rupees for a month. This constituted virtually half the population in January 1978. Instead of the rice ration, food stamps are said to have been issued to those whose family incomes are below Rs. 300 per month;

(viii) handed over partially to private sector bodies, such as agency houses, the management of publicly owned enterprises, e.g. textile—or entered into joint ventures with foreign companies, e.g. Tyre Corporation, National Milk Board, etc.;

(ix) sought assistance from World Bank and the IMF and other donor countries for its economic development scheme like the Mahaweli, Housing, Free Trade Zones, as well as to generate foreign exchange support necessary to maintain an open economy.

From the select check list of the various steps taken by the government, it becomes apparent that trade, foreign investments and aid are the key variables for growth in the current policy. However, the total commitment of the regime to growth-manship, the GDP shows a decline in its growth rate after initial rise as shown by the Table 1. In terms of constant price at 1970 level, it shows that after 1978, there has been continuously decline leading to fall in the growth rate of per capita income also.[7]

Table 1. Growth rate of the economy (Rs. in million).

|  | 1977 | 1978 | 1979 | 1980 | 1981 | 1982 | 1983 |
|---|---|---|---|---|---|---|---|
| GDP at current factor cost prices | 34686 (23.7) | 40479 (16.7) | 49789 (23.0) | 62246 (25.0) | 79337 (15.5) | 91643 (15.5) | 111353 (21.5) |
| GDP at constant 1970 factor cost price | 16079 (4.2) | 17401 (8.2) | 18501 (6.3) | 19575 (5.8) | 20706 (5.8) | 21756 (5.1) | 22824 (4.9) |
| GNP per capita (a) Current price | 2470 (22.1) | 2836 (14.8) | 3424 (21.7) | 2194 (22.5) | 5187 (23.7) | 5900 (13.7) | 7017 (18.9) |
| (b) Constant price | 1143 (2·8) | 1221 (6.8) | 1274 (4.3) | 1320 (2.6) | 1353 (2.5) | 1398 (3.3) | 1432 (2.4) |

Figures in parentheses are percentage growth rates.
SOURCE: Central Bank of Ceylon Annual Report, 1983.

To understand the emerging socio-economic tensions of Sri Lanka, it will be relevant to look at the composition of the national wealth and the changes that have occurred during these years. From the available estimates of income distribution, it appears that there has been significant erosion of income for the lowest group, while the highest group has increased its share from 29.9 per cent to 39 per cent between 1973 and 79. A few significant points that emerge from Table 2 are: predominance of the trade over manufacturing, phenomenal rise of imports, and quantum jump in allocation for the public administration and defence. Ironically, despite its efforts to boost exports, the share of exports processing in the manufacturing declined from 35 per cent to 25 per cent between 1977 and 1983. As pointed out by the Annual Report of the Central Bank of Ceylon, the manufacturing sector grew by less than one per cent in 1983. What is more alarming is the increasing volume of outflow of net factor income abroad. It shows a rise by more than 42 per cent in one year alone between 1982 and 1983. This has been largely on account of repatriation of dividends and profit accruing to the private foreign capital. The increasing burden of this can be felt by the fact that in 1977 net factor income from abroad was −252 million rupees, while in 1983 it was −3164 million ruppees.

Table 2. Sectoral composition of GDP at constant (1970) factor cost price in percentage 1977 and 1983.

| Sector | 1977 | 1983 | %change |
|---|---|---|---|
| Agricultural | 24.7 | 21.8 | 25.6 |
| Mining quarrying | 14.6 | 13.0 | 55.3 |
| Manufacturing | 14.6 | 13.0 | 26.3 |
| Construction | 3.8 | 4.5 | 65.3 |
| Trade | 18.6 | 19.7 | 50.1 |
| Imports | 3.2 | 4.6 | 103.5 |
| Exports | 4.1 | 3.5 | 20.1 |
| Domestic trade | 11.3 | 11.7 | 46.0 |
| Public admn. and Defence | 4.9 | 6.3 | 81.9 |
| Service | 13.1 | 12.9 | 41.3 |

SOURCE: Central Bank of Ceylon Annual Report, 1983.

Increasing pressure of global obligations on Sri Lanka economy can be seen by the mounting debt burden and debt services payments. The total external public debt outstanding including undisbursed is estimated at $3403.1 million in 1982 of which only $1833 million was disbursed. Though there has been rapid rise in aid commitment since 1977, the disbursement rate has been quite low. While disbursement rate has been 100 per cent in case of food aid, and near-complete in case of commodity aid, it has been going down in case of project aid from 26.2 per cent in 1978 to 14.7 per cent in 1981. Several reasons have been identified for this. What is not sufficiently brought out is that such conditions are created by the so called donor countries to have more manoeuvring power with them. This leverage gets further enhanced in view of the rising burden of debt service payments faced by Sri Lanka. The World Bank estimates are that by 1986 the debt service payment will touch a figure of $460 million as against $108.5 million in 1977, i.e. more than four times (Table 3). The projection does not include debt services on loans that is likely to be contracted, after 1983. To that extent it underestimates the debt service liability. Under two different sets of assumptions, it is calculated that this service burden will range between 21.2 to 26.8 per cent of total exports of Sri Lanka. Even commitment is not likely to be as high as it has been so far. "The prospects for foreign aid, however are much less propitious than they have been in the past and there are doubts as to whether Sri Lanka would in future receive foreign aid on the same scale as before."[8]

Table 3. External debt services payment 1977–1986 (in $ million).

| Year | Debt service | Year | Debt service |
|------|--------------|------|--------------|
| 1977 | 108.5 | 1982* | 257.0 |
| 1978 | 122.2 | 1983* | 245.0 |
| 1979 | 113.0 | 1984* | 290.0 |
| 1980 | 121.8 | 1985* | 365.0 |
| 1981 | 116.3 | 1986* | 465.0 |

*Projection.
SOURCE: World Bank Report on Sri Lanka, 1982.

The repaying capability of Sri Lanka is tied up with exports, which is dominated by three commodities, namely, tea, rubber and coconut accounting for more than 50 per cent of the total exports. Given the nature of the global market of these products, Sri Lanka cannot conceive of meeting its future obligation only with these exports, particularly when the trade balance has been showing a continuous increase in deficit since 1978. Though the rise in global tea prices have been helpful, yet the fact cannot be ignored that in volume Sri Lanka's tea export was lowest recorded since 1956. Similarly, there has been decline in exports of rubber in volume-term. On the import side, the share of consumer goods remains the critical item, increasing its share of 21 per cent in 1982 to 26 per cent in 1983. While there has been decline in the share of intermediate and investment goods from 50 per cent to 48 per cent and 28 per cent to 27 per cent, respectively. The increase in consumer goods has been also due to increased import of sugar and items such as food products and textiles.

In view of the structural deficiency in the export-import sector, it is argued by the World Bank that at least in the short run Sri Lanka's Government should tighten its budget. Since it would not be desirable to cut the investment, so it is the consumer subsidies and transfers that should be cut drastically. Taking cue from the World Bank, the Government has reduced the food subsidy and has introduced a scheme of food stamps. The share of food subsidy/ stamp in the government revenue has come down from 23.6 per cent to 10.5 per cent between 1977 to 1981, though the total subsidy remains 18.9 per cent compared to 35.7 per cent during the same period. Subsidy by itself cannot be taken as a criterion of welfare, in fact, it has been used by the ruling classes as an instrument to appease the people. The point that needs attention is that even this capability and choice no more remains with the ruling classes of Sri Lanka. Subsidy on fertilizers have however been increased to meet the rising prices. It is observed that the new variety of the paddy is highly sensitive to fertilizer, hence any cut in fertilizer intake is likely to influence the yield. Since the consumption of fertilizer is also related to the element of subsidy, it has, therefore, become essential for the ruling regime to continue to subsidize the fertilizer to maintain the paddy output. The so called self-reliance in the paddy sector is thus achieved by creating a new structure of dependency.

The government in Sri Lanka is constructing fertilizer plants and warehousing facilities with the help of foreign companies and technology as is being done in other Third World countries. The successful running of these units cannot be guaranteed in a socially disturbed situation and in the absence of adequate maintenance facilities. The production of state-owned urban factory at Sapugaskanda fell by 41 per cent in 1983 compared to 1982. According to the Central Bank of Ceylon Annual Report 1983: "This drop was mainly due to the frequent failures with interrupted production in the first half and the complete shut down of the plant from October through mid-November for maintenance."[9] It is important to note that in one stage in 1981 even the financial viability of the factory was in question after commencing production. Thus, imports became the only alternative. The weak infrastructure of distribution has further forced the economy to rely on foreign companies. The Ceylon Bank Report further says; "The work initiated in collaboration with local and foreign participation to improve the distribution of fertilizer at retail-level made good progress in 1983 as did the construction of retail fertilizer stores in different parts of the country with the assistance from Federal Republic of Germany and the Food and Agricultural Organization."[10] It is estimated that imported inputs account for 40 per cent of the paddy production cost and 60 per cent of cash cost, and 50 per cent of the agriculture budget is based on foreign aid. To understand the dynamics of emerging conflicts and contradictions in the agriculture sector of the economy it becomes necessary to make its brief appraisal.

The export-led regime has further enhanced the critical significance of plantation sector in Sri Lanka. Ironically, despite the total support from the State and the World Bank, the tree crop sector has been showing a continuous decline from 1977. As Table 4 shows, both tea and rubber registered negative growth rates. It is only the paddy which has been maintaining a secular rise except 1982.

In terms of social dynamics, this variation in the growth rate between the plantation and the paddy sub-sector suggests reversal of power balance when compared to period 1970–77. The average growth rate of paddy in 1970–77 was only 0.5 per cent as against 6.4 per cent in 1978–83. In contrast, the average rate of growth for plantation sector was 2.1 per cent in 1970–77 and 0.4 per cent in 1978–83. This obviously suggests the gains of the new regime have gone more in favour of peasant sector than plantation sector.

Table 4. Growth rate of agriculture and its main components 1977–83 (at constant 1970 factor cost prices).

|  | 1978 | 1979 | 1980 | 1981 | 1982 | 1983 | Average 1978–83 |
|---|---|---|---|---|---|---|---|
| Agriculture | 5.4 | 1.9 | 3.1 | 6.9 | 2.6 | 5.1 | 4.16 |
| (a) Tea | −4.3 | 3.5 | −7.5 | 9.9 | −10.7 | −4.5 | −2.3 |
| (b) Rubber | 5.6 | −0.8 | −13.0 | −6.7 | 0.5 | 8.8 | −.9 |
| (c) Coconut | 15.4 | 6.3 | −11.0 | 11.5 | 11.3 | −7.8 | 4.3 |
| (d) Paddy | 12.7 | 1.4 | 11.9 | 3.6 | −3.3 | 12.3 | 6.4 |

SOURCE: Central Bank of Ceylon Report 1983.

The poor performance of the plantation sector has been attributed by the World Bank to "past neglect during years of uncertainty associated with the anticipation and then implementation of nationalization and land reform, continued managerial and industrial weaknesses and failure to fully implement liberalization and producers' incentives policies."[11] Consequently, it has suggested further liberalization and strengthening of incentive policy, streamlining of management particularly of public sector corporations which are responsible for about 80 per cent of total tea production and about one-third of rubber output. Some other salient features of the agriculture policy of the regime include greater inflow of foreign and private capital into the sector specially in the dry zone, promotion of agro-based industries, and greater intensification in the use of land, water and other resources.

## II

STRUCTURAL changes initiated during last six years of export-led regime are now impinging on polity and society at various levels in different dimension. Paradoxically, the regime which came into power on the agenda of growthmanship is facing declining trend in the size of national produce itself. After the initial rise, the growth rate has been going down progressively from 1979 onwards. In 1977-78 the incremental value of the gross national produce at

1970 constant factor cost was Rs.1395 million, but in the year 1982-83 it came down to Rs. 847 million only, i.e. a fall by more than 60 per cent in six years. Certainly an underdeveloped plural society like Sri Lanka does not have the resilience to bear this sharp fall. More important is the fact that even the present growth is due to imports than exports. The share of imports in the GDP has gone up, while that of exports have come down. While exports have gone up by 20 per cent during this time interval, the imports have shown a rise of more than 100 per cent. The impact of the open door regime on industrial sector so far has been negative. While the industrial structure built under protected regime has suffered adversely due to penetration of foreign commodities, the export-oriented industries have yet to show a sign of vitality despite the investment paradises. In 1977-78, the manufacturing sector had maintained a growth rate of 8 per cent but in 1982-83 it came down to only 0.8 per cent. This growth rate was largely because average capacity utilization increased from 60 to 70 per cent. In contrast, the decline in growth rate of trading sector was not so sharp—i.e. from 9 per cent to 5.3 per cent in the same period. Within the manufacturing sector, factory industry shows a decline from 13.2 to 2 per cent and export processing sector shows a negative growth rate in 1981-82 and 1982-83. The industries which are facing market erosion are water coolers, footwear, motor spares, suitcases, plastic toys, etc. Some industries are even facing closure; these include textile printing, radio assembly, sweaters and jerseys, etc. Light engineering goods, bicycle, and automobile components have been exposed to the problem of dumping.[12]

The economy is further polarized by the adverse affect of open competition on small scale industry. It is pointed out by a Survey of Small Scale Industrial Establishment conducted by the Central Bank that a number of small scale units were closed down because of their inability to face competition. Their inability to obtain capital further contributed to their decline. The most affected industries include paper, fabricated metal products, pottery and cane products.[13] The significance of these units needs to be seen in their employment generation potential and usage of local raw materials as against high import content of the modern units.

As pointed out earlier, foreign investment is a critical factor in export-led regime, The government undertook a number of measures to attract foreign capital. Free Trade Zones were created to provide advantage of cheap labour and raw material. A number of Investment Protection Agreements were signed to create confidence among the prospective investors from USA, UK, South Korea, Singapore, Switzerland, etc. Greater Colombo Economic Commission (GCEC) and Foreign Investment Advisory Committee (FIAC) are in charge of maintaining the inflow of foreign capital. As Table 5 shows, there has been a steady rise in the investment as well as in employment.[14]

Table 5. Investment promotion zone—employment and export earnings.

|  | 1979 | 1980 | 1981 | 1982 | 1983 |
|---|---|---|---|---|---|
| Employment | 5884 | 10581 | 19921 | 22606 | 26053 |
| Gross export earning (Rs. mn.) | 152.1 | 524.3 | 1108.7 | 1653.1 | 2419.5 |

SOURCE: Central Bank of Ceylon Report, 1979 to 1983.

However, in the absence of data, it is difficult to say as to how much is the net gain for Sri Lanka. The World Bank estimates are that most of the plants that have come up in these zones have very high import content. "Nor is there any evidence that any of the existing or agreed projects will make much contribution to the technological capability in Sri Lanka, since the requirements are confined mostly to unskilled or semi-skilled machine minding, assembling or basic tailoring labour. The overall contribution to employment is also expected to be modest."[15] According to one estimate, of the Rs. 152.1 million gross earning in the year 1979, the value added only 26 per cent, i.e. Rs. 30.7 million, the balance 74 per cent was the cost of raw material imports. From the 26 per cent value added Sri Lanka earned about 16 per cent, i.e. Rs. 19 million. Thus out of gross export earning of Rs. 152.1 million, it is only Rs. 19 million that comes to Sri Lanka. This minimizes the foreign exchange earning capabilities of these FTZs.[16]

Similarly, it is difficult to say that the FTZ's have helped in allocating foreign investment and in diversifying the industrial base. The dominant industry in these FTZ's are the garment industries accounting about 79 per cent of export earnings in 1983. The garment industry developed in Sri Lanka much before the FTZ came into existence. With the establishment of these zones, the local producers started to make use of the facilities given in their zones.[17] The World Bank Study also maintains that the range of industrial activities in these zones does not suggest that any new kind of industries have come up. "It could be argued that it is Sri Lanka's natural economic advantage (low wages, educated labour, raw materials and location) which interest foreign investors, and that the removal of constraints such as import and exchange controls and removal of the anti-private and especially anti-foreign investment bias was in itself sufficient to stimulate the inflow of foreign investment. If this is correct, then the only significant factor affecting the decision as to whether to seek GCEC status would appear to be the possibility of maintaining majority control and possibily freedom from personal tax for expatriate working for GCEC units. If so, the GCEC approach, with its special infrastructure and administration would appear to be an *expensive method of attracting* just these firms which insist on majority ownership."[18] (emphasis added) From the kind of industries that are coming up in the region, it appears that a major breakthrough is still a distant possibility, only redeeming feature is the cheap labour. As Table 6 shows, wages in Sri Lanka are the lowest when compared with other labour abundant economies of Asia.

Table 6. Average labour cost (US $ per hour).

| Country | Unskilled | Labour cost Semiskilled | Skilled |
|---|---|---|---|
| India (Santa Cruz) | 0.14 | 0.20 | 0.29 |
| Malaysia | 0.28 | 0.31 | 0.62 |
| Philippines | 0.21 | 0.24 | 0.25 |
| South Korea | — | 1.30 | — |
| Sri Lanka | 0.13 | 0.16 | 0.19 |
| Taiwan | 0.52 | — | 0 60 |

SOURCE: Jean Currie, "Investment, the Growing Role of Export Processing Zones," The Economist Intelligence Unit Ltd., London, June 1979.

Given the proper climate, industrial production process from Korea and Taiwan are likely to move to Sri Lanka because these two economies are restructuring their industrial base by vacating labour-intensive production processes in favour of capital-intensive process. However, the process of shifting of these units is linked with the global market conditions. Since there is not enough evidence to suggest an early and speedy recovery of the Western economies, the prospects of restructuring are not very bright. Thus, a new crisis situation is emerging in Sri Lanka, where the domestic industrial base is getting eroded without any substitution from export-oriented industries.

Since flow of foreign capital is dependent on cheap labour, hence it has become obligatory for government to keep the wages frozen irrespective of price level. This puts the government in a dilemma—if it freezes wages, it loses politically and any upward movement of wages affects her economic survival. If the present trends are any indication, the regime is likely to weigh its decision in favour of former which means political structure of the society will have to be adjusted to meet the economic needs. In passing it may be mentioned that most of the successful free trade zones are located in those countries where state structure is not democratic, e.g., South Korea, Singapore, etc. Ironically today UNP's Sri Lanka is far from the tranquility which is so dear to foreign capital.

Impact of these structural changes can be seen on the employment generating capability of the economy. Agriculture is the primary source of employment, accounting for more than 45 per cent of labour force, followed by manufacturing providing jobs to about 12 per cent of the labour force. The available estimates indicate that after maintaining significant rise in the initial year, there is a tendency towards decline. In fact, during the year 1982, there was a negative growth of about 8 per cent as against more than 9 per cent rise in 1977-78.[19] This decline has been because of fall in employment generation in the private sector. This suggests that the impact of open economy on employment has not been significantly positive. Even the state sector shows a marginal growth. The employment potentials of the FTZ are also not very definite. According to one estimate, cost of one job creation in the zone is about Rs. 45,000.[20] In a country like Sri Lanka, where literacy rate is very high, with the past experience of 1971, a regime cannot afford to ignore the employment situation.

The growth strategy has also magnified the structural weakness of the labour market by creating new demands for skilled manpower. According to the survey conducted by the Manpower Planning Division of the Ministry of Plan Implementation, the economy is facing shortage of skilled manpower, particularly in executing high skilled intensive projects like Mahaveli Development Project. The outflow of skilled labour, which is encouraged by the high wages in the Gulf market, is reported to have got new impetus due to ethnic crisis prevailing in the country. It is observed that "one of the biggest problems for development here is going to be the human flight."[21] Thus, a new kind of pressure is developing which adds to the constraints faced by Sri Lanka in implementing its export-led strategy.

The impact of export-led regime has been rather more decisive in sharpening the contradictions of agriculture sector in Sri Lanka.[22] It has exposed the obsolescence of the plantation sector and exploded the longstanding myth about the efficiency of the plantation sector. Studies on the subject have shown that the efficiency of the plantation sector has been dependent on wages. Once wages started moving up, there has been a decline in producer's margin even recording negative gains. In contrast to the colonial period when the plantation workers were better placed than the peasant sector, the trend has been reversed. Today, wages are lower in the plantation sector where Indian Tamils are the major work force than in the peasant sector where Sinhalese dominate. Though the discriminatory trend can be traced back to earlier period, it was in 1982 that the Wage Board reversed the pattern by fixing wages for tea worker at Rs. 18.50 from Rs. 4.51, while that of rubber worker was revised from Rs. 2.65 to Rs. 19.76. In fixing allowances also, the Tamil workers are put in a disadvantageous position. Plant workers are paid 3 cents for every 1.8 point increase in the cost of living, while workers in other sectors are paid Rs. 2 per point increase. In 1967, when all daily paid workers were paid 40 cents as an Interim Devaluation Allowance, plantation workers got it at 30 cents. Similarly, for rubber workers price-wage supplement was fixed in 1971, but for tea workers in April 1975. It was fixed 30 cents per day when the price of tea was Rs. 6.60 per kg, but since then it has increased to Rs. 70 per kg, but it is still fixed at the 1975 prices.[23]

Consequently, the plantation sector is facing crisis. While it has been stagnating in terms of area under cultivation, the production has been declining touching an all-time record of only 179 million kg in 1983 compared to 214 million kg in 1975. Productivity too has been declining. Though wages are under revision and the workers have successfully got interim raise through their strike in April this year, this sector has been facing the problem of labour shortage since the signing of Srimano-Shastri Pact. The ethnic riots have accelerated the process. Government's efforts to attract Sinhalese workers in the plantation sector has not been succesful. Moreover, to attract the Sinhalese workers, the wage structure will have to be at par with the market wages which the sector cannot sustain. One method, it is suggested, of checking the migration of Indian Tamils could be to convert plantation into petty commodity production unit but this will not be accepted due to political reasons.

In the peasant sector, availability of modern inputs and methods have accelerated the process of differentiation of peasantry. Though family labour continues, yet the farmer has to go to market to procure the modern inputs which forces him to participate in market exchange. It is expected that this will contribute in promoting capitalist mode of production. Since the government is trying to initiate this process with the help of foreign capital, the nature of capitalist development is dependent on international capital. It is obvious this also makes the sector sensitive to global price structure. Imported inflation is likely to further skew the uneven distribution and contribute to the process of pauperization of small farmer. This is seen in more definite terms in case of coconut, which has been the monopoly of Sinhala middle class farmer. An export-led regime has to, by its logic, live with the fluctuation in global price structure over which it has no control. In Sri Lanka roughly half of the price indices are said to be comprised of traded goods. Thus, the movement of global price index and exchange rate have very decisive bearing on the domestic economy.

The poor performance of the export sector and inadquate flow of international investment has further widened the resource gap of the economy. The increasing reliance of the economy on foreign finance can be seen from Table 7. In 1977, the share of foreign finance in the budget deficit was 59 per cent, but it is likely to reach 86 per cent in the year 1984.[24]

It is significant to note that this budget deficit has been increasing despite the heavy cut made by the government in food subsidy and other social welfare activities like education and health. In 1977,

Table 7. Foreign finance as percentage of budget deficit (Rs. million).

| | 1977 | 1978 | 1979 | 1980 | 1981 | 1982 | 1983 | 1984 |
|---|---|---|---|---|---|---|---|---|
| 1. Budget deficit | 3074 | 7165 | 8791 | 16274 | 14866 | 20091 | 23385 | 16543 |
| 2. Foreign finance | 1779 | 4454 | 4237 | 6735 | 8208 | 8794 | 14024 | 14175 |
| (2) as % of (1) | 58.5 | 62.1 | 48.2 | 41.4 | 55.2 | 43.4 | 59.9 | 85.6 |

SOURCE: Central Bank of Ceylon Annual Report, 1983.

the government spent Rs.1424.1 million on food subsidy but in the year 1982 it is reported to be around Rs.100 million, which means 21.7 per cent of the total current expenditure in 1977 and 0.51 per cent in 1982. Similarly, share of health and education have also gone down from 6.09 per cent to 4.92 and 13.13 per cent to 10.56 per cent, respectively during the same years.[25] The inference that flows from these policy decisions is quite obvious. The resource gap is being reduced by cutting the costs of social benefits. The political consequences of such policies are likely to be quite decisive because, unlike many third world countries, in Sri Lanka, food subsidy and other social services are being given since the Second World War days and have become highly politicized issues over the years. Subsidies have been used by the ruling governments to minimize the impact of global cyclical changes on people's consumption, "a protection which present policy, with IMF prodding, precludes."[26]

Conflict situation thus has emerged in the economy largely due to the constitutional limitation of Sinhala merchant capital, which has of late gained the ascendancy. It has not been able to create and promote institutional structure to accommodate the emerging forces of underdevelopment in a plural society. On the contrary its solvency is eroding very fast as can be seen by its incapability to mobilize domestic resources and increasing dependence on foreign finance. It has sought collaboration with the international capital at a time when the economies of the North are not in a position to extend all the wherewithal which is needed to sustain the export-led regime. Unfortunately for Sri Lanka, its geo-strategic location is not comparable to the so called Newly Industrialized Countries of Asia which have, it seems, influenced the policy planners in Sri Lanka. Naturally, Sinhalese chauvanism remains the only instrument of political legitimacy when it is finding difficult to meet the developmental aspirations of the people.

The present ethnic crisis has further confounded the situation by projecting the weakness of the ruling government even as a law and order administrator. The economic regime of Sri Lanka, since the days of independence has been favourably disposed towards Sinhalese merchant capital and to rich peasantry. The hostility towards Indian Tamils can be traced back to the colonial days. As pointed out by one Indian Tamil activist: "The poor Indian estate labourer is viewed as having been an instrument and an abetter through whose help the Britishers managed to develop those lands and to continue a profitable proposition the planting industry of the island."[27] It is argued that the Tamils of Sri Lanka faced the economic deprivation because it was they who gained the most out of the 'modernization process' introduced by the Britishers particularly the English education system. Therefore, they were the main loser when Sinhalese became the national language with all its ramifications. Thus "the character of the Tamil demand on the nationality issue has been determined by the necessity for the middle class Tamils to stay outside the Tamil areas because of their employment, trade or profession. The deceasing opportunities for such gainful occupation coupled with the realization of the economic potentials of the Tamil area, especially after the boost, the cultivation of subsidiary crops received in the seventies, are tending to make even such groups support for demand for a 'Separate Existence'."[28] As pointed out earlier, the wage structure has been made biased against the Tamil workers. The ethnic bias of the State policy can be seen again by the areas where the subsidies are given for fruit crop development. Areas like Kurunegala, Manaragala, Kalutura Badulla, Ratanpura, Ganpana, where Sinhala population is about 70 per cent, are the major beneficiary of the scheme. The first two districts where Sinhala population is more than 90 per cent alone account for more than 50 per cent of the scheme.[29]

The adverse effect of these ethnic conflicts has started becoming visible on the economy. The wholesale price index has gone up from 283.3 in 1982 to 354.1 in 1983, making a growth rate of 25 per cent. The item which recorded the highest rise was petroleum products followed by food items like vegetables, meat, coconut, etc. On the other hand, the sources of income like the tourism have shown a decline from Rs. 3,050 million in 1982 to Rs. 2,500 million in 1983, i.e. a decline by 18 per cent.[30] It is reported to have further decreased by 50 per cent in the first six months of 1984. This was the first time since 1971 that the positive trend in tourist traffic growth was reversed. Though there has been some decline in rate of growth, however this sharp fall has pushed it down to the sixth place as foreign exchange earner. The Central Bank of Ceylon in the Annual Report for 1983 admits that this has been due to July disturbances. "The effect of the July disturbances on arrival figures is clearly evident by the fact that during the first six months of 1983 tourist arrival increased by 10 percent compared with the same period of the previous years but decreased by 45 percent for the latter six months." The hotel occupancy during December-January 1985 was only 55.1 as against the expectation of 80 per cent. According to the World Bank assessment the loss of "Industrial machinery, plant and equipment alone was about $75 million, total damage including retail outlets and housing may have amounted to $300 million."[31] The adverse affect of civil disturbance on the investment climate has also started becoming visible. The figures from Foreign Investment Advisory Committee, an agency which works for attracting foreign capital, recovered that in 1984 the number of approvals given by FIAC was down to 56 as against 98 a year earlier. The investment in 1984 is reported to have dropped to Rs. 3 billion from Rs. 7.5 billion in the previous year. Reports regarding postponement of investment are also coming. Coastal fisheries which accounts for 85 of annual catch has also been affect by the disturbances. The economic consequence of the ethnic disturbance is best summed up by the finance Minister: "We cannot continue like this. Our earning from tourism have already declined. Foreign investment will decrease. Foreign aid will become more and more difficult to obtain. As a result there will be unemployment and economic distress."[32]

As against the declining solvency the burden of maintaining law and order has increased in exponential proportion. It is estimated that during 1984, the capital expenditure on defence was nearly 60% higher than the 1983 provisional figure, which itself was 82.7% higher than the 1982 expenditure. It is obvious that this shift in resource allocation is taking place at the cost of welfare expenditure.[33]

Sri Lankan economy, it can be concluded under, the export-led regime has got further tied up with the fortune of the global economy on which it has little control. The domestic economy is losing its strength; hence for its survival it will have to increasingly surrender its national autonomy to get the necessary resources to underwrite the needs of the system. But there is no certainty, at least in the near future that it will be able to get incorporated into the global market system. On the contrary the economy has got further segmented and differentiated by sharpening the ethnic and class division.

### NOTES

1. See for details George L. Beckford, *Persistent Poverty* (New Delhi, 1964).
2. Satchi Ponnambalam, *Dependent Capitalism in Crisis: Sri Lankan Economy 1948-1980*, p. 23.
3. See for details, Kumari Jayawardena, "Some Aspects of Class and Ethnic Consciousness in Sri Lanka in the late 19th and early 20th Century" in Ethnicity and Social Change in Sri Lanka. Collection of papers presented at Seminar Organized by the Social Scientists Association, Dec. 1979, Colombo, 1984.
4. A.R.M. Masihur Rahman, Political Economy of Income Distribution: An Enquiry Into Social Change and Public Policy in Sri Lanka. Unpublished thesis submitted to the Flectcher School of Law and Diplomacy, Princeton, 21 Oct. 1980, pp. 311-312.
5. H.N.S. Karunatillake, "Income and Wealth Distribution Strategies in Sri Lanka," *Central Bank of Ceylon Staff Studies*, Vol. 6, No. 1, 1976.
6. T. Balasurnya, "Sri Lanka Economy in Crisis," *Logos*, Vol. 20, No. 2, June 1981, pp. 31-32.
7. Central Bank of Ceylon Annual Report 1983.
8. "Sri Lankan Economy," *Economic Review*, Jan-March 1984, Colombo, p. 14.
9. Ibid., p. 28.
10. Ibid., p. 28.
11. World Bank Report on Sri Lanka, 1982, p. 33.
12. "Sri Lanka: Policies and Prospects for Economic Adjustment," World Bank Document, May 1981, p. 90.
13. Ibid., p. 93.

14. Central Bank of Ceylon Report 1979.
15. Note 12, p. 96.
16. Tissa Balasuriya, "Our Free Trade Zone: A National Liability?" in *Free Trade Zone, Logos,* Vol. 19, No. 2, April 1980, p.107.
17. Sunil Bastian, "Garments Industries in the FTZ: Some Preliminary Observations," *Logos,* Vol. 19, No. 2, April 1980, pp. 96-97.
18. Note 12, p.87.
19. Central Bank of Ceylon Annual Report 1983, pp. 57-58.
20. T. Balasuriya, "Our Free Trade Zone: Is it Development!" Logos, Vol. 19, No.3, 1980, p.8.
21. *Newsweek,* 27 August 1964, p.9.
22. See for details N. Shanmugaratnam, "Sri Lanka's New Economic Policy and Agriculture," *Social Scientist,* Vol. 3, No. 3, March 1984, pp. 3–35.
23. *Lanka Guardian,* 15 July 1984.
24. Note 22, p. 23.
25. Central Bank of Ceylon Annual Report, 1983.
26. W.H. Wriggins, "Sri Lanka in 1980: The Years of Constraints", *Asian Survey,* Vol. XXI, No. 2, Feb 1981, p. 211.
27. Quoted in Vijaya Samaraweera, "Land Labour, Capital and Sectional Interest in National Politics of Sri Lanka," *Modern Asian Studies,* Vol. 15, No. 1, 1981, p. 139.
28. K. Sivathamby, "Some Aspects of Social Composition of Tamil of Sri Lanka" in *Ethnicity and Social Change in Sri Lanka,* (Colombo, 1984) p. 143.
29. *Tribune,* Colombo, 31 March 1984.
30. Central Bank of Ceylon Annual Report.
31. "Sri Lankan Economy: Disturbing Trends," *Tribune,* 20–27 October 1984, p. 9.
32. *Far Eastern Economic Review,* 21 Feb. 1985, p. 42. "Sri Lankan Economy: Disturbing Trends, "Tribune, 20–27 October 1984, p. 9.
33. Ibid., p. 7–8.

## CHAPTER FOUR

# Economic Disparities in Pakistan

### B. M. Bhatia

ECONOMIC disparities in Pakistan that have developed and grown over the years have their roots, firstly, in the genesis of Pakistan as an independent sovereign state and, secondly, in the development strategy that the country followed in the formative stage of its economy.

### I Growth of Capitalist Class and Concentration of Economic Power

PAKISTAN gained its independence direct from colonial rule with much hope for betterment of the quality of life of the Indian Muslims who had been left behind by the majority Hindu community in the race of modern education and foothold in modern industry and commerce. The struggle for a separate homeland for Indian Muslims in pre-independence period was led by an elite consisting of Muslim landlords, traders and businessmen. The small educated middle class did not form a conspicuous part of the leadership of Pakistan movement, though with the culmination of the struggle into the achievement of the goal, this class represented by the civil and military bureaucracy in the undivided India came to the forefront and assumed charge of civil administration of the new-born dominion as also of the preservation of its integrity. In course of time this section of the elite became the dominant part of the country's ruling class. The other two components of that class, the big landlords and newly emerged industrialists, became the allies of the civil-military bureaucracy which has remained in command of the country's affairs since inception of Pakistan.

The composition of the ruling class on the one hand and the overpowering desire to achieve parity with India not only in armed might but in all fields of human endeavour on the other hand dictated the development strategy and economic policies of the country in the early post-independence period.

In its initial stage that covered a period of roughly the first decade of the country's existence, the strategy favoured the development of industries which offered secured market and the greatest profit earning scope to the capitalist class through adoption of a policy of national autarchy. "Pakistan would seek in the first instance", stated government's policy resolution on the subject, "to manufacture in its own territories, the products of its raw materials. in particular jute, cotton, hides and skins, etc. ... for which there is an assured market whether at home or abroad. At the same time, to meet the requirements of the home market, efforts will be made to develop consumer goods industries for which Pakistan at present is dependent on outside sources."[1] This would not merely benefit the nascent capitalist class of Pakistan but would also serve the important, though unstated purpose, of severing all the complementaries that existed, before the Partition, between the territories now constituting separate entities of India and Pakistan. Almost the entire task of industrialization was entrusted at that stage to the care of private enterprise with the government assuming the paternalistic role of "assisting, guiding and controlling industrial development through wise import and capital issue policies, selective tax incentives and other salutary devices."[2] At the same time, "fiscal policy was designed to provide powerful incentives to private enterprise and investment in industry ..."[3]. Direct taxes were kept at low levels and for revenue earnings of the government, increasing resort was made to commodity taxation. Even this rather narrow tax base left the country with annual budget surpluses at least uptill 1955. These were utilized to increase defence expenditure rather than in capital formation or investments in the public sector.[4]

Yet another policy instrument deployed to promote capitalist enterprise was the establishment of the Pakistan Industrial Development Corporation (PIDC) in 1952 with the avowed object of promoting industrial enterprise by providing finance in the form of either loan capital or through equity participation to private industrial ventures. Where private capital was not forthcoming PIDC started industrial ventures of its own with, of course, a clear understanding that as soon as economic viability and profitability of an enterprise started by it was established, the Corporation would turn it over to private hands. Thus of the forty-three large industrial projects completed by the West Pakistan Industrial Development Corporation in the first thirteen years of its existence, twenty-four were converted into public limited companies and nineteen were turned over to private management.

On account of low rate of savings, the country was faced with severe constraint in regard to availability of the needed capital resources. This difficulty was sought to be overcome by (a) obtaining foreign aid and (b) policies aimed at income redistribution in favour of the capitalist industrial sector, which, in fact, meant squeezing agriculture to finance industrial development.[5]

These policy measures were instrumental in laying the foundations of perennial dependence of Pakistan economy on foreign aid on the one hand and increasing concentration of economic power in a small number of business houses within the country, on the other. The first had the effect of drawing Pakistan close to USA not only in terms of latter's military alliances in West Asia but in terms of economic ideology and thinking of the country in developmental matters. American economists together with the new crop of Harvard trained young Pakistani economists, took charge of the country's planning and opinion-formation through their research and development model-making. This powerful group of economists was responsible for inculcating the philosophy of promoting a class of "Robber Barons" and giving them all incentives for leading industrial revolution of the country on the model of the nineteenth century European capitalism. These economists insisted that through incentives, subsidies and foreign exchange endowments, a capitalist class capable of achieving high rate of savings for purposes of investment could be created. That this would lead to increasing inequalities and exploitation of the labouring classes as also of the agriculturists for the sake of capitalist class was well recognized. But it was justified on the ground that:

> ... economic growth is a brutal, sordid process. There are no short cuts to it. The essence of it lies in making the labourer producing more than he is allowed to consume for his immediate needs and to invest and reinvest the surplus thus obtained.... It would be wrong to dub the consequent emergence of surplus as exploitation: it is justification of economic growth.[6]

The policy measures forged and initiated in the first decade of foundation-laying were pursued vigorously during the Ayub era which has been called Pakistan's "Development Decade". The much publicized growth of this period was the result of artificial props provided by the government in the form of the introduction of system of multiple foreign exchange rates, sale of import licences at the officially highly over-valued rupee rate of exchange and allowing generous rates of bonuses on exportables. All this was done in the name of the nationally appealing goal to bring about the maximum degree of "import substitution" in Pakistan economy. For the time being in the glare of high growth rates attained, the disastrous social consequences that these inequitous policy measures would produce, was forgotten. The economic inequalities were allowed to deepen and mass discontent was allowed to build up.

However, by the mid-sixties second thoughts on the inequitous character of the strategy of development adopted, began to make their appearance. In 1965, while making his budget proposals for the year 1965-66, the then Finance Minister M. Shoaib noted that "there is growing discontent in the country about increasing concentration of income and wealth and economic power in the hands of a few."[7] A.R. Ibrahim in the course of a paper presented by him to RCD colloquium on "Common Problems of Economic Growth" referred to the common knowledge in Pakistan that:[8]

> the rich have certainly become richer indeed, and persons and families which were worth millions a decade ago are now worth a hundred of millions ... the same family groups own industrial undertakings, banks, insurance companies, consultancy offices, construction firms, distribution trades, etc. so that not only is there a horizontal but also a vertical concentration of wealth and a tremendous concentration of economic power.[8]

Concern over growing inequalities of income and wealth and concentration of economic power in a few hands was also voiced by the country's planners. The Third Five Year Plan stated that one of the primary objectives of perspective planning in the country would be:

> to distribute incomes equitably both between East and West Pakistan and within each region. The current disparity in per capita income of East and West Pakistan has to be completely removed over the next twenty years preferably in a shorter

period. The prevailing wide disparities in personnal incomes, particularly in the urban areas, must also be contained within limits and incomes distributed more equitably.[9]

It was left to Mahbubul Huq, the apostle of the system of free enterprise to come out with some of the most condemnatory statement about the growth of inequalities and concentration of economic power to which the set of policies earlier advocated by him and his kind, had given rise. In his address to the West Pakistan Management Association in April 1968, he mentioned that twenty families in Pakistan had come to own by then 80 per cent of Pakistan banking, 97 per cent of its insurance business and 66 per cent of all the industrial capital.[10] Of the remaining 34 per cent of industrial capital, more than half was owned by foreign firms. These results obtained further confirmation in Lawrence White's study in Industrial Concentration and Economic Power in Pakistan that relates to 1968 but was published in 1974. White restricted his enquiry primarily to concentration in the industrial sector though some rough estimates of the extent of concentration in insurance and banking sectors were also given by him. He found that there were 197 non-financial companies listed on the Karachi Stock Exchange in 1968. These companies had total assets of Rs. 9726 million and covered practically the entire spectrum of "large scale industry in a broader sense than just manufacturing" and included gas and electric utilities, transportation, construction, mining, storage and trading besides manufacturing.[11] Of the total 197 companies listed with the stock exchange 98 with total capital assets of Rs.5165.7 million or 53.1 per cent of the total assets of all the listed companies were owned by 43 families. The largest four[12] of these families controlled one-fifth of the total assets of all the listed companies, the 10 largest controlled over a third of total assets and the thirty largest controlled over half. If, however, government controlled and foreign controlled firms are excluded from the account, concentration ratios become still more striking. Of the exclusively Pakistani-owned firms, the four leading firms, controlled over a quarter of the assets, the ten leading families controlled under half of the assets and all the forty-three families and groups controlled 73.7 per cent of the assets.[13]

The country had not to wait long for the manifestation of mass discontent over the income and wealth disparities, and concentration of economic power to which economic policies of the government had led it. The turmoil of 1968 that ultimately brought down the Ayub government and the Bangladesh crisis that resulted in the dismemberment of the country were the direct consequences of these policies.

The abortive Fourth Plan (1970–75) that came after the downfall of Ayub but before Bangladesh denouement, conceded that the past strategy which "was based on the premise that capital was shy and that enterprise needs to be brought up with the help of special incentives in the form of subsidies, tax concessions and protection" had ruinous consequences. "The cost of development under this strategy for the private sector" the plan document stated, "continued to rise." "This cost," the document went on to add, "is to be measured in terms of maldistribution of income in the economy, concentration of ownership and economic power, and growing social tension."[14] The document was more specific on the charge of squeezing agriculture to benefit a small group of industrialists and the disastrous consequences which that strategy had produced:

> There was a considerable transfer of savings from the agricultural to the industrial sector...as terms of trade were deliberately turned against agriculture through such policies as licensing of scarce foreign exchange, earned primarily by agriculture, to the industrial sector, compulsory government procurement of foodgrains at low prices to subsidize the cost of living in the cities, industrial incentives for commercial agricultural investment. *The vast majority of the Pakistan population probably has a lower standard of living today than when the country achieved its independence in 1947.*[15] (Emphasis added.)

One could not think of a stronger indictment of development policies pursued by the Pakistan government in the first twenty-three years of the country's existence, than this authoritative statement from the country's own Planning Commission.

This realization, however, failed to turn the tide or reverse the earlier trends. For a study by Khalid Sharwani covering the period 1967–1973 on concentration ratios in various industries showing, among other things, that concentration ratios were fairly stable and even showed a small increase over the period of the study,[16] reveals that the exercise of monopoly power and restrictive trade practices by all industrial giants had increased over the period, with the result that their profits had shown a rise while utilization of installed capacity by them had gone down.

Bhutto made a feeble attempt to break the monopolistic hold of big private business houses on the industrial sector of the country. Under its "Economic Reforms" programme, in January 1972 the government took control of 31 industrial units in ten basic categories: iron and steel, heavy engineering, heavy electrical goods, electricity generation, gas, etc. In March 1972 the management and control of 32 life insurance companies were also taken over under a Presidential Order. From January 1974, Pakistani scheduled banks which were the major constituents of the banking sector were nationalized under the Banks (Nationalization) Act. In every instance, compensation was assured to the former owners and each time it was emphasized that the government believed in "mixed economy" rather than socialism. This was, of course, true for the most important private sector industry of the country, viz. cotton textile, remained untouched by the nationalization programme. Government steps in that direction were more symbolic than representing a genuine desire on its part to dislodge capital from its dominant position in the industrial structure of the country. In the end, the nationalization measures proved more to be a blow for the "morale of the bourgeoisie than to their entrenched position in the economy."[17] For all that happened as a result of this "socialist" endeavour of the government was to send private capital on the sideline of investment activity in large scale industry. The share of private sector in the industrial sector showed a precipitate decline in 1970s and since the growth in public sector investments could not fully compensate for the decline in private sector investments which was of the order of 7 per cent per annum during the decade, the volume of aggregate investments in that sector showed a disconcerting fall. Though the situation improved appreciably after the fall of Bhutto, yet the volume of private investments towards the end of the decade was still much less than that attained during the early seventies.[18] The present government has gone all out to restore the private sector to its pre-Bhutto position. For some time the new government had to contend against the psychological barrier that Bhutto had created among the private industrialists but it now appears to be succeeding in winning over capitalist class to its side and inducing it to resume its investment activity at the former scale. These efforts seem to be succeeding; private sector investments in large scale manufacturing sector that were stagnating in the range of Rs.1526–1569 million during 1976/77–1978–79 shot up to Rs.3291 millions in 1980–81, Rs.3596 millions in 1981–82 and Rs.3877 millions in 1982–83. Big business and industry, thus, appears to have regained its earlier, position not only in the economy but also in the power structure of the country.

## II. Inequalities in the Rural Sector

IF IT WAS the development strategy of the country that was largely responsible for concentration of economic power and growth of disparities in the industrial sector of the economy, it was initially held strong position in the country's elite of the landowning class that was responsible for not only sustaining but even strengthening the hold of that class on the rural sector of the economy. The development strategy actually ran counter to the agricultural interests in the earlier stages of the country's development: it favoured the building up of the industrial sector with the help of surpluses drawn from agriculture.

The refusal to devalue the currency in September 1949 following devaluation of pound sterling was on the face of it an anti-agriculturists act. But on closer scrutiny of the case it is found that it is largely the agricultural interests of East Pakistan, the producer of jute which was the most important agricultural export commodity of the country at the time, that bore the main brunt of this policy decision. The landlords in West Pakistan had to bear much smaller share of the burden on agriculture imposed by that policy decision. Even for that they had their compensation: many of them branched out into the industrial field by setting up agro-based industries like cotton-ginning, flour milling, rice husking as also into trade and transport. Also the landowning class in West Pakistan developed, from the very beginning, close connection with the military: the officer class mainly came from the class of landed artistocracy. At the same time the British system of rewarding military men with grants of land was continued with the result that many retired military men found their way to the landed aristocracy rank. Landowners in West Pakistan, were, thus, able not only to protect their economic interests but also preserve their pre-eminent position in the country's ruling class even at the time when economic policies of the country ostensibly seemed to be going against their interests.

In 1955 the rupee was devalued and agriculture was relieved of the disadvantage from which it had suffered for six long years as a result of over-valuation of the currency. Henceforth, the interests of the landed class converged on those of the newly emerged industrialists' class. Legislation aimed at redistribution of land, with a view to reducing disparities in the ownership of this most important productive asset in the country, was merely of symbolic character. In practice, it had only nominal effect on land distribution in the country. The land reform measure under Ayub Khan in 1959 affected no more than 1.6 per cent of the cultivated land.[19] The law fixed the ceiling on individual holdings at 500 acres of irrigated or 1000 acres of unirrigated land. A person could hold more than the prescribed limit if production from the prescribed size of holding fell below 36,000 produce index units. There were several other exemptions apart from this which made the law practically useless so far as the goal of achieving equitable distribution of land and reducing disparities was concerned. But as the Land Reform Commission on whose Report the reform was based itself admitted, the aim in view in fixing the ceiling limit had not been social justice so much as "causing minimum necessary disturbance of the social edifice, lead to a harmonious change over, and at the same time by providing incentives at all levels conducive to greater production."[20]

Bhutto introduced a new measure of land reform on 1 March 1972. The ceiling of 500 acres of irrigated and 1000 acres of unirrigated land was lowered to 150 and 300 acres respectively. However, provision was made for a number of adjustments and exemptions in determining the ceiling in an individual case so that the effective ceiling on operational holding came to range between 318 acres in the Punjab to 519 acres in Sind depending on land productivity.[21] A study published $2\frac{1}{2}$ years after the enactment showed that less than one per cent of the cultivated area, had been redistributed as a result of the reform: the total area resumed under the reforms by 31 October 1974 was 879,000 acres which is a little over a third of the area resumed under the 1959 reform.[22]

The reform of January 1977 announced by Bhutto government had three significant features, the first of these being that the ceiling on landholding was now brought down to 100 acres of irrigated and 200 acres of unirrigated agricultural land; or in terms of PIUS the ceiling was fixed at 8,000.[23] The implementation of this measure, unlikely in any event, would have made some difference to the feudalistic hold of big landlords on agricultural property. But the measure turned out to be no more than an election gimmick and was never implemented. That landowners and other social forces at work like rapid population growth, and growth of employment outside of the agricultural sector have made little impression on distribution of land among big and small farmers can be seen clearly if we compare the Agricultural Census data of 1960 and 1980 censuses. In 1960, distribution of land among different farm size groups was as given in Table 1.[24]

Table 1

| Farm size | % of the total number | % of the total farm area occupied |
|---|---|---|
| *Position at the 1960 census* | | |
| Small farms (under 5 acres) | 49 | 10 |
| Medium farms (5 to 25 acres) | 43 | 48 |
| Large farms (25 acres and above) | 8 | 42 |
| *Position at the 1980 census*[25] | | |
| Small farms (below 5 acres size) | 35 | 6 |
| Medium farms (5 to 25 acres) | 57 | 53 |
| Large farms (above 25 acres) | 8 | 41 |

The share of large holdings both in respect of their numbers and the area occupied has practically remained the same between 1960 and 1980. However, medium size holdings have gained both in numbers and in their share of total farm area. This has been at the cost of small farms that have lost ground both in numbers an in the share of land occupied. Thus the emerging trend is towards further concentration of landownership into fewer hands rather than towards more egalitarian and widespread distribution. The most striking fact brought out by the Census data is that big landlords have succeeded in retaining their dominant position in the agricultural economy of the country despite all the agrarian reforms measures of successive governments.

Another factor relevant to the discussion on trends in concentration or otherwise of economic power in the rural area is the far-reaching changes in the degree of mechanization and use of modern technology that Pakistan's agricultural has gone through over the last two decades. In this connection a distinction is some time made between feudal landlords and capitalist farmers. The latter are regarded as progressive farmers who were quick to grasp the opportunities thrown open by the introduction of high yield varieties of seeds and offer of big incentives to them by the government in the Ayub era for construction of tubewells and purchase of tractors. The rapid mechanization of agriculture particularly in Punjab, in the 'sixties and seventies', it is agreed, threw up a class of "middle peasants" who belonged to middle class only in terms of the size of their holdings, but in affluence and position in the rural power structure, they had begun to equal, if not really, surpass the position earlier occupied by the feudal landlords. A typical representation of this view is contained in Burki's paper on "The Development of Pakistan's Agriculture."[26] Burki contends that as a result of farm mechanization and introduction of modern technology in agriculture, a new class of middle class farmers, or agrarian capitalists has emerged in the countryside displacing the old feudal class who used to employ sharecroppers. These new middle class farmers, he suggests, are those who own between 50 and 100 acres (in our definition they are, in any case, big farmers). He associates the Ayub coup, supposedly a revolution, with the rise of this class. This view has been challenged, among others, by Alavi who thinks that Burki's thesis is built on "fictitious data and fractured logic."[27] The farm mechanization data, Alavi persuasively argues, suggest that the big landlords themselves were in the forefront of farm mechanization—86.5 per cent of the cultivated area of mechanized farms was in the hands of owners with holdings above 100 acres, of this no less than 43 per cent with owners of 500 acres and over size holdings. By contrast, Burki's category of those who own between 50 and 100 acres who are supposed to have taken over land from big landowners (who, he says, are investing outside agriculture) accounted for no more than 10 per cent of the cultivated farm area in the mechanized farm sector.[28]

However, whether "middle peasants" are taking over the top positions displacing the previously entrenched feudal landlords in the economic structure of rural Pakistan is not very relevant to our present discussion. What is really important to note is that mechanization has strengthened the trends towards concentration of wealth and incomes in the rural areas and widening of disparitie between feudal-cum-capitalist owners of land and the ru al proletariat. The use of tractors and other farm machinery has resulted not only in dispossession of share-croppers, but also in loss of employment to the rural labour. But for the fact that Pakistan has been able to find a lucrative export market in the Middle East for its surplus labour mostly from the rural areas, it would have been faced by this time with a serious problem of rural unemployment.[29]

### III. Continuing Regional Disparities

REGIONAL DISPARITIES in income levels and growth rates between the two wings of United Pakistan brought about the dismemberment of the country even before it could celebrate its twenty-fifth birthday. One should have imagined that after that traumatic experience every effort would be made to bridge the wide gap that exists in income and development levels between the four provinces of the country. But, unfortunately, this does not appear to have happend. Baluchistan, the second largest province in the country in respect of area remains the least developed among the four provinces. The North Western Frontier Province has the smallest area of the four provinces but like Baluchistan it remains poor as ever. Agriculture in both these provinces remains poor, mostly because of inhospitable soil and climatic conditions. Of the total area of 34.8 million acres, net sown area in Baluchistan was

0.5 million or 1.3 per cent of the total in 1948-49. The position has not changed very much since then. In the North Western Frontier Provinces, the percentage of cultivated to total area was about 30 (2.5 million out of total of 8.7 million acres) but want of irrigation made its agriculture of primitive nature. Industry was practically non-existent in these two provinces before the partition: of the total 1547 joint stock companies registered in West Pakistan with a paid up capital of Rs. 127.1 million in 1947-48, 17 with a paid up capital of 30 million were in North Western Provinces and 5 in Baluchistan with a paid up capital of 1½ million. In contrast, Punjab had 1204 companies with a paid up capital of Rs.70.8 million and Sind 31 with paid up capital of Rs. 26 million. Partition made Punjab and Karachi in Sind the growth centres of industry and commerce in Pakistan so that in 1969, of the 22 largest business houses, 21 were located in either Karachi or Punjab. It is interesting to note in this connection that most of the business families located in Karachi were migrants from India. Karachi attracted them because firstly it was the then capital city of Pakistan and secondly the major port city of West Pakistan. Punjab and Sind have been able to retain the initial advantage they had in the development of modern industry and trade and income gap between two provinces on one side and North Western Provinces and Baluchistan on the other has continued to widen with the passage of time.

Till recently, not much was being done to reduce regional disparities through planning and relatively liberal allocation of development funds to the less developed regions. There is now some evidence of a little more of resources being made available to Baluchistan and the North Western Provinces for developmental purposes. For instance, per capita capital expenditure in 1980-81 in Punjab was Rs.39.48, in Sind Rs.43 88, in North Western Provinces Rs.50.23 and in Baluchistan Rs.82.25.[30] However, per capita capital expenditure figures in the four provinces may convey a misleading impression. It can be legitimately argued that it is the total expenditure that matters. On that basis Punjab is still seen to be occupying dominating position in the total picture. Out of the total capital development expenditure of Rs.3593.1 million in 1980-81 for all the four provinces put together, Punjab accounted for Rs. 855.9 or 51.65 per cent of the total, Sind Rs.831.9 million or 23.15 per cent, NWFP Rs.546.8 million or 15.22 per cent and Baluchistan Rs.358.6 million 9.98 per cent. Punjab and Sind thus claimed 75 per cent and the other two provinces 25 per cent of the total development expenditure.

Among the objectives of the Sixth Plan (1983–88) is "to embark upon special programmes aimed at fostering growth and development in some of the poorer regions such as Baluchistan."[31] How far this aim is translated into action and realized remains to be seen.[32]

Regrettably concrete information on condition of the people in the four provinces separately for each province is not available in the Federal Government publications in Pakistan. Pakistan Economic Survey does not give any information on Provinces except population and budget figures. In the absence of such information, it is difficult to say whether any progress towards reduction of regional disparities in incomes and living standards of the people is being made or what the trends are in that matter.

### IV INCIDENCE OF POVERTY

ALL THE available evidence suggests that there was a sharp increase in inter-regional and inter-personal inequalities of income and wealth in Pakistan in the first twenty years of the country's existence.[38] Partly this was the result of belief entertained widely at the time that growth of inequalities in the initial stages of economic growth in a country was a prerequisite of industrialization. It was thought not only expedient but even necessary to promote actively through fiscal measures a high-income sector as a means of raising the rate of savings in the economy. To finance the growth of manufacturing sector, it was considered necessary to squeeze agriculture. In the case of Pakistan, as things turned out, it also meant at the time squeezing agricultural East Pakistan to promote industrialization of West Pakistan.

In the fifteen year period 1949–50 to 1964–65, the rate of increase in per capita income in real terms in Pakistan was less than 1 per cent per annum. Over the same period, the output of the modern manufacturing sector increased at an average rate of 15 per cent per annum. This extraordinary growth rate of industry could not have been financed in the ordinary way because of the low saving potential of the economy. What was done, therefore, was to encourage industrialists to reinvest their extraordinary high profits from the newly started and heavily protected industries in further growth of industry. It is estimated that 75 to 80 per cent of the profits in the manufacturing sector were annually reinvested in that sector during the period and that rural areas transferred annually Rs.3,600 million or 15 per cent of the annual gross produce of the agricultural sector to the urban sector of the economy to finance latter's development.[34]

The constant drain imposed on the rural sector for the benefit of the urban sector had the effect of the impoverishment of the farmer. Thus while per capita income for the country as a whole improved from Rs.311 in 1949-50 to Rs.370 in 1964-65 in real terms, the per capita income in rural areas declined from Rs.207 in 1949-50 to Rs.194 in 1959-60 and then began to improve gradually reaching the 1949-50 level of Rs.207 again in 1964-65. Another indicator of condition of the people is per capita consumption of foodgrains. This was 16 ounces per day in 1948-49, fell to 12 ounces per day in 1955-56, remained around 13 to 14 ounces over the next 8 years and stood at 15 ounces in 1964-65.[35] Table 2 shows dispersion of incomes among four income groups.[36] The figures are in terms of 1964-65 constant prices.

Table 2. Estimate of income distribution in Pakistan at the time of Third Five Year Plan.

| Per cent of total population | East Pakistan (Rural) Rs. | West Pakistan (Rural) Rs. | Karachi Urban Rs. |
|---|---|---|---|
| 5% lowest income group | 186 | 203 | 80 |
| 45% lower middle | 222 | 276 | 211 |
| 45% upper middle | 368 | 398 | 624 |
| 5% highest income group | 686 | 995 | 2165 |
| Average Income | 309 | 363 | 488 |

Even in 1959-60 which year marked the beginning of the country's development decade there was distressing degree of income inequalities.

The income disparity was less pronounced in rural East Pakistan than in rural West Pakistan and more in urban Karachi than in the rural West Pakistan though the incidence of absolute poverty was far greater in East Pakistan and Karachi than in rural areas of West Pakistan. Taking Rs. 250 per capita per annum income as the cut out point to determine the incidence of poverty, we find that at least 50 per cent of the population in East Pakistan and in Karachi lived below the poverty line.

It is in the decade following the benchmark year, 1959-60, that income disparities and inequalities assumed threatening proportions and began to cause concern and attract wide attention. Policy makers and planners began openly to express dismay over undue concentration of economic power in the hands of a few industrial newly rich families. The accumulation of riches by the new rich was largely made possible by the fiscal and economic policies pursued by the Government at the time, or, to put it simply, the result of the strange economic philosophy of the Government. But partly it also reflected exploitation of labour by the capital inasmuch as while profits rose steeply during 1959-69 decade, real wages of industrial workers showed a decline to begin with. There seems to have occurred some improvement after 1963-64 when real wages in all industries per worker on an average stood at Rs.870.6 compared to Rs.966.2 in 1954 and Rs.936.7 in 1959-60.[37] But the real break came after 1967-68 in the wake of political turmoil that helped labour unions to raise their voice for better deal at the hands of the capitalist. They were able to get substantial wage increases during the last year of the Ayub era through strikes and other trade union action. The upward trend in real wages in organized sector of the economy continued during the Yahya Khan and the Bhutto regimes.

The breakaway of East Pakistan in December 1971 might have caused a serious setback to this trend because of decline in demand for labour on account of loss of captive Bangladesh market to the West Pakistan industries. Just then some new factors entered the scene. The first was the liberal attitude that Bhutto had to adopt towards labour due to political compulsions of a democracy. The second and more important of these was the sudden demand for Pakistani labour in Middle East countries following price hike of crude oil caused by OPEC action in 1973. Since then emigration of labour has played a notable part in sustaining Pakistan's economy.

At the same time by causing shortage of skilled labour at home, it has helped to push up wage rates only not of highly skilled but even of the relatively skilled/unskilled labour in Pakistan. This has had the effect of not only reducing the incidence of poverty in the country but also of reducing somewhat inequalities of incomes also. Similarly, the green revolution which has again gathered momentum after the overthrow of Bhutto has worked in the same direction. The small and medium farmers have been enabled to use modern inputs and farm technology to raise their incomes. Mechanization of agriculture, instead of displacing labour, seems to have actually increased employment and led to rise in wages of rural worker. The combined result of all these developments is that interpersonal and class disparities of incomes in Pakistan are today less pronounced than in 1967–68. The percentage of population living below the poverty line also seems to have fallen over the last 15 years.[38]

However, regional disparities have grown in recent years precisely because of these reasons. Impact of green revolution has remained confined to Punjab and Sind with the North Western Provinces and frontier Baluchistan having little share in it. Labour export has also been largely from Punjab and Sind. These two provinces have consequently grown still richer compared to the underdeveloped North Western Provinces and Baluchistan.

## V. Twin Threats to Political Stability

RECENT TRENDS in income disparities in Pakistan show that threat to political stability and national integrity comes more from wide disparities in incomes of people in various regions rather than those in personal incomes in the country as a whole. Pakistan has developed into a consumer society. The poorest in Pakistan have better access to food than their counterparts in other South Asian countries. Irfan's study in 1980 showed that the percentage of those below the poverty line taken as a per capita consumption level of Rs. 250 per annum in 1959–60 prices was 22 per cent in the formal and 34 per cent in the informal sector of employment.[39] Condition of the poor in Pakistan has thus shown considerable improvement over the last 15 years. There are, however, indications of demand for labour in the Middle East tapering off and flow of incomes in the form of remittances from abroad flattening out.

The boom caused by international price hike of oil seems to be coming to an end. At the same time Pakistan's economy has grown in dependence on foreign aid not only for developmental but even for part of its current expenditure. This dependence has already reached dangerous proportions. It constitutes the other threat to future of Pakistan economy and political stability.

As late as in 1978, Mir Ghous Bakash Bizenjo, a front rank Baluch politican and former governor of Baluchistan said in an interview: "The most important issue Pakistan has faced from the very beginning is that its national identity has not been established. So long as the concept of a national identity does not strike root in the country. the prospect of a bright future cannot be encouraging."[40] Islam is being used as the cementing force for national integration. How far this succeeds in overcoming regional conflicts in the country remains to be seen. Recent happenings in Sind province do not encourage hope in that direction.

Pakistan has thus to contend against two threats, one from within and the other from outside. The first relates to acute disparities of income, wealth and availability of public services between the developed Punjab-Sind region and the still largely backward Baluchistan-North Western Frontier region. Fear has been expressed in some quarters that a situation similar to the one that led to the break-up of the country in December 1971 may once again be developing due to unequal distribution of not only wealth but also political power among the four provinces. The have-nots among the provinces are increasingly getting alienated from the "haves" among them. Punjab has come to be singled out even by Sind for attack on the ground of its dominance over the rest of the country both in economic and political spheres.

The inordinately heavy dependence on foreign aid that Pakistan has developed in recent years poses the second serious threat to future integrity and stability of the country. Total outstanding external indebtedness of the country as on 30 June 1982 stood at US $8.8 billion and total debt service charges in 1982-83 came to $866 million which constitutes 34.1 per cent of the country's merchandize export earnings. In 1981-82, the gross aid received was $809 million while the net amount received was $175 million, the rest $634 million accounting for debt repayment charges. In 1974-75 net transfers of capital as percentage of gross disbursements stood at 75; by 1982-83 the figure had come down to 15 per cent only. Of the total Federal

Government Capital disbursements of Rs.34.46 billion in 1982–83 (budget estimates) Rs.17.26 billion or 50 per cent of the total came from external sources, mostly as loans. This is too much of foreign dependence for any independent country to live with. Any interruption in foreign aid flow which may come any time due to any change in international situation or in the foreign policy of the USA could spell disaster for Pakistan economy resulting in disaffection and discontent among the people.

## Notes

1. Pakistan Government, *Pakistan Year Book 1953*, Karachi, p. 30.
2. Pakistan Government, Planning Commission, *The First Five Year Plan 1955–60*, Karachi 1956.
3. Pakistan Government, *The Economic Report 1953-54*, Karachi, p. 57.
4. *Pakistan Economic Survey 1964-65*, Rawalpindi 1965, p. 34.
5. The decision in 1949 not to devalue Pakistan rupee following devaluation of £ sterling and Indian rupee was probably promoted by the desire to deliver a mighty blow to the Indian economy. But the desire to promote the interests of manufacturing industry at the cost of agriculture might have been another important factor contributing to that decision. The action helped Pakistan to command better price for its exports of jute and cotton, particularly to India. It also encouraged the establishment of cotton and jute manufacturing industries in Pakistan. At the same time, however, over-valuation of Pakistan currency in international markets meant less receipts in rupee terms for exports to the agriculturists by about 33 per cent and correspondingly low rupee payments by importers of machinery and high profits for them. The non-devaluation of the rupee and its over-valuation that continued till 1955 was thus one of the important mechanisms employed in the early years of Pakistan's development for squeezing agriculture to provide resources for financing industrial development.
6. Mahbubal Haq, *Strategy of Planning: A Case Study of Pakistan*, Oxford University Press, 1963, pp. 20, 30.
7. Budget speech of Finance Minister, 14 June 1965. Government Press, Rawalpindi, Para 40.
8. "The Pains of Economic Development" cited in K. Griffen and A.R. Khan (eds.) *Growth and Inequality in Pakistan*, Macmillan, London, 1972, p. 40.
9. Pakistan Government, *The Third Five Year Plan*, p. 28.
10. *Business Recorder*, Karachi, April 1965, p. 1.
11. Lawrence J. White, *Industrial Concentration and Economic Power in Pakistan*, Princeton, New Jersey, 1974, p. 58.
12. The four richest families or business houses were Dawood, Saigol, Adamji and Jalil (Amin).
13. White, op. cit., pp. 58-59, 62.
14. Government of Pakistan, Planning Commission, *Fourth Five Year Plan*, Karachi 1970, p. 81.

15. Ibid., for details see Chapters 1 and 2, pp. 1-18.
16. Sherwani, Khalid, "Some New Evidence on Concentration and Profitability in Pakistan's Large-scale Manufacturing Industries," *Pakistan Development Review*, Autumn 1976, vol. XV, no. 3, p. 279.
17. Hamza Alavi, "Class and State" in Hassan Gardezi and Jamil Rashid (eds.) *Pakistan: the Roots of Dictatorship*, Oxford University Press, 1983, p. 53.
18. Syed Nawab Haider Naqvi and Khwaja Sarmad, *Pakistan Economy Through the Seventies Islamabad*, 1984, p. 62.
19. Hamza Alavi, op. cit., p. 60.
20. *Report of Land Reforms Commision for West Pakistan*, Lahore, January 1959.
21. Joost B.W. Kuiten Brouwer, *Self Reliance without Poverty—An Analysis of Pakistan Fifth Five Year Plan 1976-82*, Bangkok, 1976 (mimeo), p. 79.
22. Ronald Herring and M. Ghaffar Choudhry, "The 1972 Land Reforms in Pakistan and their Economic Implications—A Preliminary Analysis," in *Pakistan Development Review*, vol. XIII, Autumn 1974 No. 3 p. 80.
23. The other two features were that holdings of less than 25 acres in size were exempted from payment of land revenue and those above 25 acres were to pay graduated income tax.
24. *Pakistan Census of Agriculture 1960*, vol. II, West Pakistan Table 3.
25. *Pakistan Economic Survey 1982-83*, Statistical Appendix, Table 12, p. 41.
26. See S.J. Burki, "The Development of Pakistan Agriculture" in R.D. Stevens, H. Alavi and P. Bertocci (eds.), *Rural Development in Bangladesh and Pakistan*. Honolulu, 1976.
27. Hamza Alavi "Class and State" in Gardezi and Rashid (eds.) Pakistan, *The Roots of Dictatorship*, op. cit., p. 45.
28. Ibid., p. 45.
29. A survey conducted by the Manpower Division of the Government of Pakistan in 1982 showed that 1.6 million Pakistani workers were living/working abroad and home remittances from them in 1981-82 amounted to US $ 2.4 billion, *Pakistan Economic Survey 1982-83*, p. 176 and *Statistical Annexure*—Table 11, pp. 178, 179.
30. Worked out from Table 8, pp. 98-99 in the Statistical Annexure of *Pakistan Economic Survey, 1982-83*.
31. Ibid., p. 24.
32. The Plan has since been abandoned.
33. For a fairly detailed discussion on the subject see Keith Griffen and Azizur Rahman Khan (eds.) *Growth and Inequality in Pakistan*, Macmillan, London, 1972.
34. Keith Griffen, "Financing Development Plans in Pakistan" in ibid., p. 44. Also see Pakistan Government, *Third Five Year Plan*, June 1967, p. 7.
35. Ibid., p. 38.
36. *Third Five Year Plan*, p. 29.
37. Azizur Rahman Khan, "What has been Happening to Real Wages in Pakistan" in Griffen and Khan, op. cit., p. 235.

38. See in this connection A.R. Kemal, *Income Distribution in Pakistan, A Review* (Mimeographed), Islamabad, September 1981.
39. Irfan, M. *Wage Structure in Pakistan*, Ph.D. Thesis submitted to Graduate School of Cornell University USA, (1980) quoted in Ibid., p. 31.
40. Interview with Sahak Baluch in *Viewpoint Weekly*, Lahore, 18 June 1978.

CHAPTER FIVE

# Economic Development and Social Changes in Bhutan

B. S. Das

IN BHUTAN, the state had been synonymous with monarchy and Lamaism. Both responded to the expectations of the traditional society which was limited in its isolation. The sixties saw a fundamental change when it shed its isolation and was exposed to modern development and external forces. The two institutions which formed the pillars of an integrated system began to come under pressures when the need arose to build a new socio-economic structure of a modern state. In a multi-ethnic society, the need for unity and integrity become the primary factor. This could be possible only if the modern economic development could preserve not only the integrity of the social fabric but cater for the identities of language, religion and region by providing equal access to resources and opportunities created by the developmental activities. Since Lamaism catered to a limited section of the people, its role took a back seat and the monarchy became the instrument of direction and interaction between diverse social groups. The emphasis shifted from a tightly controlled Buddhist social order representing Bhutan's identity and culture to nationhood with a Bhutanese national consciousness.

Bhutan emerged as a political entity only in the seventeenth century. Its historical development has been moulded to a large extent by its geographical location in the Himalayas, and a landlocked area. It was one of the reasons for its isolation from the rest of the world. The process of social change in Bhutan, therefore, has to be viewed in context of its traditional isolated existence and the later attempt to break out, establish contacts and modernize.

The founder of the nation state of Bhutan was Nawang Namgyal a Drukpa monk,[1] who consolidated the political boundaries between 1616 and 1648 subduing the rival Buddhist sects settled in Bhutan since the sixth century. To govern, he established a theocratic system acquiring himself the supreme powers, secular and religious, with the title of Shabdung. The system was inherently unstable. The Shabdungs, like the Dalai Lama, being reincarnates, led to long gaps in succession. During the 250 years of theocracy till 1907 when monarchy was established, there were only seven Shabdungs leading to long periods of turmoil and struggle for power amongst the interim rulers like the Druk Desi (the secular head), the Penlops (governors) and the Dzongpens (regional heads). Power ultimately passed on to the most powerful of Penlops which led to the establishment of monarchy in 1907 and Ugyen Wangchuk, the Governor of Tongsa becoming the first King. The intervening period between Nawang Namgyal and the first King was one of instability, conflicts and turmoil.

Continuous conflicts for power over these three centuries inevitably involved the small population whose entire psyche was formed on sheer struggle for survival. The social structure gave little opportunity for self-expression or change. The economy both for reasons of terrain and internal turmoil, remained stagnant and confined to inter-dependence of a barter system which prevailed till the mid-20th century. Self-sufficiency of the economic system, moreover, did not encourage contact with the outside world, thus closing the avenue of exogenous social change. The need to oped out hardly arose till the events in Tibet after 1949. The socio-economic perceptions of the Bhutanese were thus confined and limited.

Emerging out of its centuries old isolation in the late fifties with a socio-economic background relevant only to 17th century if not earlier, the time capsule for economic development had to be condensed in a manner as to be relevant in modern terms of a developing country. Bhutan started from scratch in 1961 when it went for economic development through five year plans. These twenty years or so have been one of dramatic changes. The entire socio-economic structure wedded to a traditional system of yesteryears has undergone and is undergoing a sea change, the effects of which would be visible only in the coming years. Therefore, the dynamics of social change, creative or destructive, has to be viewed not in the South Asian context per se but in Bhutan's historical origins, its theocratic and ethnic content. Significantly, the structure of political and economic power is still wedded to the traditional system.

Bhutan's ethnic and cultural diversity, its geographical and demographic content have contributed to the social and economic tensions and inner contradictions. An estimated population of 1.2 million in an area of approximately 46,000 sq km, provides one of lowest density of population in Asia.[2] The economic pressures with adequate land and consequently food, hardly existed till the country opened out for modernization in the fifties. Yet, the ethnic diversity and cultural contradictions created their own socio-economic tensions. To understand this, one has to consider the geographical and ethnic divisions.

Three main ethnic groups classified as Sharchops, Ngalops and Nepalese form the population of Bhutan. The Sharchops were the earliest inhabitants mainly residing in eastern Bhutan. Their origins can be traced to the tribes of north-east India and north Burma. The Ngalops were the migrants from Tibet and brought Buddhism with them. Nepalese, mostly Hindus, came much later in the late 19th century as labourers to work in the inhospitable climate of southern Bhutan. Each of these groups had their distinct culture, religion and identity. The Ngalops became the rulers subduing the Sharchops and integrating them through conversion to Buddhism and inter-marriages. The Nepalese were confined to the south not being permitted to migrate or own property in the upper regions. The country's geographical zones generally cover the ethnic distribution, the Sharchops living mostly in eastern Bhutan, the Ngalops in the west and central Bhutan and the Nepalese in the south.

One sees a clear division of the country on ethnic lines in the geographical and historical context. Despite the rigid power apex, each ethnic community was, by and large, left to itself in its social and cultural context. The economy was such where interaction between regions was minimal, confining the ethnic groups to their traditional way of life. It was only in matters relating to monastic order that the entire Buddhist community was under a rigid control exercised by the ruling group of Drukpas.

The Bhutanese protected and confined in this environment were suddenly confronted with a new situation when China occupied Tibet and became a powerful neighbour. Happenings in Tibet, China's claims on Bhutanese territory and the fear of communism, all contributed in Bhutan's opening out to the outside world for its security. Though liberal trends had started emerging in the fifties with the late King Jigme Dorji Wangchuk setting up a National Assembly in 1952 and abolishing slavery, Bhutan was still living and thinking in the past, a rigid and traditional way of life. Even the very small presence of Indians who came to assist the Government in the late fifties and subsequently was looked upon with suspicion despite the threat from the north. The Drukpa dominance and the traditional culture could only be maintained through the policy of isolation and there was a general tendency to shun foreign contacts or presence. Had the events of 1959 and the Sino-Indian war of 1962 not taken place and a threat not perceived to their traditional way of life, Bhutan would have preferred to remain in isolation with minor changes in economic perceptions. The realization came only in late fifties that a major change in the socio-economic structure was inevitable with acceptance of Indian aid and developmental activities, specially communications network which would expose them to the outside world. Earlier it took days from the capital to reach the Indian borders. The people from west to east or vice versa hardly travelled making them insular to the goings on within their own country. In fact, that was one way of maintaining the Drukpa hegemony over others and retain their culture and traditions.

The developments in Tibet in the fifties and Bhutan's rapid economic development as a consequence, had a far reaching effect on the socio-economic structure of the country. The self-sufficient agricultural economy with a barter system came under stress. From 1961, money economy began to replace the traditional barter system with the induction of Indian aid, opening up of communications and employment opportunities. A middle class unknown earlier, emerged forming the nucleus of the new power elite involved in social and economic activities of the State. This class was educated, young and less traditional and its power was rooted in money and professionalism. It now forms the key factor in Bhutan's social structure replacing the traditionalists and the monks who earlier dominated the psyche of the people. The young King while maintaining the balance between traditionalism and modernity, has come to depend on the new class to implement the new directions towards making Bhutan a modern State with a nationalistic fervour.

Like any middle class, it seeks, to assert its personality, the institution of monarchy providing the source of power and leadership. It is now the back-bone of governance and national consciousness which is emerging as a consequence of the country's economic and political independence. Realizing the tremors it has created in the clergy which formed and regulated the social structure for centuries, the King is seeking to educate and modernise the established monastic order. A special cell has been set up to attune the clergy's thinking to social and economic changes taking place. The monks themselves are being involved in development programmes giving them a consciousness of the importance of their new role as an important segment of the country's development and new image. It is a unique experiment of creating a new society zealously upholding its traditional values fitting into a new structure of modern social consciousness.

While Bhutan continues with its laudable efforts towards a new direction, the task is a difficult one with its ethnic stresses and strains and absence of a well knit and credible institutional system so nesessary for support in such a major change. The time capsule itself poses a challenge of its own kind. Every new effort must neutralize or balance the Drukpa supremacy vis a vis the other ethnic groups if success is to be achieved. An unenviable task for any ruler whose traditional source of strength has been the ruling Drukpa community and Lamaism both of which now need to be pruned and modelled to suit the new image based on national strength involving all segments of the people.

The new focus is now on the Nepalese who have multiplied in numbers to the extent of some even claiming parity in numbers. With all the ingredients of distinctiveness vis a vis the Drukpas in terms of language, religion and culture, their sheer numbers pose a potential threat to the hegemony of the ruling race. The rate of population growth of the southerners is estimated to be about 2.8% as against less than 2% of the rest[3]. This imbalance is a serious cause for concern. Officially, the Government cannot force family planning in one region based on ethnicity. Yet, to retain the supremacy of the ruling community, it needs to offer incentives for higher rate of growth of the Drukpa population on one hand and control rate of the southerners to maintain a balance on the other. It is a dillemma not easy to resolve. Bhutan is one of the very few countries, if not perhaps the only one, where it needs a larger population for its economic growth and yet it faces a unique problems of its cultural and historical identity being eroded due to an imbalance in ethnic population growth ratio. The example of Sikkim haunts the Bhutanese.

Representation of the southerners in the political and economic institutions does not correlate to their numbers. This is despite the efforts of the late King and a very major effort on the part of the present King to integrate them with the rest and create a national consciousness. Increasing representation is now being given to them in the services and economic activities. Priority is being given in developing southern Bhutan in which through decentralization of developmental programmes, they would be involved directly and consequently have a sense of participation at the national level. Religion and language become the rallying ground for minorities especially if they feel suppressed. Emphasis is now being laid by the Government on encouraging the Nepalese to project their culture and social activities. Major Hindu festivals are being declared holidays with the Royalty participating in them. The National Day of Bhutan is celebrated not only on one day at the capital but in southern and other regions also with the King being present to meet the people directly.[4] Inter-marriages are being encouraged and a percentage of students from one region are being educated in another. The King's own sister is married to a Nepalese Bhutanese, a very positive step towards integration. The young King's efforts in creating Bhutanese national consciousness amongst the southerners is indeed commendable and to a degree, it has achieved some positive results. More and more young Bhutanese of Nepalese origin are being inducted into economic and administrative bodies at the national level and involved in major decision making process.

Yet, these measures are inadequate palliatives when the major contradictions in the socio-economic structure are seen. For such differing ethnicity, integration and a national consciousness can only be built if the political and economic institutions cater to them on the basis of equal opportunities. The contradiction lies in Bhutan's culture and image being linked to Buddhism and its Tibetan origins. Minus this image, Bhutan's identity stands eroded. It has no powerful secular and connected institutional base. Though the Committee for Integration headed by no less a person than the King's own sister with a Nepalese husband exists, the issues are emotional, cultural and religious and go deeper into the psyche of the people who rule the country. Power, economic or political, can be shared upto a point. Beyond that the entire structure of the existing society and the social fabric could break and Bhutan exposed to a turmoil.

Monarchy and the Lama heirarchy are the only two institutions as of today which can sustain Bhutan's cultural and historical identity. The integration of southern Bhutanese will not be an easy task and is likely to pose a major problem in the coming years. As Bhutan is exposed more and more to the outside world through economic development, public consciousness and political awareness would rise. The conflict of economic and social disparities would generate a debate on equal rights. One has to view the ethnic contradictions in economic and political terms and prepare to meet them in the correct perspective of the coming decades.

The stability of a system lies in the institutional framework which caters for change. Bhutan, despite this incipient development, is still a highly tradition-bound society with a system of archaic values. For instance, the economic, political and religious institutions as they exist today do not cater for the ideas and approach of a new social structure. The National Assembly is still tradition bound despite its occasional postures of criticism or debate. The representation is lopsided without incorporation of the new class. It does not encourage public debate on economic or political issues, which cannot remain suppressed for very long. The judicial system or the executive still rest on old concepts while the thinking and attitudes of the new class and the problems of growth are very contemporary. The economic institutions are even more tricky. With external aid and infrastructural needs of development, it will require considerable debate, discussion and cogent policy formulations. The present system of decision making based on assessment and thinking of a small elite may be adequate for the moment, but in the coming years this process will be inadequate. Frustrations, failures and setbacks will create serious economic and political complications for the Government. Unless the old institutions are restructured and new ones created with economic and political participation of the people assured, the country will face similar problems as in other developing countries. The class division of 'haves' and 'have nots' is rapidly emerging with portents of future imbalances and consequent social conflicts. Ethnicity will then come into full play and may be taken advantage of by outside elements. However, whatever changes may take place, they will be within the framework of a monarchical system, it being the only stabilizing factor in contemporary Bhutan.

## II

BHUTAN'S economic development, though controlled to avoid any serious imbalance, could at best be called patchy. Prior to the sixties, the economic structure was stable with the ratio of land to labour being well balanced. Exposure to outside influences was minimal. Since the sixties, while the rural structure has not changed radically, a new modern sector has now emerged which is tightly controlled so far. The result has been that its overall economic impact has been limited. Planned development involves a clear conceptual framework of minimum acceptable level of growth. In Bhutan, even though the Fifth Five Year Plan is underway, the non-availability of basic socio-economic data—even the size of the population and its economic and social needs, both in terms of region and ethnicity, prevents any accurate assessment to be made of the functioning or impact of the economic system's development.

With the resource availabilty being scarce, the effective utilization of this in terms of equitable benefits becomes a critical issue. To overcome this problem, the Government has undertaken a lot of socio-economic statistical work related to census of population, livestock census, national agricultural survey, nutrition surveys and preparation of estimates of the national accounts and balance of payment.

Development planning efforts trace back to 1959 with Indian assistance. Starting from 1961 when the First Five Year Plan was formulated, Bhutan has completed four Plans upto 1980/81. Table 1 gives the outlays and financing.[5]

The First Plan was critical, the priority being transporatation infrastructure to plan a communication network for opening up of Bhutan. The outlay of 66 per cent on this included major road network connecting India. Basically, it was an infrastructural Plan to cater for the subsequent Plans. The major constraint, which still persists, was the shortage of manpower and technical skill. The Second Plan priorities extended to social services, education getting 18 per cent agriculture 14 per cent and health 8 per cent. Transportation went down to 41 per cent .[6] The two Plans laid the foundations of planned developement.

Table 1. Financing of Five Year Plans (Rs. millions).

| Source of financing | First Plan (1961-62 1965-67) | Second Plan (1966-67 1970-71) | Third Plan (1971-72 1975-76) | Fourth Plan (1976-77 1980-81) |
|---|---|---|---|---|
| Govt. of India | 107.2 | 200.00 | 426.6 | 853.00 |
| UN and other international agencies | — | — | 15.8 | 193.7 |
| Internal resources | — | 2.2 | 32.8 | 59.5 |
| Total | 107.2 | 202.2 | 475.2 | 1106.2 |

The period from 1961 to 1971 saw significant changes—in fact, major ones. The barter economy gave way to money economy affecting a very large segment of economic activity and interaction between the inaccessible regions. A middle class emerged which began to acquire a say in the country's governance through the developmental process. The need of development also led to major changes in the administrative set up. The Cabinet system with a Council of Ministers was set up in 1968. Doing away with the earlier system of a Prime Minister, the King assumed the roles of head of Government and State. This brought him directly into the process of governance, economic development and social changes. The most important event, however, was Bhutan's joining the United Nations in 1971, opening out to econamic aid from sources other than India. The political and economic stance changed and serious efforts began to be made to diversify dependence—economic or political. It was a turning point in the traditional pattern of relationship between Bhutan and India.

The Third Plan not only brought in foreign aid of Rs. 15.8 million (besides India) international agencies like UNDP and others found presence in Bhutan, for the first time opening it out in later years to more diversified field of economic activity. Consequently political role of Bhutan as an emerging Third World country in the South Asian and international context became clear.

The foreign aid rose to Rs.193 million during the Fourth Five Year Plan. The Fifth Plan, which is a six year plan, envisages an outlay of a very large figure of Rs.3396 million under which besides India's contribution of Rs.1340 million, the other committed foreign aid is Rs.521 million.[7] Diversification of aid and reduced dependence on India has now come to be accepted as a major policy thrust of the Government. The role of the Planning Commission of India has been substituted by Bhutan's own Planning Commission which has now three key divisions of planning, resources and statistics.

The trends of the first four Plans are indicative of the process of development. From an infrastructural First Plan, the second one with an almost doubled outlay, went into an implementation stage giving priority to social services, education and agriculture. The efforts to spread the social benefits of economic development were visible with social services, education, agriculture and health getting over 40 per cent of the outlay. The Third Plan with an increased outlay of almost 135 per cent over the First Plan was the take off point in terms of economic goals and achievements. It could be called the forerunner of a new directional approach to planning correlated to the social needs and Bhutan's growing independence both economically and politically. Along with social benefits, education got top priority to create a cadre of people for meeting the development commitment. The Third Plan was interesting in another way. For the first time, the UN system contributed 3 per cent of plan expenditure and internal resources were generated to the extent of 7 per cent. Till then, India met the entire burden, both plan and non-plan expenditure.

The Fourth Plan with an outlay as large as Rs.1106 million brought about major changes in the pattern of economic perceptions. While economic growth remained the prime goal with increased emphasis on agriculture (an outlay of 29%—the highest so far), industry, hydropower and forestry, the emphasis changed to multi—dimensional project planning fitting into a progressive image of Bhutan as an international entity forging its way to interaction with the outside world. There was a six-fold increase in overseas finance—mainly from the UN system—from 3per cent to 18 per cent. In economic terms, however, the major failure lay in mobilization of internal resources which went down from 7 per cent envisaged to 5 per cent of total financing.

## III

BHUTAN entered a new phase in the economic and political spheres after 1981. It took steps to extened its relationship externally on both fronts. This move fitted into the policy of active involvement in international relations. Trade Agreements with Bangladesh and Nepal, financial assistance from Kuwaiti Development Fund, membership of World and Asian Development Banks, setting up Consulates in Singapore and South Korea were some of the steps taken. The role of international agencies like UNDP, FAO, WHO UNESCO, etc. increased substaintially. SARC became a major platform for Bhutan to project its regional image in the South Asian context.

Internally, a major thrust was made in formulating the Fifth Five Year Plan which was not only vast in its dimensions, it also involved people's participation at the grass root level. The emphasis and the keynote was decentralization going to the village level with a substantial contribution of voluntary labour to meet the large commitments and save scarce resources. For this, each district had its own Plan based on expressed district priorities and projected available financial resources. Each was discussed and approved by the National Assembly. To these, district level components were added to such projects which would come under the central implementation. These included major projects such as large public industries, national road and power projects and higher level education. Table 2 gives the broad framework of the Fifth Plan and its financing.[8]

Table 2. Fifth Five Year Plan

| Sector | Outlays | Internal resources and Govt. of India grants | Committed International assistance | Resource gap | Gap as % of total Rs. millions |
|---|---|---|---|---|---|
| Non-developmental | 532 | 526 | 6 | — | — |
| Developmental | 2210 | 1,436 | 464 | 310 | 23 |
| Sub-total | 2742 | 1,962 | 470 | 310 | 23 |
| Commercial industrial | 1596 | 520 | 51 | 1,025 | 77 |
| Total | 4338 | 2,482 | 521 | 1,645 | |

The macroeconomic objectives of the Fifth Plan are to achieve an overall growth of 8.5 per cent. Areas of rapid growth are expected to be power, industry and tourism. Agriculture is expected to grow at the rate of 12 per cent per annum. These are estimated figures. On the covering of the unfinanced gap, the picture is not clear. Even the revenue expenses of the Government are not expected to be covered until 1986/87 despite fiscal reforms introduced in 1982/83.

To cover a large gap in funding is not an easy task. It is expected that public investment will rise from 16 per cent of GDP in 1980/81 to an average of 30 per cent during the Fifth Plan period peaking at over 45 per cent of GDP during 1984/85. This can at best be described as an ideal with little prospects of achievement with Bhutan's very limited economic growth over the four plans. One can visualize a serious possibility of the Plan being considerably pruned and revised. As of today, there are no indications of this large financing gap being covered either by India or by international finance. The saving grace is that the Plan includes only estimated costs of the projects without any detailed appraisal. As and when each of such centrally controlled project is considered in detail for being taken up, the question of financing will come up and steps then taken to raise the resources. To that extent, the financing gap is flexible and subject to major revisions.

## IV

FOR A COUNTRY whose internal revenues are limited such a huge Plan has several implications. Can Bhutan sustain such a pace of development with its internal resources extremely limited? Can it absorb the huge doses of external aid with its small population and lack of infrastructure? Can the social fabric sustain the pressures that would be generated through external aid of such magnitude and exposure it would be subjected to? Will it be possible for the country to create the institutional support on a permanent and credible basis to meet the new economic, social and political challenges that this massive developmental activity will throw up? Could the multi-ethnic content of the country be moulded into the Bhutanese national mainstream in the long run with only one source of power, guidance and control? And lastly, would Bhutan, exposed as it is to a totally new concept of its personality in economic terms, be able to retain its cultural identity as reflected by its Buddhist socio-religious traditonal background?

Answering the problem of internal resources and external aid, Bhutan expects that with the limited scope that exists for increasing domestic savings, increased levels of investments will have to come from external sources. Unless additional aid materializes many of the investments proposed cannot be carried out. Though the development strategy is basically sound and worthy of support, such aid will be limited and on highly concessional terms. Bhutan being one of the least developed country of the world would need all the support by the donors. But, no country gives charity and expects either repayment in financial or political terms. Financially, it will be beyond the capacity of Bhutan to repay with its inability to service convertible currency debt. That leaves only India as the major donor country for times to come. Financing the costs of some of the larger projects is likely to be beyond the means of any individual donor country. That brings in their political interests. Here Bhutan unless very cautious, could fall into a trap where its economic and political independence may come under severe pressure. Once the pace of development takes a particular momentum it becomes extremely difficult to control it.

So far Bhutan as a policy has avoided large scale bilateral aid from any other country except India. Most of the committed external assistance is through international agencies. It has also sought to support with vigour the South Asian Regional Cooperation SARC to promote regional assistance and cooperation, specially in the field of projects and technical assistance. The SARC Declaration of August 1983 not only describes the objectives but spells out the institutional framework for defining its programmes and financial arrangements to implement them. Bhutan is a signatory to this. Its efforts are to promote intra-regional trade and better utilization of opportunities among South Asian countries with the large reservoir of technical manpower. To what extent Bhutan can draw financial and technical assistance from the member countries to meet its developmental and non-developmental commitments will depend very much on the resource availability of the member countries, Bhutan having little to contribute with its severe limitations. However, SARC is a platform for Bhutan to project its independent personality on the basis of political equality. Dependence on India economically will remain a fact of life for

Bhutan to live with but with SARC as a regional body, some of this dependence could be channelled through SARC giving a psychological comfort to Bhutan. SARC's role in the South Asian economic development context is still at a nebulous stage. In economic terms, therefore, Bhutan cannot base its development strategy on SARC's efforts at regional economic assistance.

If one views Bhutan's economic development in retrospect, one can say that progress has been substantial and even laudable in some respects. That this has happened in such a short time and in an environment which was almost three centuries old till three decades ago without any serious imbalance or social upheavals, is a matter of legitimate pride. Bhutan has developed an impressive stock of basic economic infrastructure and enjoys a standard of living which belies its very low per capita income. In the context of South Asian contruies, its expenditure on education as percentage to the total recurrent budget is the highest. From zero adult literacy rate in 1960 to 10 per cent in 1977–80 is again an achievement. Same goes for technical training and skilled manpower. In agriculture and related activities, a steady average annual growth of 7.7 per cent has been maintained since 1980. In industry and power the growth has been 23 and 88 percent respectively.[9] The consumer price index has been managable. Most of all, the exposure through economic development has not led to any economic or political instablity or social upheavals. The institution of monarchy has emerged as the key factor in guidance, liberalization of institutions and evolving a national consciousness. Traditional pattern of life has been moulded so far to suit the modern concepts and challenges. The contradictions that prevail in other developing countries in terms of economic opportunities, social behaviour and class distinctions and conflicts are minimal. Undoubtedly, Bhutan has a small population with no problems of pressure on land or property. But, these advantages have been maximized through effective and balanced utilization so far. Foreign influence and pressures so marked in other aid receiving countries have been controlled. Priorities in economic and political relationships are balanced.

However, with all these plus points, the country has some serious problems. The constraints of technical and managerial manpower, shortage of manual labour, low productivity, the terrain an inadequate communication network, serious shortages and gaps in material and financial resources and increasing dependence on foreign aid cannot be easily resolved. With the momentum of planning to achieve ambitious economic goals, Bhutan's dependence will increase. Domestic resources will never be adequate to match or even reach anywhere near the projected targets. Despite external assistance from international funding agencies, the dependence on India for finances, manpower, material and markets will continue to grow if Bhutan has to make a headway in terms of its economic goals. Any ill-conceived external assistance could have serious overall economic and political consequences. Bhutan's ability to service convertible currency debt is extermely limited. It has no major export potential. The scope of concessional finance in foreign exchange is very limited.

Dependency development has proved beyond doubt that it does not resolve the bane of underdevelopment. As yet Bhutan has not reached the critical point. India is not included in this dependence for obvious reasons. The mutuality of interests precludes such pressures as would cause serious worry. It would not be true of other external assistance. Both Bangladesh and Nepal evolved their development strategy based on receipt of foreign aid with unfortunate consequences like debt trap rather than economic growth. What kinds of development and social arrangements are opted for is basically a question of value. If the human organization can be effectively used, variety of design can be worked out. Here the major concern is the role of the people at grassroot levels in the development process so that the new emerging elite does not establish its hegemony which may act as a divide between them and the people, specially in the complex problem of southerners and the rest. The new elite is basically of Tibetan stock and it would not permit sharing of power and influence on equal terms with others. The King has an awareness of this problem and hence his efforts towards integration and decentralization.

V

IN TODAY'S context, the King provides the leadership and motivating force for the people of every faith. The challenge he faces is one of integration, motivation and creating an awareness of needs of Bhutan in the national context. Realizing this, the King has given primary importance to integrating the different sections of the people and for that the National Council for Social and Cultural

Promotion was set up in 1980, the objectives of which are broadly defined as follows:[10]

(i) Organization and promotion of social, cultural and educational activities to indicate a feeling of a national community transcending regional loyalties.
(ii) Establishing programmes/schemes for the youth to instil a sense of national identity and dedicated service to the King and the country.
(iii) Initiating plans/programmes to emphasize social, cultural and spiritual aspects of life to integrate youth with the national development programmes at the rural levels.

All the three objectives highlight national integration, a national consciousness and a national identity. These indicate that modernization has created an imbalance in the old social order. In such a situation, the sharing of economic power and the interaction between the State and the new class or the interaction between the various ethnic groups becomes critical. So far the only institution to guide and resolve the emerging contradictions is the monarchy. The question of prime importance, therefore, is whether this leadership which by any account is the most progressive, dynamic and stable today can shoulder the burden of the socio-economic change all by itself without viable supportive institutions. There is no second line leadership even within the Royal family.

The monarchy is the sole stabilizing factor in the absence of any other political or people's platform. No doubt, the National Assembly is much more aware of and participative in the national problems today and the King shares with it the formulation of official policies. The Royal Advisory Council has been given a more active role as a watch dog in overseeing the implementation of government policies. But, they all derive their strength from the monarchy alone. The new class of civil servants and technocrats which forms the elite is limited by its very nature to public response. None of those institutions are capable yet of handling the emerging socio-economic and political problems of the coming years. What answers will emerge to the problems of regional identity, the emerging rural consciousness and ethnic militancy is a question mark.

Bhutan has changed and the old social fabric is too fragile to last. The divide between the 'haves' and 'have nots' will increase with large economic inputs. The value system will change with traditional roots of the past passing away. The exposure to the outside world and coming in of an age of diversification of relationships with neighbours and other countries, the flow of foreign funds from several external sources, the pressures that are bound to arise as a consequence are factors which cannot be lost sight of. The coming years will be a period of immense changes and challenges. The major factor with which the King himself is concerned is the national integration. The rest will flow out of it. For this, grassroot and local leadership at the rural level will have to be built up fitting into the national integration programme and mobilization of manpower resources for fulfilment of economic goals. That is what the King is striving at through his decentralization scheme which is basically motivational.

Motivation comes through sharing of economic benefits and equal opportunities. The economic planning and consequent social benefits must correlate to environment of a country. So long as these factors are kept in mind which are critical, there is hope that the leadership of the King will provide the necessary motivation, guidance and response to the problems the country is likely to face in the coming years.

## NOTES

1. Nirmala Das, "Bhutan" in *World Focus*—47-48 Fourth Annual Number —November-December issue 1983.
2. Fifth Plan 1981-87, Royal Govt. of Bhutan.
3. Approximation based on calculation of 1981 population figures ethnic wise.
4. Aims and Objectives—National Council for Social & Cultural Promotion, Royal Govt. of Bhutan
5. Fifth Five Year Plan, Royal Government of Bhutan—Main Document.
6. Ibid.
7. Ibid.
8. Ibid.
9. Ibid.
10. Write up on Annual Plan and Budget for 1984-85—Planning Commission, Royal Government of Bhutan.

# BIBLIOGRAPHY

PRIMARY SOURCES

Government News Publications Kuensal from 1968–81.

UNITED NATIONS DOCUMENTS

"Bhutan: Development in a Himalayan Kingdom"—World Bank, 1983.

GOVERNMENT DOCUMENTS

Fifth Plan 1981-1987, Main Document—Royal Government of Bhutan.

SECONDARY SOURCES

Books

Pradyumna, P. Karan, *Bhutan: A Physical And Cultural Geography*, Lexington, Ky, 1967.

V.H. Coehlo, *Sikkim and Bhutan*, New Delhi, 1970.

Nagendra Singh, *Bhutan—A Kingdom in the Himalayas*, New Delhi, 1978.

Ram Rahul, *The Himalaya As a Frontier*, New Delhi, 1978.

Leo E. Rose, *The Politics of Bhutan*, Ithaca and London, 1977.

Claude White, *Sikkim and Bhutan, Twentyone Years on the Northeast Frontier 1887-1908* (London, 1907).

CHAPTER SIX

# Ethnic Conflicts in South Asian States

Urmila Phadnis

THAT THE ethnic factor is one of the many impulses of social conflicts is a fact nobody can or will deny. However, what needs to be enquired into is as to why ethnic impulses assume a salience over others. This is particularly so in view of the fact that no ethnic group is a monolith. Inherent in its structure are many cleavages—horizontal as well as vertical. In other words, the question is how does it happen that one component of an ethnic identity at a given time assumes pre-eminence, insulating if not subsuming for a while, built-in cleavages?

The question has even a greater salience in the context of the political experiences of the multi-ethnic societies of South Asian states. Ethnicity, for instance, has been a critical variable in the formation and reformation of the state structures in the region as is evident by two partitions of legitimized state in less than half-a-century. Furthermore, over the decades, even in cases where ethnic conflicts have been managed, such a conflict management has been shortlived, erupting again after a while. An interrupted continuity has thus marked the old inter-ethnic group tensions, with new groups being added to it and a relatively wider segment of the various communities getting increasingly involved therein.

As such, it is not merely the conflictual dimensions of inter-ethnic group relationship per se, but also the fact of its magnitude—in terms of scale as well as space that requires an explanation.

Added to this have been the complex patterns of ethnic group mobilization and its variegated demands—for 'affirmative' discrimination, autonomy and secession. A noteworthy trend in South Asian states in this respect has been an increasing constellation of separatist movements since the 70s many of which were, earlier, mainly autonomist. Though varying in intensity and strength, such movements symbolize a revolt against the state and its power structure at various levels. Insurgency and counter-insurgency, violence of the terrorists and violence of the state-apparatus thus underline the phenomenon of a protected 'internal war' between a segment of the civic society and the state encompassing many more groups in the region than perhaps ever before.

Furthermore, in South Asia the pressure and pulls of some of these movements have not been confined to the territorial boundaries of the state in question but have had transnational dimensions too. In particular, a spill-over effect of some of them in India's relations with its neighbours has its own implications. This has been particularly pronounced because of the Indo-centric character of the region under which criss-crossing trans-border affinities of certain ethnic groups have befuddled the content and context of 'neighbourhood' and 'nationhood'.

In sum thus, whether in terms of magnitude, scope, scale or patterns, the ethnic tensions, turmoils and conflicts in South Asian states appear to be increasingly variegated and also, on the ascendancy in the years to come, having thereby critical implications for India's bilateral relations with the neighbours in general and, in particular, for the systemic contours of South Asian States.

If the issues pertaining to the causes and consequences of ethnic conflicts are pertinent so is the issue relating to the very definition of the term ethnic. Interestingly while the term has been very much in vogue in recent times in popular parlance as well as in the vocabulary of policy makers and social scientists, its definitional ambience has grown. What does it encompass and what does it leave out? This is a question which may attract the attention of more and more social scientists in the years to come for, an analysis of ethnic conflict will, *suo motto*, require a clearer boundary delineation of ethnic group than has been done hitherto.[1]

I do not intend to discuss the issues pertaining to the definitional dimension in this paper in detail as such an exercise has been done elsewhere.[2] Briefly stated, an ethnic group can be viewed as a historically defined aggregate of people with shared objective traits and symbolic referents connoting its distinctiveness vis-a-vis similar groups and regarded to be so by others. The definition thus has as its major components: (a) historical antecedents; (b) objective cultural markers, e.g. race, descent, language, religion, region, or a combination of some of them; (c) subjective awareness of belonging to a group provided by a cultural core: and (d) the recognition by the others of the group-distinctiveness (the we-they paradigm).

A heightened sense of group awareness takes the form of an ethnic community. Providing the community a quality and a character ethnicity is a process in identity formation which involves the select use of ethnic markers/symbols for socio-cultural and politico-economic purposes and thereby connotes the assertion, mobilization and/or sustenance of the group identity and distinctiveness in consensual, competitive or conflictual modes of interaction with other ethnic groups.

If conflict is the overt manifestation of coercive interaction between two contending social collectivities, then ethnic violence is a conflictual manifestation of the patterns and processes of interaction between two or more ethnic groups. However, as such a conflict is aimed basically towards the sharing of societal rewards and goods it automatically follows that the nature and character of the institutions of power and authority (in ethnic as well as non-ethnic terms) epitomized by the State and its apparatus at various levels, assume a criticality in appraising the bases and manifestations of ethnic conflict.

In other words, as both the 'dominant' and 'subordinate' groups (in terms of power and status) in a civic society perceive the state as a "gate-keeper of the contradictions and the controller of conflict,"[3] there is, consequently, a perennial need on the part of various social collectivities for either exclusive or participant power over and in a state apparatus. One of the modes of such manifestation is politicized ethnicity.

However, not all the ethnic groups acquire a conflictual mould. Nor all the multi-ethnic societies turn out to have ethnic 'explosions.'

In this respect, several questions confront us in the South Asian context. Why is it that in India ethnic conflicts on the one hand have been contained in some cases but have conflagrated in others? Why is it that in Sri Lanka the conflict is being exacerbated over the years and in Pakistan, led to its bifurcation? Why is it that even after its bifurcation ethnic movements of the minority communities continue to persist? Why is it that in Nepal and Bhutan, despite their respective poly-ethnic social structures, inter-ethnic cleavages have been, by and large latent and have not manifested themselves in violent terms?

Moving from the region-based questions, a number of issues of broader concern arise. In the multi-ethnic societies, why is it that ethnic demands and competition involve some groups and not others? Under what condition ethnicity of a particular group progressively becomes demanding, competitive and conflictual? Under what situations does an ethnic commmunity assert its status as a 'nation' and what are the requirements for its success? What are the various approaches pursued by the power wielders to cope with the challenges of plurality?

Finally, as with social conflicts in general, an ethnic conflict has the potential of being creative as well as destructive. The moot question is: What is being created and what is being destroyed? What have been its ramifications in terms of patterns of interaction amongst ethnic groups in general and ethnic group versus state structures in particular?

An attempt to answer some of these questions has been made in this paper by providing: (a) a critique of the various approaches towards ethnic groups and conflicts and their relevance in the context of the experiences of South Asian States; (b) an appraisal of the preconditions for ethnic conflict; (c) role of the institutions of power and authority therein; (d) the transnational dimensions of these conflicts; and (e) the implications of these conflicts for the South Asian State's systems at present and in years to come.

## II

THE BURGEONING literature, having a bearing directly or indirectly on the phenomena of ethnic cleavages, competition and conflicts brings to the fore a number of contending perspectives and approaches. Some focus on its 'cultural core' and thereby emphasize on its perseverance and tenacity. Others have postulated that with the development of the industrial societies, ethnic identities will in due course wither away.

In between the two opposite perspectives are a host of others. In this paper, I propose to critically evaluate a set of four approaches: primordialist, cultural pluralist, developmentalist and neo-marxist.

As for the primordialists, their basic focus is on culture. To them ethnic identities are not 'chosen', they are given, i.e. they proceed inexorably from the cultural givens of the past with the cultural markers being descent, race, language, religion, etc.

The emphasis laid by the primordialists on certain attachments in the cultural sphere as part of the personality formation and development which persist with them through life either consciously or unconsciously is well taken. There is no doubt that such affiliations provided the impetus and impulses for social and political mobilization.

Even so, ethnic identity is a significant but not a sufficient prerequisite to explain ethnic cleavages and conflicts. The very recognition of the primordialist sentiments and consequently differentiated character of ethnic groups for example does not explain as to why inter-ethnic group relationship has been harmonious at one time but not at another and still in some cases remains muted.

Besides, the cultural markers have their fluidities and variabilities in one's own life. What is more, the assumption of a primordialist core in the form of cultural attachment tends to be not only static but also ambivalent. For, among the various components of such a cultural core one may assume a pre-eminence at a time but may be supervened by another as the focal point of group identity assertion. The shift in emphasis from Muslim Bengalis to Bengali Muslims during the national movement of the erstwhile East Pakistan (now Bangladesh) describe it aptly.

Furthermore, underlining the premise of primordial ties is also the premise that these ties being 'particularistic', they have the potential to be road-blocks in the process of national-cohesion. Secondly, since ethnic attachments pertain to the 'non-rational' domain of the human personality, they lead to social turbulence and violence and thereby tend to be dysfunctional in the developmental process of the civil society.[4]

As for the latter, one needs to ask the question: Development for whom? Development for what? If the ethnic turbulence is the manifestation of a protest or revolt against the structural inequalities inherent in the existing social framework (e.g. the position of low castes and some of the tribes) in which a certain segment has continued to be disadvantaged, then such conflict should be viewed as mobilization-effort on the part of such groups for distributive justice and thereby functional in the developmental processes.

As regards the former, there is no doubt that the impulses for mobilizing the groups may be primordialist. And yet, empirical evidence in South Asian contexts has shown that the demands and mechanisms of such mobilization has been anything but primordial in a large number of cases. If anything, such demand articulation and aggregation has tremendous potential to widen the mediating structures and broadbase the democratic institutions of a pluralistic society. It is in such a context that the nature of power structure at the local and central levels assume salience in coping with the aspirations and demands of multi-ethnic collectivities. And in this respect, the approach of cultural pluralists provide a noteworthy explanatory framework.

Initially evolved by Furnivall[5] and subsequently refined and modified by Smith,[6] and others, the cultural pluralist approach has been an advance on the primordialist frame with their emphasis not merely being on the ethnic distinctiveness of a group as such but on the dominant-subordinate patterns of interaction amongst the various ethnic groups.

Briefly stated, Smith's cultural pluralism encompasses within a single society, the coexistence of various groups having institutional systems (i.e. social structures, value systems, belief patterns) which are 'mutually incompatible'. In such a culturally divergent situation, the structural requisites of a political order leads to the subordination of one group to the other. In the process, characterized as these societies are by domination, separation and instability they are "defined by dissensus and pregnant with conflict."

Here again, the dominant-subordinate syndrome does not take note of the intra-ethnic group cleavages. Nor does it inform us as to why in such a society 'impregnated with conflict', inter-ethnic group harmony exists. Finally, if the degree of cultural difference amongst the groups is the critical variable then it will be difficult to explain as to why inter-ethnic group conflict has often been led by the segments of the people that are culturally most similar "specifically, among the 'westernized' strata which have been engaged in the greatest amount of social and cultural interchange."[7]

If the cultural pluralist approach has posited the source of conflict in mutually incompatible values of various groups, the marxist/neo-marxist approach explains ethnic conflict as emerging: (a) at a general level in which ethnicity is viewed as a device in the hands of the vested interests, and (b) in a situation where there has been a 'cultural division of labour'. When members of an ethnic group are systematically assigned to a subordinate position within a given state (internal colonialism) or in global context (international division of labour).

Though conceived within the broad gamut of the theory of imperialism and that of dependency theorists, the proponents of internal colonialism have attempted to place "peoples rather than classes" as the central point of their approach.

Writing in 1965, Casanova maintained that "internal colonialism corresponds to a structure of social relations based on domination and exploitation among cultural heterogeneous, distinct group."[8] A decade later, taking the case of North Ireland, as his empirical universe, Hechter maintained that ethnic groups could be subjected to an internal colonialism in their subjugation to the core. The maintenance of ethnic divisions in the stratification system was not perceived as an abberation but as a systematic arrangement between the core and the periphery. Such a 'cultural division of labour' was defined as a system of stratification where objective cultural distinctiveness are superimposed on class lines. Given the convergence of ethnicity and economic status in the stratification system, the salience of ethnic distinction and awareness was likely to increase.[9]

The combination of economy and culture in the analysis of internal colonialists implies a rather limited realm: an 'internal colony' must have a geographically defined area and its relationship with the centre should be that of the dominant subordinate, exploiting-subjugated one.

However, in South Asia many areas can be specified in which despite the existence of the conditions mentioned above, inter-ethnic group conflict or the centre-periphery conflict have not occurred. While on the one hand, one does discern conflict prone areas fulfiling the requisites of 'internal colonialism' (e.g. Bangladesh, Baluchistan and to some extent Assam), there are many others fulfiling the prerequisites but not being conflict prone (e.g. South Bhutan, Arunachal, etc.).

Furthermore, the internal colonial model has a limited salience and does not provide an explanatory framework for either the ethnic violence in Sri Lanka or the recent turbulence in Punjab.

In sum thus, though in the evocation of ethnic conflict or ethno-nationalism, underdevelopment (real or perceived), has a strong emotive component, it can only partly explain the ethnic conflictual phenomena. Alongside the economic denominators, the socio-cultural concern for status and prestige coupled with the stakes in the political arena of the elites are equally critical in harmony as much as conflicts in ethnic terms.

Significantly, the internal colonial model by implication points to the perseverance of ethnic identities. As such, it seems to be shorn of the value premise prevalent in the other Marxian writings in which, ethnic conflicts have been viewed as a tool in the hands of the vested interests, ethnicity thus being perceived as antithetical to class. Some of the recent Marxian writings, however, not only, concede it as a significant part of the social base and social formations but also ascribe it a certain degree of autonomy, resilience, perseverance and dynamism as 'ethnos' (peoples) and nationalities.[10]

In contrast to this has been the much criticized approach of the development and communication theorists vis-a-vis ethnicity.[11] In such a perspective, as it emerged in the 1950s and 1960s, ethnic affinities were perceived as a residual phenomena. It was postulated that with the differentiation of division of labour and extension of capitalist market, ethnic attachment will be undermined, diffused and dissolved. However, not to speak of the third world, the continued assertion of ethnic pluralism in the USA, the devolution debate and the Ulster crisis in the UK, the issue of autonomy versus self-determination in Canada and the endemic nationalities question in the USSR have proved the assumptions of the developmentalists to be erroneous.

In fact the processes of 'modernization' and development have been caught up in the dialectics of their own dynamics; combating ethnic loyalty on the one hand and stimulating ethnic consciousness on the other. Consequently, whatever be the level of the development of the state, ethnic conflicts need to be viewed as parts of an ongoing process which have to be coped with and managed but cannot be resolved once and for all except through the total assimilation or elimination of a particular group. While the former has not been a large scale success as evidenced historically, the latter can be only genocidal and therefore an affront to human values and dignity.

In sum, thus, the various approaches discussed above provide valuable insights towards the understanding of ethnic conflicts but only partially. As for the attempts towards a general theory of political conflict, that of 'relative deprivation' has attracted the attention of many scholars in this respect. While economic explanations based on relative deprivation (real or perceived) do have a certain degree of explanatory value, 'relative deprivation' per se is a questionable device given the fact that there are a number of economically worse off ethnic groups who do not revolt and there are cases of relatively well off people who also do.[12]

As such, what I propose to do in the rest of the paper is not to present a neat model of ethnic conflict lest its neatness may belie empirical realities but to dwell on a cluster of variables which may not obtain in equal measure in all the cases. Nonetheless, they tend to be the prerequisites of ethnic conflict, its management or exacerbation.

In the process, I maintain that though having both the dimensions of identity and interest, ethnicity is basically a device in the pursuit of collective goals, through competition and interaction. The causes for its exacerbation lie in: (a) the linkages of ethnic consciousness to broader processes of social change; (b) the continuing trend towards expansion of state activities and following from it, the increasing intrusion of the institutions of power and authority in the form of domination (perceived or real), competition, threats or advantages in the ethnic realm.[13]

### III

THE SOUTH Asian canvas, whether in terms of the number or the web of inter-ethnic group interactions is perhaps one of the most varied and complex in the world. All the major religions have their followers in the region. About 20 languages have a recognized status as official languages at Central/State levels added to which are innumerable dialects spoken in various parts of the region. A substantial number of castes/tribes and sects criss-cross in between religion, race, language and region.

In such a context, an attempt to provide a checklist of ethnic groups at all-country level in various South Asian States can at best be tentative at a given time. Not only this, it has to reckon with the fact of: (a) the non-monolith character of an ethnic group, and (b) the changing locus of interaction at the various political-administrative tiers below the centre, i.e., the state/provinces/districts/divisions/villages. To this needs to be added the urban-rural divisions too.

Keeping these points in view, the broad categories of ethnic configuration in power terms may be as follows:[14]

1. A politically dominant majority vs. a subordinate minority or several such minorities: Sri Lanka (Sinhalese⟩ Tamils, Moors, Burghers); Pakistan (Punjabis⟩ Sindhis, Pathans, Baluchis); Bangladesh (Bengalis⟩ tribal groups).
2. A politically dominant minority vs. a subordinate majority as in most colonial situations. Bhutan (tribal groups⟩ Nepalis); Nepal (Valley Hindus⟩ Tarai people, Newaris, tribal groups).
3. A multiplicity of ethnic groups of various size and power confounded by a multiplicity of loci of contacts among them to the extent that ethnic configuration in terms of politically dominant and subordinate groups at the state level becomes well nigh impossible. India falls into this category. However, the locus of ethnic political interaction, on ethnic lines assume the dominant-subordinate configuration and even stratification—a criticality in the federal polity at the tiers below the central authority.

Besides, such a pattern is not static but may vary over time, e.g. the ethnic configuration in the pre-partition Pakistan stipulated the position of Bengalis and tribal groups as subordinated groups. This changed after 1971. Similarly till 1975, in the erstwhile monarchical system of Sikkim, the Lepchas/Bhotias had a political pre-eminence vis-a-vis Nepalis. Such a situation was virtually reversed particularly after its merger with India.

However, such a typology does not take us very far in explaining as to why some groups tend to be more volatile while others do not. It is here that the variable clusters—demographic, psychological, social, political and economic—take us a step ahead.

As for the geographical factor, the greater is the concentration of an ethnic group within a territorial confine, the greater is its potential for demand articulation and aggregation, e.g. the East Pakistan-West Pakistan conflict, the Sinhalese-Tamil conflict in Sri Lanka, the Tamil Nadu, Nagaland, Punjab and Assam situation in India.

Alongside spatial dispersal or concentration, the numerical dimension of an ethnic group has also some relevance (e.g. Newars in Nepal, tribal groups in Bangladesh, Moors in Sri Lanka) for, spatial dispersal and numerical weekness limits the capacity of the group for manoeverability, bargaining and conflict with the Centre.

Notwithstanding the numerical dimension, if an ethnic group has been historically insulated and has consequently perceived its stakes to be limited in the Centre then such a historical insularity has the potential to be an additional input in its demands for greater autonomy or self-determination. The people in the northeastern India, the Baluchis and Pathans and the tribal groups in the Chittagong Hill Tracts do discern such tendencies in asserting their identities and in perceiving the 'mainstream' as non-representational vis-a-vis them in cultural as much as in power terms.

Furthermore inequality in power terms amongst two ethnic groups need not per se invoke conflict. The preconditions of such a conflict are: (a) a socially mobilized population; (b) the existence of a pool of symbols connoting its distinctiveness; (c) the selection, standardization and transmission of such symbol pools to the community by the leadership; (d) presence of a group with which an adversary relationship is perceived and a sense of relative deprivation (real or perceived) is engendered.

Depending upon the position of the reference group in the various tiers of politico-administrative structures, the levels of inter-ethnic group cleavages can be identified. In cases where the centre and the reference group in question are perceived as virtually synonymous, the conflictual points reduce the capacity of the centre (e.g. Sri Lanka and Pakistan)—an option which may be available to it otherwise, depending upon the nature of linkages which it has with the units in question (e.g. Assam and the Punjab tangle in India).

This brings us to the crux of the question: the nature of power structure in ethnic/non-ethnic terms, the extent of stakes which the various ethnic communities have in the political system. What is their share in the power cake? Who gets what? From whom? Whose cost is perceived as another's gain?

The issue of the nature of state structure is equally closely related to the level of political development as much as the pace of social change within a state. Thus, if the overall political-economic development is low and the pace of change is far too graduated then it follows that conflicts may not rebound to disturb the status quo in violent terms. The inter-ethnic group experiences in Nepal and Bhutan provide some significant clues in this respect.

As for the power structure in Nepal, it has been by and large oligarchical with a small and dominant minority, pertaining to 'client families' and having three dominant caste groups (Brahmin,

Khatriyas and Newars), residing in the valley and belonging to small set of families, with the monarch at the apex. In the Terai area too, a small minority controls a "large share of the national wealth; much of the best agricultural land of the country, much of the small scale industry, a significant share of the large scale industry and trade between Nepal and outside world."

If the economic resources have been controlled by a minority of the Terai people, the hill echelon (notwithstanding the general poverty of the hill areas) has centralized political power in both the hills and the plains through the institution of monarchy, the control of state apparatus and the induction of Panchayat system under which the very dynamics of its operation keeps it somewhat fragmented leaving the umpire position of the king virtually unfettered.

Notwithstanding the polyethnic character of its society and regional differentiation, the political institution which has provided an overarching identity to the system has been that of monarchy. Consolidating the country into one state only about two centuries ago, the monarchy has not only had an emotive edge in political integration but vital stakes in it too for its own survival. As such, the induction of a partyless panchayat system in which even earlier, when special weightage was provided to 'class organizations' the tribal category as such was not recognized therein. Administratively, too, the formation of the development zones which unlike the districts have vertical, not horizontal divisions, have been presumably a device to blur regional distinctions.

Presumably, education, economic development and ballot box politics might have generated a certain amount of stir if not an upheaval. However, direct elections have been inducted only a few years ago and that too within the vortex of the panchayat system. The economic development has gone on at a snail's pace. The level of literacy is low. Consequently, the culture of politics has been dominantly a subject political culture in which the attitude of a few are acceeded to by the acquiescence of many. As such, issues of language and citizenship evoked by the Terai people at times have been contained, and have not exploded firstly because of the interlocking interests of the elites of the Terai and valley and also presumably because of the non-availability of alternatives.

It needs to be noted that because of its vicinity, terrain and other facilities, the Terai Hindus have been the biggest beneficiaries of aid from India. If they perceive merger with India as the alternative (apart from New Delhi's attitude which is a critical variable in such alternate-decision-fructification) they not only lose their identity but also the aid which comes to them primarily because they are part of Nepal!

As such, in the oligarchic set-up of the land locked kingdom, the inter-ethnic group divergence complex has a constellation of congruence areas in the context of which the interests of the elites of both the groups find expression in a competitive but not a conflictual frame of politics.

Juxtaposed as they are, between caste, class and tribe, ethnic group identities in Nepal seem to have effectiveness only under the canopy identity of region or race or tribe. As for the tribal groups, apart from their spatial dispersal and levels of underdevelopment in most cases, the 'notables' of several ethnic groups have been co-opted in the power structure.

In sum thus, the latency in inter-ethnic group conflict has been because of the tardy pace of social change and the non-competitive character of polity and economy. However, as and when the participatory character of its civic society advances in politico-economic spheres, demands in ethnic terms may be evoked with greater stridency. In the social terrain of Nepal, however, as and when such ethnic group mobilization takes place, the smaller under-privileged group leadership of the various tribes may demand greater share in societal rewards and goods by harping on "affirmative discrimination". As for the Terai Hindus, such group demand may be for greater politico-cultural autonomy for reasons referred to earlier.

As for Bhutan, its cultural pluralism has envisaged a relegated position to its minority Nepali community which has been by and large underdeveloped. However, in its case, the ethnic situation seems to be akin to that of the erstwhile Sikkim, with the power structure firmly entrenched in the hands of the hill people. So far, the relative inaccessibility of the landlocked kingdom has resulted in a slow pace of change. This however is being eroded gradually with the external pressures and pulls—in the form of aid and ideas impinging upon it. At present the polity seems to have a consociational mould which is basically an elitist frame. However, the durability of such a framework not only depends upon the continuing fact of the elites of various communities sharing enough in common to maintain a top level coalition but also have legitimacy vis-a-vis their respective communities as their leaders.

However, with the development of its physical infrastructure as well as communicational networks, and its gradual efforts to shed its age long isolation and insularity, the process of social change may assume a greater momentum so as to disturb its existing social order and its normative framework.

Three alternative scenarios can be envisaged in future in this respect:

(a) a gradually and relatively ordered process of social change capable of containing the pressures and pulls of development in general and cultural pluralism in particular;

(b) a somewhat trubulent political order in which the competitive edges of its socio-political order get sharpened in ethnic terms leading to a conflictual (though intermittently so) situation, in which the centre's 'holding operation' may not allow it to go out of control;

(c) an overtly conflictual situation in which the Nepalese ethnic loyalties get mobilized to pose a challenge to the capabilities of the non-Nepali dominated centre. The last alternative seems to be least likely at present. Nonetheless it should be kept in view particularly in the context of the irredentist and at the moment somewhat inchoate demand of 'Greater Nepal' or 'Gurkhaland'.

In contrast to the latency of ethnic conflict in Nepal and Bhutan, in Bangladesh, the tribal conflict, though showing an ascendancy in the late 1970s and early 1980s, seems to be somewhat muted at present. However, the impulses for the resentment of the tribal people in Chittagong Hill Tracts seem to be more or less similar to the several other tribal ethnic groups in the region: fear of loss of identity as a result of 'Bengalization' of the area, colonization, disturbance in the traditional mode of agricultural production and shrinking employment avenues. This is followed by a medley of constitutional/extra constitutional measures on their part to keep the centre out. The tribals have hardly succeeded in doing that, partly because of inter-tribal division, clash of leadership, sparse population and manpower personnel and last, but not the least, the presence of the coercive apparatus of the state. They have thus, registered their protest in ethnic terms vis-a-vis the centre but are too small a group to withstand its intervention in various forms.

Finally, the very fact that across the border, the tribal movements in Mizoram and Tripura have been perceived as hostile by the governments of the two States also implies the absence of succour from the governments across the border, a facility which they are alleged to have enjoyed in the pre-partitioned Pakistan.

## V

As with the other states of the region, an appraisal of the nature and tenor of the ethnic conflicts in India, Sri Lanka and Pakistan needs to be viewed in the context of their inherited situation, the nature of the states' systems, the perspectives of leadership and the impact of the uneven pace of development and change on its various ethnic groups.

Thus, during 1947-48, the challenges confronting the post-colonial states demanded on the one hand, a strong viable centre; on the other, their highly segmented social structures necessitated the involvement of a heterogeneous complex into a common undertaking and mould. Diversity needed to be harnessed for the state unity and dissent needed to be accommodated in a consensual frame.

The imperatives of state and nation-building were thus common; the strategies of leadership, however, were not. The nature and tenor of the post-independence power structure partly accounted for this divergence and so did the ideological heritage of its governing elites.

A segment of such an ideological heritage was that of the Eurocentric model of a 'nation-state' in which not only was a tendency to synonymize, erroneously though, the state with 'nation', but often to view the ethnic communites at best as 'sub-nation' having narrow parochial outlook and manifesting 'sectional nationalism'.

Such a perception of the 'nation' was at best that of a 'state-centric nation' in the making. Its juxtaposition with ethnic nation or nationalities not only confused the issues of state and nation-building, but also led to the pre-eminence of one over the other instead of harmonizing the pressures and pulls of both.

The agitation, debate, turmoil and conflict in these states indicated the pulls of identity and interest along with such ideological pulls in the vortex of which, generally speaking the Pakistan and Sri Lankan central elites appeared to veer towards the 'integrationist' approach while those in India seemed to oscillate between an integrationist and pluralist approach.

The integrationist approach implies the recognition of individuals' rights, obligations and privileges with the differentiated corporate entities being given a pretty low premium and an assimilation of the entire state population into a common identity. The pluralist perspective entailed the recognition of corporate sections along with individual rights and privileges and envisage for diversity a role in the development of personality of the state.[14] In other words, while the integrated perspective aims at unity of diversities, the pluralist perspective envisages the unity in diversities.

Added to such a differentiated perspective has been the systemic divergence in the three states. Thus, as for Pakistan the very nature of its power structure, moving from a week and fragmented political institutional base to a 'garrison state' gave a unitarian thrust to its federal framework.

The impulses for the break-up of Pakistan is already a well-documented area. As for the truncated Pakistan, such a unitarian thrust has been further compounded by the perception of the Punjabi domination at the Centre. However, while the movement in Sind has been nascent, that of the Pathans and Baluchis have been long-drawn. And even between the Baluch and Pathans, the feeling of alienation and the relative sense of deprivation appears to be far more intense amongst the Baluchis than amongst the Pathans in view of the fact that in the power cake, while the Pathans do have a certain representation, the Baluch share has been negligible. Even so, the very dynamics of the military regime has been such as to leave little leeway for protest and dissent. Consequently, as in the past, the process of 'state-building' has been such as to hamstrung the power dispersal and consequently an emphasis on the responsiveness of the multiple ethnic collectivities. As a result, the structures of ethnic conflict management in Pakistan seem to have been increasingly weakened through the virtual negation of the federal structure, provincial autonomy, electoral processes as well as the dynamics of party-politics.

However, the electoral processes and party politics need not necessarily operate as mediating structures and processes unless and until correlated to the legitimacy of authority structures. The ethnic turmoil in India and Sri Lanka aptly demonstrates this.

In both the cases, while on the one hand the processes of social change and development, buttressed by a participatory framework operated through fairly regularly held elections has given way to new impulses and demands, the very modalities and mechanisms to cope with them have either tended to be integrative or redundant in many instances. Thus, if the electoral processes have provided the legitimacy to the democratic framework of the states of India and Sri Lanka, the governmental processes have weakened the authority of such a legitimacy. If the constitutional framework of the two states provided some leeway for power dispersal, the very mechanisms and public policies have rendered it increasingly centralized and narrow-based in varying degrees. Furthermore, in the case of Sri Lanka, an adversarial concept of politics in a highly competitive and volatile political ethos, coupled with an increasingly bland affirmation of majoritarian principle in a multi-ethnic society and maldeveloped economy has brought in a deep ethnic divide.

As for India, the erosion of the Congress 'system' and the fragmentation of the opposition parties, coupled with the increasing mediation of vested interests at various levels has relegated the state to the position of a 'clay footed colossus' with its sociopolitical dynamic permeated by a 'low key violence', eruption of intermittent explosions of various sorts, whether they be in Assam or in Punjab.

With the very mechanism of power-management getting increasingly centralized and highly personalized, the mediating structures of the yore which provided anchorages and cushioning for conflict management at various levels have lost their initiative. And the lesser effective has been their clout the greater have been the interlocking situations between the Centre and its various socio-political collectivities. And in situations leading to direct confrontations, the more frequent has been the use of the state apparatus the greater has been the political vulnerability of the power wielders in terms of the authority of their legitimacy and lesser has been their flexibility for the various options—structural and non-structural—for conflict management in the ethnic sphere.

## VI

THE LEVEL of conflict management is also related to the nature of the demands of an ethnic group. This may be: (a) for affirmative discrimination (e.g. some of the tribal groups in Nepal), (b) greater autonomy and power without questioning the systemic sanctity (e.g. Centre-State debate in India, language reorganizations, demand for regional autonomy by the Tamil moderates in Sri Lanka); (c) autonomy demand related to that of systemic change (e.g. moderate groups in NWFP, Baluchistan and Sind); (d) secessionist (e.g. Baluch, Pathan militants in Pakistan and Tamil militants in Sri Lanka, pro-Khalistan elements in Punjab, National Socialist Council of Nagas Tripura National Volunteer Front); and (e) irredentist (demand for Pakhtunistan),

By and large, the continued neglect or mishandling of the initial demands for linguistic accommodation, regional autonomy, inequitious treatment in educational or employment avenues turns the autonomists into secessionists. Even so, at any given time, within the same ethnic community, one may find the votaries for autonomism, secessionism and irredentism, the classic example being that of Pathan and Baluchis in Pakistan.

As for the ramifications of secessionist and irredentist movements, added to their domestic sources of stresses and strength are also the transnational implications within the region and also beyond.

So far as its intra-regional implications are concerned, alongside the Indo-centric character of the region, the socio-cultural continuities in many cases spill over the territorial confines of its neighbourhood. As such, the ethnic violence in the neighbourhood brings in its wake refugees as well as political activists providing them the sanctuary or the base or mere moral support in India as the case may be.

To this needs to be added the support with the separatist/irredentist groups may get from other countries, e.g. the support to the Nagas and Mizos by China and by Pakistan before its break up and the linkages of a segment of Punjabi terrorists with Pakistan. Finally, the separatist/irredentist movement can also get succour of sorts from the expatriates as is the case of the Tamils in Sri Lanka.

Such support may provide them sustenance and a moral boost but the goal of separatists or irredentists is not easy to realize. In the former, it is not possible except through military intervention of another state and in the latter, the very irredentist character of the movement may bring more than two states together to contain it.

## VII

IN SUM THUS, progress in science and technology, widening of communication network, demographic changes, maldevelopment in the economic sectors. intended or unintended consequences of the participatory turned plebiscitory electoral-political processes have tended to be the catalysts of the process of social change in South Asian states, though in varying degress. To some extent, such processes have affected the normative order of the existing social framework in positive terms by questioning at times its stratificatory order and generating in the process social conflict with ethnic conflict being one of its many manifestations. Thus, contrary to the beliefs of the modernization and developmentalist theorists, ethnic conflict has been concomitant to the processes of change and development.

Further, as the South Asian experience has shown, with the institutions of power and authority playing a critical role in the processes of social change, the nature of states' system assumes a criticality in engendering conflict in ethnic terms as much as in its management.

Alongside the nature of the state structure, the level of development, aspirations and capabilities of its leadership in the process of negotiations and bargaining has been equally important. Furthermore with inter-ethnic group cleavage being basically political, the ethnic conflict is mainly the competition for power sharing and its management. As such, the greater is the relative distribution of ethnic communities in the competition for societal resources and opportunities, the greater are their stakes in the institutions of power and authority at various levels with the apex being the centre.

However, if at a given time, a particular ethnic community perceives the centre domination and control as being partisan and discriminatory vis-a-vis its own identity and interests and thereby resents its own peripheral status (either real or imaginary), it may develop a higher stake in its own ethnic identity. In such contexts, the lower is the capability and will of the central authority to match if not transcend such ethno-centric stakes of a community, the greater will be the structural strains on the political system, its extreme manifestation being a separatist movement.

The demand-conversion from separatism to autonomy can come only if the power wielders at the centre are prepared to give primary, not to the coercive apparatus of the state but to negotiated settlement which basically implies, and necessitates power-dispersal not its concentration failing which ethnic conflicts may tend to be endemic, expansive and in some cases, protracted in the South Asian region in the years to come.

## Notes

1. For example, writing as late as 1974, Isajiw rightly complained that in their empirical research on ethnicity, out of 65 studies by sociologists and anthropologists only 13 of them included some definition of ethnicity: 52 had no explicit definition at all. Wsevolod W. Isajiw, "Definitions of Ethnicity," *Ethnicity*, vol. 1, 1974, pp. 111-124. Also see Eugene Obidinski, "Methodological Considerations in the Definitions of Ethnicity," *Ethnicity*, vol. 5, 1978, pp. 213-228. The most comprehensive exposition of ethnic plurality in India is provided by R.A. Schermerhorn in *Ethnic Plurality* in India (Tucson, 1978). However, authors like Weiner, Kalzenstein and Lewandoski who have done empirical work on the subject have treated the definitional dimension of ethnic group and ethnicity rather cursorily. See, Myron Weiner, *Sons of the Soil: Migration and Ethnic Conflict in India* (Delhi, 1978): Mary Katzenstein, *Ethnicity and Equality: The Shiva Sena Party and Preferential Policy in Bombay* (Cornell, 1979); Susan Lewondowski, *Migration and Ethnicity in Urban India: Kerala Migrants in the City of Madras 1870-1970* (Delhi, 1980).
2. In the South Asian context, the methodological and definitional complexities have been touched in my paper entitled "Ethnic Movements in Pakistan" in Pandav Nayak, ed., *Pakistan: Society and Politics* (Delhi, 1984), pp. 182-211 and "Ethnic Dimensions of Nepalese Politics" in *Changing South Asia: Development and Welfare* (London, 1984).
3. Joseph Rothschild, *Ethnopolitics: A Conceptual Framework* (New York, 1981), p. 4.
4. For a succinct account and critical appraisal of the primordialist approach, see Paul R. Brass, "Elite Groups, Symbol Manipulation and Ethnic Identity among the Muslims of South Asia" in David Taylor and Malcolm Yapp, eds., *Political Identity in South Asia* (London, 1981), pp. 35-43. Also see in the same volume by Francis Robinson, *Islam and Muslim Separatism*, pp. 78-112. Robinson provides cultural factors a primacy in his presentation on the Muslim separatism. Brass adopts the instrumentalist approach in explaining the same phenomenon.
5. Furnivall, *Colonial Policy and Practice* (London, 1948).
6. M.G. Smith, *The Plural Society in the British West Indies* (Berkeley, 1965).
7. For a critical appraisal of the concept, see, Donald Horowitz., "Multiracial Politics in the New States: Towards a Theory of Conflict", mimeo. Also refer to several contributors in Vera Rubin, ed., "Social and Cultural Pluralism in the Caribbean", *Annals*, vol. 83, 1960, Leo Despres, "The Implications of Nationalist Politics in British Guiana for the Development

of Cultural Theory" in Reinhard Bendix, ed., *State and Society: A Reader in Comparative Political Sociology* (Boston, 1968), pp. 502-28. For a far more composite view of 'Cultural Pluralism', see Crawford Young, *The Politics of Cultural Pluralism* (Wisconsin, 1976).

8. Gonzalez Casanova, "Internal Colonialism and National Development," *Studies in Comparative International Development*, vol. 1, no. 4, 1965, p.33.
9. Michael Hechter, *Internal Colonialism: The Celtic Fringe in British National Development* (London, 1975).
10. e.g. see the writings of Yulian Bromkey, "The Object and Subject Matter of Ethnography," *Problems of the Contemporary World*, no. 49, (Moscow, 1978), pp. 7-23. Also see, "The Dialectic of Class and Tribe" in Saul, *The State and Revolution in Eastern Africa* (New York, Monthly Review Press, 1979), cited in Crawford Young, "The Temple of Ethnicity" (A Review Article), *World Politics*, vol. 35, no. 4, July 1983, p. 659.
11. e.g. see Daniel Lerner, *The Passing of Traditional Society: Modernizing the Middle East* (New York, 1958) and Karl Deutsch, *National and Social Communication* (Cambridge, 1966).
12. For a detailed exposition of the concept of relative deprivation as well as its merits and limitations, see, various contributions in Ted Robert Gurr, ed., *Handbook of Political Conflict* (New York, 1980).
13. Young, n. 10, pp. 659-60.
14. For an elucidation of these perspectives in analytical terms see Paul R. Brass, *Language, Religion and Politics in North India* (Delhi, 1975), pp. 119-81. An elucidation of these approaches in the context of South Asian States has been attempted by me in "Politics of Language in South Asia," Paper presented at the Eighth European Conference on Modern South Asian Studies, Tauberg, Sweden, July 1983.

CHAPTER SEVEN

# Ethnic Conflict in Sri Lanka

## V. Suryanarayan

WHEN SRI Lanka (formerly known as Ceylon) became an independent country on 4 February 1948, it was relatively a peaceful country in contrast to the orgy of violence that accompanied the birth of its two northern neighbours, India and Pakistan. D.S. Senanayake, the first Prime Minister, was not only the leader of the majority Sinhalese community, but he had also the tacit support of the minority groups. As such, many political commentators felt that the country was well on the way to attain political stability and the major ethnic groups would get integrated into one nation.[1]

Thirty-six years later, the political system has undergone a fundamental transformation. During the last three and a half decades not only have the bridges been burnt, the chasm dividing the Sinhalese and the Sri Lanka Tamils has widened. There are very few Tamils in the two major political parties, the United National Party (UNP) and the Sri Lanka Freedom Party (SLFP). The Sri Lankan Tamils have moved to the other extreme. Thwarted in their repeated attempts to find an honourable solution within the multi-ethnic state of Sri Lanka the leaders of the major Tamil political party, the Tamil United Liberation Front (TULF) raised the demand for a separate Tamil Eelam in Vaddukaddai in May 1976. In the general elections held in May 1977, the TULF obtained an overwhelming endorsement from the electorate in Northern district and considerable (but less than that in the Northern district) support in the Eastern district, which is generally considered to be the traditional homeland of Sri Lankan Tamils. Law and order situation began to deteriorate soon. Since Jayawardene assumed power, first as Prime Minister in 1977 and then as President in 1978, communal riots have taken place at regular intervals. Masterminded by the lumpen sections of Sinhalese population and abetted by the armed forces and the police, riots have broken out in 1977, 1981 and 1983. The winter discontent continues unabated in Tamil areas with the Sri Lankan armed forces going on rampaging spree and attacking innocent civilians at regular intervals since July 1983. The riots have brought in their wake a trail of untold misery and suffering to the Tamil minorities and has put the clock back as far as Sri Lanka's political, economic and social progress is concerned. Compounding the complex situation is the presence of a determined group of Tamil extremists, popularly known as Tamil Tigers. Disillusioned with constitutional niceties, they have taken to the cult of the bomb and the bullet to attain their goal of Tamil Eelam. Sri Lanka today is at the cross-roads. The Tamils and the Sinhalese are sitting on the top of a volcano that can erupt at any moment. The next few months would unfold whether President Jayawardene and Prime Minister Premadasa would rise to the occasion and make necessary accommodation to arrive at an amicable settlement with justice and fair play to all, or whether the Republic would plunge into a state of continuing civil war like Lebanon and Ulster, or even end up dividing itself into two states either by consent or by surgery.

What are the underlying causes of Sinhalese-Tamil conflict? What are the roots of Tamil separatism? Does the demand for Tamil Eelam have the support of other minority groups like Indian Tamils and Tamil Muslims? Would the establishment of Tamil Eelam lead to a solution of the Tamil problem in Sri Lanka? These and other questions are naturally being raised in India, especially in Tamil Nadu, by all sections of population. A modest attempt will be made in the succeeding sections to analyse the problems of contemporary Sri Lanka.

### POPULATION STATISTICS

SRI LANKA is a large island of 65,609 square kilometres and is situated 20 miles away from the southern tip of India. Like India, Sri Lanka is a multi-ethnic, multi-religious and multi-lingual country. According to the official census estimates for 1981, the total population of Sri Lanka is 14,850,001 of which the Sinhalese number 10,958,666 or 74.0 per cent; Sri Lankan Tamils 1,871,535 or 12.6 per cent; Indian Tamils 825,233 or 5.5 per cent; Sri Lankan Moors 1,056,972 or 7.1 per cent; Burghers 38,236 or 0.3 per cent; Malays 43,378 or 0.3 per cent and others 28,981 or 0.2 per cent.[2]

69.3 per cent are Buddhists (Sinhalese); 15.5 per cent Hindus (Sri Lankan Tamils and Indian Tamils); 7.6 per cent Muslims (Ceylon Moors, Tamil Muslims and Malays) and 7.5 per cent Christians. (Sri Lankan Tamils, Sinhalese, Indian Tamils and Burghers). As is obvious, Sinhalese speak Sinhala language, Sri Lanka Tamils, Indian Tamils and Tamil Muslims speak Tamil while the Burghers speak English or Sinhalese.

### Sinhalese Fears

THE SINHALESE comprise a group of people who speak an Aryan language called Sinhala. According to tradition, the first Sinhalese migrants led by Prince Vijaya and his 700 followers migrated from Eastern India to Sri Lanka some 2,500 years ago.[3] They gradually took roots in different parts of the Island, and got assimilated with the aboriginal inhabitants and also more substantially with later migrants from Malabar coast and other parts of India. Gradually, they developed a distinct identity of their own; this process was further hastened when all of them embraced the Buddhist faith around the third century B.C. As time went by, the Sinhalese subscribed to the view that Sri Lanka is *Sinhaladvipa* or the land of the Sinhalese and *Dhammadvipa*—or the land of Buddhism. Based on a prosperous agricultural economy, the Sinhalese established their powerful kingdoms, patronized the Buddhist faith and erected impressive Buddhist monuments. The Sinhalese hegemony in Sri Lanka began to decline as a result of systematic invasions from South India, which led to the abandonment of their great centres of civilization like Anuradhapura and Pollanaruva. In the beginning of the sixteenth century, there were three independent kingdoms in the island; the Sinhalese kingdoms of Kandy and Kotte (near Colombo) and the Tamil Kingdom in Jaffna peninsula. It must be kept in mind that the historical experience of Tamil-Sinhalese conflict has produced a pattern of mythical history, which lies at the heart of the Sinhalese perception of their own destiny and also the role of the Tamils in the island. The Sinhalese argue that the invasions from South Indian Tamil Kingdoms and the consequent Sinhalese-Tamil conflict have led to the developmnt of two antagonistic identities, Sinhalese and Tamil. Allied to this was another dangerous doctrine which portrayed the Sinhalese as the defenders of the *Sasana* (Universal Buddhist

Church) and the Tamils as the opposers of the *Sasana*. As Gananath Obeyesakere rightly points out, these theories are not always, in accordance with historical facts.[4] Tamil kings who ruled over Sinhalese kingdoms often took upon themselves in the traditional role of the Sinhalese rulers as the upholders of the Buddhist faith: few Sinhalese kings pillaged temples and robbed monasteries of their wealth. Yet these myths are important because these explain how the Sinhalese perceive their role and, in times of national crisis, these myths become the rallying points of Sinhalese nationalism.

The religious and cultural efflorescence that took place in the late nineteenth and early twentieth centuries reinforced these tendencies further. Anagarika Dharmapala and other exponents of Buddhist revivalism resurrected the glories of the Sinhala-Buddhist past, underscored the necessity to safeguard Buddhist religion, a duty believed to have been ordained by Lord Buddha himself and safeguard the pristine purity of the Sinhala-Aryan race from the corrupting influences of un-Aryan elements. Thus emerged the concept of Sinhala-Buddhist hegemony, which should be protected at all costs from the inroads Dravidian Tamil groups. Kumari Jayawardena quotes a recent Sinhalese chauvinist publication, *Kauda Kotiya* (who is the Tiger) which states:

> The Sinhalese race has a clearly documented unbroken history of over 2500 years. There is no history older than the history of the Sinhalese in Sri Lanka. That Sri Lanka belongs to the Sinhala race is not based on mythology or fables handed down from mouth to mouth. Ancient rock inscriptions, inscriptions in gold, huge viharas and dagobas, huge statues of Lord Buddha sculptured out of rocks, huge tanks and irrigation systems all bear unshakeable witness to the heritage of the Sinhala race and Sinhala country.... .[5]

The close identification between Sinhala race and Buddhist religion and the necessity to be united and vigilant against "anti-Buddhist barbarians" comes out vividly in another Sinhalese publication, *Sinhaluni, Buda Sasna Bera Geniw* (Sinhalese, Save the Buddhist Religion):

> The link between Sinhala race and Buddhism is so close and inseparable that it had led to the maxim. "There is no Buddhism without the Sinhalese and no Sinhalese without Buddhism". This

is an undeniable fact. The literature of the Sinhalese is Buddhist literature. The history of the Sinhalese is the history of Buddhism. The language of the Sinhalese is enriched by the doctrine of the Buddha. The 'era' of the Sinhalese is the "Buddha era". The culture of the Sinhalese is Buddhist culture. The flag of the Sinhalese is the Sinhala Buddhist flag... Yet, from a few years ago, there has been an organized movement of anti-Sinhala, anti-Buddhist barbarians to destory our invaluable archaeological ruins and Buddhist shrines. It is undoubtable that the future generations, as well as our forefathers who sacrificed their lives for the freedom of their race and for the glory of their religion, shall curse us for our silence. At least, now, in the name of our race, in the name of our forefathers and in the name of unborn generations, let us all direct our attention to this situation.[6]

Though the Sinhalse comprise nearly three-fourths of Sri Lankan population, they do not look at the Tamils as minority groups but as those who have special links with India and no loyalty to the island Republic. A Sinhalese publication, *Sinhalayage Adisi Hatura* (The Unseen Enemy of the Sinhalese) states:

The Sinhalese have no motherland other than Sri Lanka. The Indian trade union leaders, the Sindhi traders and most Tamil workers use Sri Lanka as a mine from which they obtain money and invest it in large houses and lands which they buy in the names of their children and close relatives, in India. All of them live with one foot in India and the other in Sri Lanka. Their only loyalty to Sri Lanka is as a gold mine. They do not have any sympathy towards the Sinhalese culture, language, Buddhism or the traditional Sinhalese people.[7]

In moments of ethnic crisis, the Sinhalese chauvinists raise the bogey of Tamil expansionism and present a nightmarish scenario of having no other homeland to migrate to and begin driven to the sea by massive hordes of Tamil invaders. Paul Sieghart, the distinguished Jurist, mentions that "even well-educated Sinhalese will construct fanciful scenarios of the State of Tamil Nadu forcing the Union of India, by threats of secession, to invade Sri Lanka in defence of Tamil interests."[8]

## Tamil Misgivings

The Sri Lankan Tamils resent and vociferously protest if one refers to them as immigrant community. They insist that they are a nation and point out that their historical tradition in Sri Lanka is as old as the Sinhalese. Without entering into the controversy as to whether the Sinhalese or the Tamils were the first to settle in the island, it can be stated beyond a shadow of doubt that the Sri Lankan Tamils are as indigenous to the country as the Sinhalese.[9] The Tamil population gradually began to increase as a result of immigration from South India. With the rise of powerful Tamil Kingdoms in South India, the island was subjected to frequent invasions. Tamil kingdoms emerged and gradually became strong largely based in the Jaffna peninsula. The Tamil kingdoms in the North and the Sinhalese kingdoms in the South occasionally engaged in warfare; otherwise they led a life of peaceful coexistence. There was also an extensive no man's land between the two kingdoms. In the keen competition of mutual bickering and slinging match between Sinhalese and the Tamils, it is generally forgotten that if there were frequent clashes between the two kingdoms, there were also notable interludes of mutual tolerance and cooperation. As C.R. De Silva, the well known historian points out, Sinhalese kings occasionally married South Indian Tamil princesses; and Tamil officials were known to hold important positions in Sinhalese courts; Tamil rulers in Jaffna are known to have assisted Sinhalese kings against their enemies. Buddhist temples gradually came to accommodate shrines to Hindu Gods within their premises.[10]

If the Sinhalese perceive that Sri Lanka is *Dhammadvipa* and *Sinhaladvipa* and, therefore, they have a greater historical and cultural claim to the country, equally it must be stated that the existence of powerful Tamil kingdoms in North and East, prior to the arrival of the Portuguese are significant motivating forces for Tamil nationalism. Though not expressly stated, the Sinhalese argument asserts that Sri Lanka is the land of Buddhist Dhamma and Buddhist institutions; it is the original homeland of the Sinhalese race and Sri Lankan nationalism and Sri Lankan nation must be based on the foundation of its Sinhalese component, especially the Sinhalese language and the Buddhist faith. According to Sinhalese fanatics, all other cultural components are alien and if they still survive it is because of the tolerance and magnanimity of the

Sinhalese. The Tamils, on the other hand, argue that they also have an authentic memory of shared historical experience which are as old as the Sinhalese component, They also wielded independent political power in the North and the East from the thirteenth to the sixteenth centuries. What is more, during this period, the Sri Lankan Tamils acquired their most important possession, the "territorial homeland," which has served to underline their distinct identity. According to the protagonists of Tamil Eelam, based on the historical promise, Tamil Eelam does not mean partition or separation; it means the restoration and reconstitution of the ancient Tamil kingdom whose death knell was struck by the Portugese in 1621.[11]

The Sri Lanka Tamils, as stated earlier, claim the Northern and Eastern Provinces—Jaffna, Mannar, Vavuniya, Mullaithivu, Batticoloa and Trincomalee districts—as their traditional homeland. According to the 1981 census, they comprise 95.3 per cent of Jaffna's population; 50.6 per cent of Mannar; 56.8 per cent of Vavuniya: 70.8 per cent of Batticoloa; 76.0 per cent of Mullaithivu and 33.8 per cent of Trincomalee.[12] The dynamics of economic development that has taken place during the British rule and in the post-independence period has led to the migration of a number of Sri Lanka Tamils away from their homeland to Sinhalese inhabited areas. Over the years, they have taken roots in these regions and have developed considerable economic stakes as professionals, white-collar workers, and businessmen traders. According to the 1981 census, 699,000 or 38.0 per cent of Sri Lankan Tamils inhabit the Southern, Central and Easern parts of the island.[13] Incidentally, it is interesting to note that among the urban areas, Colombo has the largest concentration of Sri Lanka Tamils. Acccording to the 1981 statistics of the Central Bank of Ceylon there are 166,400 Sri Lanka Tamils within the city and suburbs of Colombo. Even Jaffna Municipality has only 112,290 Sri Lankan Tamils.[14] As a result of frequent communal riots, many Indian Tamils have migrated to the predominantly Tamil Northern and Eastern districts. According to the 1981 statistics, they constitute 19.4 per cent of Vavunia, 13.8 per cent in Mullaithivu and 13.3 per cent in Mannar.[15] Due to the diminution of employment opportunities aggravated further by the blatant pro-Sinhalese recruitment policies of successive governments in Colombo, a large number of Sri Lankan Tamil academicians, doctors, engineers, scientists, technologists, accountants and other skilled personnel are migrating to United States, Canada, Western Europe, Middle

East, Australia and New Zealand. Smarting under an acute sense of deprivation in their own motherland, these educated elite are the greatest protagonists of Tamil Eelam. They also provide considerable financial and material support to the cause of Tamil Eelam.

### Sri Lankan Tamils—not a Homogeneous Group

ONE SHOULD be cautious and not fall into the convenient trap that the Sri Lankan Tamils are a homogeneous group. Depending on their geographical location, economic organization, social structure and level of development, they have responded differently to crucial issues of ethnic politics.[16] Broadly speaking the Sri Lankan Tamils could be divided into three groups. First, Jaffna Tamils. They are numerically the largest and politically the most volatile; they have provided the leadership and dedicated following to the TULF and Tamil militants. The chief attribute of the Jaffna Tamil, according to Dr. Sivathamby, is that he is Jaffna-centric; even when he works outside the Jaffna peninsula, he has displayed a sense of exclusiveness and pride in his Jaffna identity.[17] In terms of social stratification, it is the Vellales who have dominated the social, economic, political and cultural setting in Jaffna. Many of the Vellala leaders have been unashamed apologists of Vellala superiority over the other depressed classes. Sir Ponnambalam Ramanathan, for example, opposed the introduction of adult franchise on the ground that it would give the depressed classes the right to vote. He also, on the same ground, opposed the introduction of equal seating arrangements in Jaffna schools. Since education was the main industry in Jaffna and public services the chief avenue of employment, the Jaffna Tamils had always been in the forefront opposing the government's policy on language, education and employment. As the London based Minority Rights Group puts it, "Nothing arouses deeper despair among Tamils than the feeling that they are being systematically squeezed out of higher education."[18] (ii) Unlike the Jaffna peninsula, the Eastern provinces are educationally backward, have mixed population with a large sprinkling of Muslims and are predominantly agricultural. As a result, the Eastern Tamils are less militant on questions like standardization. On the other hand, the district-wise quota system for admission to universities introduced by the present UNP government has been welcomed by large sections as they stand to gain from it. It is also interesting to note that in terms of political behaviour, while the TULF swept the polls in the 1977 elections in the Jaffna peninsula, it could win only four out of ten seats in the Eastern districts. Devenayagam, a Cabinet Minister, won on the UNP ticket from Kalkuda constituency. C. Rajadurai, a senior Vice-President of the Party, won the Batticoloa seat, but deserted the TULF, joined the UNP and became a Cabinet Minister. K. Kanagaratnam, elected on the TULF ticket from Pottuvil, defected and joined the UNP. (iii) Large sections of Tamils have made Colombo their permanent home as professionals, civil servants, business executives and white-collar workers. Working with the Sinhalese closely, they have a vested interest in the survival of Sri Lanka as a united country and have developed a great amount of tolerance than their Jaffna counterparts. Many of them voted for the UNP in the 1977 election and were pressurizing the TULF to come to an understanding with the government. A clue to the political behaviour of the Colombo Tamil is provided by the Tamil lawyer, Dr. Neelan Tiruchelvan, the former TULF MP, who has been mediating between TULF leaders and the President. In other words, the solid support for a separate Tamil Eelam comes mainly from the Northern districts, especially the Jaffna peninsula. All said and done, one should not ignore the winds of change affecting all sections of Tamils, especially after the riots of July 1983. In the new situation all of them share the same feeling of insecurity and this factor can provide a new sense of solidarity among them.

## Indian Tamils—Most Vulnerable Section

Though the Indian Tamils share the common bonds of ethnicity and language with the Sri Lankan Tamils, the problems that they face and the aspirations that they entertain are in many ways different from their kinsfolk in the Northern and Eastern parts of the islands. The Indian Tamil component in Sri Lanka's population has been speedily declining. According to the 1971 census, they numbered 1,174,606 or 9.3 per cent of the population; but in 1981, their number came down to 825,233 or 5.5 per cent of the island's population. The reduction has been due to the repatriation of Indian Tamils as a result of the implementation of the Sirimavo-Sastri pact. The Indian Tamils are concentrated in the plantations located in the Central, Sabaragamuva and Uva provinces. They constitute 47.3 per cent of the population of Nuwara Eliya; 9.3 per cent of Kandy;

6.8 per cent of Matale; 2.1 per cent of Badulla; 3.3 per cent of Monaragala; 11.1 per cent of Ratnapura and 6.4 per cent of Kegalla.[19] Unlike the Sri Lankan Tamil settlements, these plantations are surrounded by Sinhalese villages and are located in the heartland of Sinhalese people. This stark reality has made them realize that both their present and future are closely intertwined with the Sinhalese and that they must coexist with the Sinhalese population. In other words, Tamil Eelam would not lead to the political salvation of Indian Tamils.

Unlike the Sinhalese and Sri Lankan Tamils, the Indian Tamils are not indigenous to the island. They are the descendants of the Tamil labourers who were brought to the island by the British colonialists to provide the much needed labour for the development of the tea, rubber and coconut plantations. They formed the bulk of the labour which turned the malaria infested forests of Sri Lanka into smiling plantations, earning the much-needed precious foreign exchange which sustains the Sri Lanka economy today.

The plantation workers was the worst victim of imperialist exploitation and after independence of the ultra-nationalist politicians of Sri Lanka. One can apply any yardstick; per capita income, living conditions, educational attainments, longevity of life, status of women—and one finds that the Indian Tamil is undoubtedly in the worst position in Sri Lanka today. As the *Economic Review*, published by the *People's Bank*, summed up: "After almost 110 years of tea industry, the life of the plantation worker is still characterized by low living conditions, illiteracy, crowded housing and suffering."[20]

Most of the Indian Tamils belong to the third or fourth generation and the younger elements know precious little of India except perhaps the names of the villages from which their ancestors originally came. According to all canons of justice and fairplay they should have become Sri Lankan citizens entitled to all rights and privileges of citizenship. In the protracted negotiations that took place between New Delhi and Colombo after independence, Jawaharlal Nehru maintained that the future of the Indian Tamils was a domestic problem of Sri Lanka and requested the governments in Colombo to speedily confer citizenship on them. The Shastri era represented a slide back from the correct stand taken by Jawaharlal Nehru. In a most unstatesmanly manner, Lal Bahadur Shastri signed an Agreement with Sirimavo Bandaranaike in 1964 by which New Delhi agreed to confer citizenship on 525,000 persons of Indian origin and repatriate them to India in exchange for conferment of Sri Lankan citizenship on 300,000 persons in the ratio of 7 : 4. The Agreement, popularly known as Sirimavo-Shastri Pact, which was concluded without taking into consideration the view and wishes of the plantation workers, was not only inhuman, but also bad precedent for New Delhi's policy towards the Indians Overseas. By a subsequent Agreement in 1974 between Indira Gandhi and Sirimavo Bandaranaike, India and Sri Lanka agreed to confer citizenship on 75,000 people more, respectively.[21]

Even though the Sirimavo-Shastri Pact expired on 31 October 1981 it has not solved the problems of the stateless people of Indian origin. The process of conferment of Sri Lankan citizenship and repatriation to India has been painfully slow. The fate of several thousands of people of Indian origin is still hanging in the balance. It must also be pointed out that the hope of starting a decent life which many people of Indian origin entertained on coming to India has not been fulfilled. Most of the grandiose schemes for the rehabilitation of repatriates have failed due to unimaginative planning, bureaucratic bungling and red tapism. For the repatriates it has been a bitter home-coming. Unwanted in Sri Lanka and unwelcome in India they are driven from pillar to post and languish in different parts of Tamil Nadu.[22]

The plight of the plantation workers is rendered worse by the fact that their basic human right, namely, protection of life, limb and property has not been assured to them. The communal carnage that took place in 1977, 1981 and 1983 clearly demonstrated the vulnerability of people living in the plantation areas and their utter helplessness against the lumpen sections of Sinhalese marauders. The police and the army stood mute and paralysed and did not take any action against the offenders. It has shaken the confidence of the people in the custodians of law and order, and has created a psychological climate of fear and insecurity. Their natural reaction, whether they belonged to the Ceylon Workers Congress or any other rival union, was to flee to India. They were aware that it is not roses, roses all they way in India, but they are convinced that in India they will not be friendless and defenceless like an uprooted tea bush.

It is the tragedy of Tamil politics in Sri Lanka that the educated elite, who provide leadership to the Sri Lankan and Indian Tamils, have not found it possible to take a common stand on many crucial issues. The only experiment at unity took place in 1972, when the

Federal Party, Tamil Congress, the Ceylon Workers Congress and Devanayagam of the UNP came together to form the Tamil United Front. With the victory of the UNP in the 1977 elections and the induction of Thondaman and Devanayagam into the Cabinet, the original basis of the TULF disappeared completely. The TULF now is an alliance of two parties, the Federal Party and the Tamil Congress, the latter splitting into two over the selection of candidates in the 1977 election, with a dissenting group under Kumar Ponnambalam leaving the TULF. Except for this brief interlude, the TULF and the CWC have taken parallel and occasionally even contradictory lines. In May 1976, when the TULF raised the demand for a separate Tamil Eelam, the CWC dissociated itself from what it considered to be an impractical and unrealistic slogan. The CWC activities also point out to the early years of independence, when sections of Sri Lankan Tamils under G.G. Ponnambalam worked hand in glove with the government in disfranchising a million Indian Tamil plantation workers.[23] The TULF attempts to get a foothold in the plantations through its trade union, *Illankai Tholilar Kalagam*, have not made any headway. On the other hand, the demand for Tamil Eelam and the violent activities of Tamil militants have made the position of the plantation workers extremely vulnerable. Dissociation from the Tamil Eelam demand has not saved them from the savage attacks by Sinhalese goons in 1977, 1981 and 1983.

It is pertinent here to ask as to what extent has the CWC been able to safeguard the interests of the Indian plantation workers? Started in 1940, the Ceylon Indian Congress (later renamed Ceylon Workers Congress) has over the years developed as the most representative organization of Indian Tamils in Sri Lanka. Savmayamoorthy Thondaman, President of the Party, is an astute politician and has a charismatic appeal to the plantation workers.[24] In the political climate after the landslide victory of the UNP in the 1977 elections, the CWC decided to reverse its opposition stance and to join hands with the UNP government. It was an act of deliberate choice, because in the political calculation of Thondaman, Jayawardene was more sympathetic to the cause of Indian Tamils than Sirimavo Bandarnaike and he would provide honourable solutions to the manifold problems facing the community. Thondaman served as a member of the Select Committee to draft the new Constitution and decided to join the government. For the first time in independent Sri Lanka, a representative of Indian Tamils was included in the government when Thondaman joined the Cabinet as Minister for Rural Industries Development. It was a clever political move on the part of Jayawardene, which brought immediate political benefits to the government by both widening the breach between the two Tamil communities and also securing the crucial Indian Tamil support in subsequent electoral battles. The support of the Indian Tamils was an important factor which tilted the balance in favour of the UNP both in the Referendum and the Presidential elections. President Jayawardene has also made certain positive gestures towards ameliorating the conditions of the plantation workers. The distinction between citizens by registration and citizens by descent has been removed. An amendment was introduced to the Local Bodies Election Ordinance as a result of which the plantation workers, for the first time in independent Sri Lanka, were entitled to participate in elections to District Councils and Local Bodies. The estate schools have been taken over and integrated with the national system of education and better housing facilities have been given in few estates. What is more important, President Jayawardene held out the promise repeatedly that he would find a lasting solution to the problem of statelessness, which has been hanging like the damocles sword over the Indian Tamils.

The critics of the CWC, especially in Jaffna and Tamil Nadu, accuse Thondaman of betraying the Tamil cause, who they feel has become a gullible victim of the Machiavellian President. The criticism is unfounded and is not based on a proper appreciation of the political realities of Sri Lanka. In the present difficult political situation, Thondaman has maximized his options as Cabinet Minister, the President of the CWC, intimate friend of Jayawardene and M.G. Ramachandran and longstanding confidant of New Delhi. The successful nine days plantation workers strike in April 1984, called by the CWC and supported by all rival trade unions (except the UNP-led Lanka Jathika Estates Workers Union), was a master stroke of an astute politician. It displayed Thondaman's ability to initiate independent action even against the government of which he was a part. It was the first successful strike in recent times and also demonstrated Thondaman's unquestionable hold on the plantation workers. Even though a Cabinet Minister, Thondaman has not surrendered his individuality, and has on several occasions, both in public and private, criticized the discriminatory policies of the government against Sri Lankan Tamils. When the Sri Lankan Parliament, in an unusual and unprecedented gesture, passed a vote of no confidence against the leader of opposition, A. Amrithalingam, in July 1982, Thondaman dissociated himself from the UNP; his speech was the only voice of sanity in an otherwise poisoned atmosphere.[25] In the Parliamentary sessions since July 1983 again, he has been forthright in his comments on the political developments in the island. In hard hitting speeches in parliament, he lashed out at the Sinhalese extremists, both within and outside the government, and underlined the necessity for the moderate elements to rally round President Jayawardene.[26]

The CWC no doubt is opposed to the demand for Tamil Eelam, but Thondaman has repeatedly pointed out that the TULF had been driven to the extreme position because of the many acts of discrimination, aggravated by military reprisals, perpetrated by the successive Sinhalese-dominated governments. Even now he believes that the hands of the moderates within the TULF should be strengthened which would make them amenable considering reasonable alternate proposals. On the eve of the 1977 elections, Thondaman arranged a meeting between Jayawardene and Amirthalingam in his house; it was as a result of these discussions that the UNP listed the Tamil grievances in its election manifesto and promised to hold an all-party conference to find out an amicable solution. Thondaman also suggested to Jayawardene not to field UNP candidates against TULF in predominantly Tamil constituencies in the North and the East. Had Thondaman's suggestions been heeded, Jayawardene-Amirthalingam relations would have taken a different course. Thondaman's visit to India and his discussions with the Indian government were the catalysts which paved the way for G. Parthasarathy's visit to Colombo and the convening of the Round Table Conference. In the new political situation in Sri Lanka after July 1983 riots, with the TULF out of the parliamentary arena, it is Thondaman who is emerging as the main spokesman for Tamil minorities. In the keen competition to whip up passions and mobilize opinion, which characterizes Tamil Nadu politics today, Thondaman has taken a statesmanlike attitude. He appealed to the politicians and the media in Tamil Nadu to exercise restraint in their comments, lest communal tensions should get exacerbated in Sri Lanka.

The announcement in October 1984 that the All Party Conference has reached a consensus to confer citizenship on 95,000 stateless people is no doubt a welcome development. However, a discordant note has been struck by the SLFP which has opposed the move and has asked the government to negotiate another agreement with India. What is more important, citizenship will have no meaning unless the basic right of the plantation Tamils for security of life and property and a decent standard of living is assured.

The most important fall-out of the 1983 riots is the fact that the Indian and Sri Lankan Tamils are coming closer together, feeling threatened by a common sense of insecurity as they do. Thondaman articulated this feeling succinctly:

Whether it is Amirthalingam, or the CWC, or Maheswaran, I told you earlier that an identification has been created by the manner in which all Tamils have been treated in the past. We have different problems but when there is a determined policy to discriminate, to harass, to persecute, to crush, then all the Tamils in Tamil Nadu or here or anywhere in the world feel that injustice is done.[27]

### Sri Lankan Muslims—Opposition to Tamil Eelam

The Sri Lankan Muslims who number 1,056,972 or 7.1 per cent of the island's population are scattered in all parts of the country. They constitute 41.4 per cent of the population of Amparai; 29.0 per cent of Trincomalee; 26.6 per cent of Mannar; 24.0 per cent of Batticoloa; 9.7 per cent of Puttalam; 6.5 per cent of Pollanaruva; 6.9 per cent of Vavuniya; 7.1 per cent of Anuradhapura; 10.0 per cent of Kandy and in smaller proportions in other places.[28]

The Muslims are noted for their entrepreneurship and hard and sustained work. As a result, they are the most business-like community in Sri Lanka today.[29] It is but natural that they should prefer a free enterprise economy, which explains their traditional support to the UNP. The Muslim identify their ethnicity in terms of religion and culture and not language. As in India, they speak the language of district in which they live and most of them are proficient in both Sinhalese and Tamil. Acutely conscious of their geographical dispersal, the Muslims have not formed any communal party of their own. Their strategy is to join hands with the SLEP and the UNP and try to win concessions from whichever party is in power. This policy has paid high dividends and the two major Sinhalese parties are vying with one another in championing the cause of the Muslims. There are three Muslim Ministers in the present UNP cabinet, with A.C.S. Hameed holding the key portfolio of External Affairs. The Muslims have bargained and wrested concessions in two spheres affecting their cultural identity, first in the area of consolidation and recognition of Muslim personal laws and second, in the field of education.

As far as the Sinhalese-Tamil conflict is concerned, the claim of the TULF that it is the spokesman of all the Tamils in the "traditional Tamil homeland" is discredited by the Tamil Muslims' refusal to join the TULF ranks. In the day to day politics, the community has hardly cooperated with the Federal Party and its successor, the TULF. In the parliamentary and district council elections, the TULF fielded few Muslim candidates, all of whom were decisively defeated. According to Dr. M.C.H. Khaleel, a distinguished Muslim leader, the Muslims are against the very idea of Tamil Eelam. If it comes about, they will become a mini-minority within a minority.[30] It must be pointed out, in this connection, that the Muslims wholeheartedly supported the language policy of the government; they are great votaries of the quota system for university admissions and would like to have ethnic quotas for recruitment to government services. In the All Party Conference, the Muslim stance falls somewhere between the UNP desire to strengthen the District Development Councils and the Regional Councils suggested by TULF-CWC combination; as Dr. Badiudin Mahmud said the Muslims feel that the most equitable and workable solution will be Provincial Assemblies.

The UNP-Muslim honeymoon has received a severe jolt by Colombo's decision to establish links with Israel and induct Mossad to assist in counter-insurgency operations. Not only has it created misgivings among large sections of Sri Lankan Muslims, who were hitherto, willing to play the Sinhalese game with alacrity, but has also put a spoke in Sri Lanka's relations with Arab countries. As is well known, Sri Lanka has been consistently cultivating the Arab countries during recent years to get maximum aid from them. The closure of the Israeli Embassy; the appointment of a Muslim as the Education Minister by the SLEP government and Minister of

External Affairs by the present UNP government, the extraordinarily warm welcome given to the Arab delegates during the Nonaligned Conference in Colombo in 1976 and the wide external publicity given to Colombo's policy towards the Sri Lankan Muslims—all these, to some extent, were intended to befriend the Arab countries. And Sri Lanka did gain enormous benefits in three specific areas: (i) bilateral aid from Arab countries; (ii) a sizeable market for Sri Lanka's export products; and (iii) job opportunities for the thousands of Sri Lankans in the Middle East and the resulting flow of foreign exchange into the country. All these are likely to be seriously affected. The Muslim community has expressed its discontent in unmistakeable terms and, though for the moment, the government seems to think that the discontent is "manageable", it is too early to say how the situation will develop within the island, especially in the Muslim areas in the East. Similarly, the Arab opposition to Sri Lanka's Israeli connection has yet to crystallize into concrete action. In this connection, it must be mentioned that the Tamil militants did receive their initial military training from the PLO; the PLO links later became tenuous, but in the present context, the possibility of the Tamil extremist groups reinforcing their links with the PLO should not be ruled out. If such a situation materializes, it may add an entirely new external dimension to the Sinhalese-Tamil conflict.

### Malays and Burghers—Insignificant Role

In the game of numbers, the Malays who number 43,378 or 0.3 per cent and the Burghers 38,236 or 0.3 per cent[31] are extremely insignificant. The Malays are scattered throughout the island while the Burghers are concentrated in Colombo and Kandy. These two miniscule minorities have a vested interest in harmonious relations with the Sinhalese population and do not welcome the idea of vivisection of the country.

### Emerging Trends

The Developments in Sri Lanka since the UNP victory in the 1977 elections have qualitatively changed the nature and intensity of the ethnic conflict. Coming into power after the long dark spell of the Emergency under Sirimavo Bandarnaike, the UNP government fired the imagination of the people by promising the establishment of a *Dharmista* society, the necessity to revert to an open democratic system, the guarantee of personal liberties, freedom from arbitrary arrest and detention, control of police excesses and upholding of the rule of law and independence of the judiciary. What is more, as stated earlier, the UNP promised to convene a Round Table Conference to find a just and humane solution to the ethnic problems which had been plaguing the country since independence.

It is the tragedy of Sri Lankan politics that far from bridging the gap, the years since 1977 have seen the chasm widening between the two communities as a result of which it has become essential for a "third party" to bring together the leaders of the two communities. The Tamil question today seems to have reached insoluble proportions. Though President Jayawardene is far more sympathetic to Tamil aspirations than Mrs Sirimavo Bandarnaike, and did make some gestures and concessions to pacify the Tamils, these were the classic illustrations of "too little, too late". The Tamils continue to be the victims of deprivation in education, language, employment, land colonization and political participation. What is more, the Sinhalese attitude has hardened over a period of time. In the perception of Sinhalese political elite, more so after the bloodbath of July 1983, the Sinhalese are the only politically relevant groups in the island today. The Sinhalese pressure groups and their drummer boys within the UNP led by Cyril Mathew, the former Minister for Industry and Scientific Affairs, are ever ready to instigate and whip up racial vendetta, as a result of which, President Jayawardene has become, to quote his own words—"Prisoner of circumstances". What is more, the high-handed repressive methods and the many acts of savagery are slowly and steadily pushing the Tamils to a point of no return and many of them are convinced, rightly or wrongly, that the only solution lies in a Tamil Eelam, a separate sovereign state consisting of the Northern and Eastern provinces.

### Insecurity Faced by the Tamils

The most important qualitative change that has taken place in Sri Lanka during recent years is the increasing insecurity of life and property as for the Tamils in non-Tamil areas. In the

Sinhalese areas, especially in Colombo and up-country plantations, the threat to security comes from Sinhalese hoodlums abetted by police and armed forces. In the northern and eastern provinces, the security forces are committing hienous crimes even against the civilian population: The Amnesty International, the International Court of Justice and the LAWASIA have, after systematic and painstaking research, documented the gross violations of human rights taking place in Sri Lanka today.[32] As stated earlier, the Tamils and the Sinhalese view themselves as endangered communities and, as a result, there had been an escalation of divisive actions and reactions increasing resort to violence by Tamil militants and counterviolence by the state. If the Sri Lankans of all communities are to accept the legitimacy of the state, the government must ensure impartial and equitable justice to all. Unfortunately in the present situation, the coercive apparatus of the state is titled against the Tamil minority groups. Colombo seems to have embarked on an annihilation strategy and wants to teach the Tamils that the violence of the Tamil militants would be matched by intensified state terrorism. The killing of the innocent in Chunakkam, the naval bombardment of Velvettiturai, atrocities on civilians in Point Pedro, Atchuveley, Thikkam, Karanavai, Adampan and Murunka and kidnapping and cold blooded murder of Tamil passengers in the bus in Puvarasankulam point to a dismal scenario of matching Tamil violence and state terrorism, the first casuality of which would inevitably be the negotiated settlement.

### LAND COLONIZATION

INTERRELATED to the issue of insecurity is the problem of "Sinhalese colonization" in the Eastern province which, as stated earlier, the Tamils consider as an integral part of their "traditional homeland". Successive Sinhalese-dominated Sri Lankan governments do not accept the concept of "traditional homeland"; on the contrary, they subscribe to and uphold the right of any community to move and settle in any part of the island. According to Colombo, the question at issue is landlessness and landlessness is more acute among the Sinhalese than among the Tamils.[33] The Tamils maintain that colonization in traditional Tamil areas should be exclusively reserved for Tamils and no attempt should be made, covertly or overtly, to change the demographic landscape of the

Eastern province. There is conclusive evidence to prove that the agrarian policies of successive governments and state sponsored land colonization schemes have definitely altered the racial composition in the Trincomalee and Amparai districts. In 1921, the Sinhalese constituted a miniscule 3.0 per cent of the population of Trincomalee; it rose to 20.6 per cent in 1946; 28.8 per cent in 1971 and 33.0 per cent in 1981. In Amparai, the Sinhalese population in 1971 was 82,280; it rose to 146,371 in 1981 showing an increase of 78.0 per cent in Sinhalese population.[34]

The Tamil critics point out that land colonization is also affecting Manner, Mullativu, Vavunia and Batticoloa districts. The compositions of the electorate in Kalkudah and Padiruppu in Batticoloa district demonstrate an adverse effect on the Tamil component. The TULF and the Tamil militants also allege that Sinhala fishermen are being inducted into Mullativu, threatening the way of life and source of living of Tamil fishermen.

Another irksome development, according to the Tamil spokesmen, has been the use of Buddhist religious symbols—the Stupa and the Bo tree—to give legitimacy to Sinhalese settlements. The sudden "discovery" of sacred relics in Seruvila and Tikavapi and the controversy over Buddha statue in Vavuniya town are cited as examples to inject religious justification for Sinhalese intrusion into Tamil areas.

Equally pathetic has been the plight of the Indian Tamils in Trincomalee and Vavuniya districts. Since the 1977 riots, there has been a movement of Indian Tamils towards the Eastern provinces and this process gathered further momentum after 1981 riots. The Indian Tamils eked out their living either as landless labourers for the Sri Lankan Tamil landlords or encroached on state lands and established illegal settlements or found a new way of life in the camps run by the Tamil Refugee Rehabilitation Organization and the Gandhiyam. The attempts made by CWC to legalize the illegal settlements did not succeed; on the contrary, the government was determined to evacuate the Indian Tamils from these areas. A close study of the July 1983 riots would reveal that the communal holocaust had its beginning in the state-sponsored attacks on the Indian settlers in Trincomalee in May-June 1983. Caught between the 'Sinhalese Lions' and the 'Tamil Tigers', the Indian Tamils became the defenceless victims of communal poison, vendetta and violence.

### ECONOMIC NEGLECT

ANOTHER deploreable aspect of the current situation is the continuing neglect of Tamil dominated areas in terms of economic development. The government has hardly exploited the economic resources of the north and one economic activity which was been doing fairly well—cultivation of subsidiary crops like potato, onions and chillies in Jaffna has been adversely hit by the introduction of free enterprise and liberal import policy by the present UNP government. The Colombo based non-communal Committee for Rational Development, after an analytical study of Sri Lankan development programmes, has come to the conclusion that Jaffna peninsula is being meted out a step motherly treatment by Colombo. The amount allocated for development in the Jaffna district budget for 1982 was only Rs. 27 million. It clearly shows the smallness of the district budget and its limited capacity to spearhead decentralized development in Sri Lanka. As far as the central budget is concerned, in 1981, the capital expenditure in Jaffna district was only Rs.260 million, i.e., 2.6 per cent of the national capital expenditure of nine billion rupees. The per capita capital expenditure in the Jaffna district was only Rs.313 compared to the national per capita expenditure of Rs.656. The foreign aid utilization for Jaffna district for the period 1977–82 was zero.[35] The callous approach towards the Jaffna peninsula is evident from the recent decision of the government to stop work on all development projects in the Tamil-dominated northern province and channel the funds for defence. The government has also decided to suspend all road repairs to minimize/eliminate attacks on the security forces by Tamil militants using land mines.

An important consequence flows out of the three grievances listed above. For the first time, the poorer classes of Tamil society are exposed to the cruel effects of ethnic conflict, which until very recently, had affected only the middle classes. Colombo can ignore the writing on the wall only at its own peril. This in not to minimize the intensity of discrimination in education and employment. Here again the position is getting worse everyday. The district quota system of admission has undoubtedly improved the chances of Tamil medium students from educationally less advanced areas like Mannar Mullativu and Batticoloa. But they generally get admission to the Arts stream. And employment is very high among the arts graduates. It must be borne in mind that the reservoir for recruitment to various militant groups among the Tamils consists mainly of GEC (AL) students and, now with more and more Arts graduates joining the market of the unemployed, the net for recruitment becomes wider. The most deplorable incident in the field of higher education was the calculated attack on Tamil students in the Peradeniya University in May 1984. With growing insecurity, the Tamil students are migrating either to Jaffna or coming to Tamil Nadu for higher education. Discrimination against the Tamils in the field of employment continues unabated and is evident from the telling figures published by the Committee for Rational Development. With 74 per cent of the population, the Sinhalese have 85 per cent of all the jobs in the public sector, 82 per cent in the professional and technical categories. On the other hand, the Tamils, with 18 per cent of the population, have only 11 per cent of all public sector jobs, 13 per cent of all professional and technical posts and 14 per cent of administrative and managerial positions.[36]

### Rise of Extremism among Tamils

The demand for separation and its extreme manifestation among Tamil militant groups has to be seen in the light of these developments. Although the Tamil militants are dismissed by the Sri Lankan government as "terrorists", it would be a grave mistake to view them in that light and write off the issue completely. Extremism is the manifestation of the disenchantment of the Tamil youth in the present political set-up combined with an intense Tamil nationalist feeling. In a letter to Prime Minister Premadasa in 1979, the Liberation Tigers of Tamil Eelam (LTTE), claimed:

> We are neither murderers nor criminals or violent fanatics as your Government often attempts to portray us. On the contrary, we are revolutionaries committed to revolutionary political practice. We represent the most powerful extra-parliamentary liberation movement in the Tamil nation.[37]

The origin and development of extremism among Tamil youth can be traced on the one hand to the effects of discrimination in language, education and employment which got compounded by state violence and, on the other hand, to growing disenchantment with the established TULF leadership and their forms of parliamentary struggle. After some sporadic violent incidents in the early 1970s, these militant youth came together in 1979 under the Liberation Tigers of Tamil Eelam (LTTE) with the objective of attaining independence through armed struggle. Gradually schism developed due to differences in strategy and tactics, ideological outlook and personal squabbles and the Tiger movement got splintered into many factions. The Tamil militants are mainly divided into five groups: (1) Liberation Tigers of Tamil Eelam (LTTE) under Prabhakaran, (2) People's Liberation Organization of Tamil Eelam (PLOTE) under Uma Maheswaran, (3) Eelam People's Revolutionary Liberation Front (EPRLF) under Padmanabha, (4) Eelam Revolutionary Organization (EROS) under Balakumar and (5) Tamil Eelam Liberation Organization (TELO) under Sri Sabaratnam. Over the last six years, these groups have committed a series of bank robberies, ambushed security personnel, assassinated policemen and security forces and have also liquidated 'informers' and 'traitors' from among themselves. Instead of isolating these extremists and trying to find a political solution with the cooperation of the moderate leadership, the government responded to the situation by massive deployment of security forces in the Jaffna peninsula, enforcing the Prevention of the Terrorism Act of 1979 and passing of the Sixth Amendment to the Constitution which even prescribed the peaceful advocacy of a separate Tamil state. The governmental measures, far from reducing the influence of the extremists, resulted in the swelling of their ranks and growing isolation of the TULF leadership. Jaffna has become a ghost city today and the prospects of a peaceful solution to the Tamil problem seem to be very dim.

Two significant features of these militant movements must be underlined. Unlike the Dravidian movements in South India, which receive sustenance from a golden age of the Tamils in the past, none of these militant groups are enamoured of past glories. The emphasis in all their publications is on discriminatory policies of Sinhalese dominated governments and the right of self-determination for Tamil nationality. Secondly, all these groups are Marxist oriented and subscribe to the path of armed struggle.[38]

Despite the ideological affinities and the common goal, attempts to unite various Tamil militant groups under one banner or even forge a united front have not succeeded so far. What is more pathetic, mutual recrimination and character assassination are the order of the day in Tamil Nadu. A few groups: like the EPRLF, occasionally create even embarrassing situations for the Tamil Nadu government as they did in the case of the kidnapping of the Allen couple. Similarly by stepping up guerrilla attacks on the Sri Lankan army, the TELO and the LTTE have created a difficult situation for the Tamils in Jaffna peninsula.

But the inexorable logic of events and the necessity to face a common enemy will have to bring the militant groups closer together with the TULF. An observer of Tamil Nadu scene can discern healthy tendencies of introspection and pragmatism among sections of TULF leadership and also in militant groups like the PLOTE. If Amirthalingam and TULF deradicalize themselves—that is a big if—and take to Gandhian forms of non-violent non-coperation, it could provide a rallying point for various Tamil nationalist groups and lead to a convergence of interests. Even an ardent advocate of Sri Lankan Tamil cause like the DMK leader, Karunanidhi, was constrained to remark a few weeks ago that unless the various Tamil groups come together under common programme and collective leadership, they will lose their credibility even in Tamil Nadu.[39]

## No Progress in Peace Talks

THE FAILURE of the All Party Conference must be viewed against the backdrop of these developments. The hopes that many observers entertained (following the mediatory role of New Delhi and the acceptance of Annexure C as the basis of negotiations) that a workable solution to the ethnic problem would emerge out of the Conference have been belied. It was due to New Delhi's good offices that the TULF was persuaded to come to the negotiating table, though the party had decided in the Mannar Convention in July 1983 not to have any more talks with the government. From their mandate for an independent state the Party has scaled down its demand to a union of states within the framework of a united Sri Lanka. The All Party Conference itself ceased to be a Conference of all recognized political parties, with a number of them walking in and out at their convenience and numerous other groups being brought in as and when it suited the government. The kernel of the TULF proposal was the formation of Regional Councils by merging the District Development Councils into Provinces, especially in the North and the East, without the necessity of the proposal being endorsed by a national referendum. The party hoped that the APC would result in the creation of a Tamil linguistic region consisting of the Northern and Eastern provinces, with developed legislative and executive powers over specified listed subjects, including the maintenance of law and order in the region, the administration of justice, social and economic development, cultural matters and land policy.[40]

Unfortunately, Annexure C has been ignominously jettisoned by the Sri Lanka government. The government is refusing to budge an inch from its earlier stand that the unit of devolution should be District Council and no more. The present proposals only permit inter-district coordination and collaboration in defined spheres of activity. There is no provision to devolve any legislative and executive power to this coordinating unit. There is no indication that this unit will be a legal person. The attempt to link devolution to the second chamber is only a calculated move to defeat the objective of devolution.

Despite the failure of the All Parties Conference, the TULF has shown admirable restraint in sticking to the path of negotiations. What is tragic is the fact that the government is simultaneously carrying on military reprisals which is taking a heavy toll of innocent lives. The emerging scenario in Sri Lanka would be like a pendulum swinging between savage bouts of communal carnage and uneasy lulls of simmering discontent.

Can India, especially Tamil Nadu, remain a mute witness to these dangerous developments next door? Nearly 40,000 Tamils have sought refuge in Tamil Nadu and more likely to arrive legally and illegally in the event of further communal orgies. Compounding the complex situation is the internationalization of the dispute and entry of external forces into Sri Lanka which will have repercussions on India's geopolitical and strategic environment. The induction of the notorious Israeli counter-insurgency set-up, Mossad, the arrangements with British mercenaries to train Sinhalese armed forces, the leasing out of the Trincomalee oil tank firm to a US proxy firm based in Singapore, manifestations of increasing US interest in Sri Lanka as is evident from the Voice of America deal—all these will have serious bilateral and regional implications. In this connection, it is worth remembering that the acquisition of Diego Garcia by the United States from Great Britain had its beginnings in the location of communication facilities, but gradually it was expanded into a full-fledged modern nuclear military base.

One can understand, and even appreciate to some extent, the natural fears and apprehensions that a small country has towards its big neighbour. But the Sinhalese politicians have developed this fear complex into a fine art and have successfully used it as a carrot to mobilize Sinhalese population and also as a stick to keep down the Tamil minority groups. They exaggerate the fears and proclaim in moments of national crisis that the Sinhalese race is fighting a last ditch battle for its survival. This tends to make their treatment of the Tamils more discriminatory which, in turn, makes the Tamils thoroughly distrustful of the Sinhalese. When will the Sinhalese diehards realize that this theory has dangerous overtones? Beyond a point, it would be counter-productive and can even boomerang on them.

## Notes

1. The first part of this essay is an abridged version of the author's article, "Sri Lanka: Ethnic Myths and Facts," *Economic and Political Weekly* (Bombay), 24 September 1983, pp. 1657-60.
2. Department of Census and Statistics, Ministry of Planning Implementation, *Census of Population and Housing, Sri Lanka 1981* (Colombo, 1981), p. 3.
3. For a good account of the Sinhalese perceptions, refer Gananath Obeysekera, "The Vicissitudes of the Sinhale-Buddhist Identity through Time and Change" in Michael Roberts, ed., *Collective Identities, Nationalisms and Protest in Modern Sri Lanka* (Colombo, 1979), pp. 279-313.
4. Ibid.
5. Quoted in Kumari Jayawardena, "Ethnic Consciousness in Sri Lanka: Continuity and Change," *Lanka Guardian* (Colombo) 15 March 1984, pp. 11-12.
6. Ibid.
7. Ibid.
8. Paul Sieghart, *Sri Lanka—A Mounting Tragedy of Errors* (Report of a Mission to Sri Lanka in January 1984 on behalf of the International Commission of Jurists and its British Section Justice) (London, 1984), p. 11.
9. For good account of Tamil perceptions on the subject, refer 1) S. Arasaratnam, "Nationalism in Sri Lanka and the Tamils" in Roberts, n. 3, pp. 500-22 and 2) K. Kailasapathy, *The Cultural and Linguistic Consciousness of the Tamil Community in Sri Lanka* (Colombo, 1982).
10. C.R. de Silva, "The Sinhalese-Tamil Rift in Sri Lanka" in A. Jayaratnam Wilson and Dennis Dalton, eds., *The States of South Asia—Problems of National Integration* (Honolulu, 1982), pp. 155-74.

11. *Resolution unanimously adopted at the First National Convention of the Tamil United Liberation Front held in Vaddukoddai on 14 May 1976* (Jaffna, 1976).
12. Census of Population, n. 2.
13. Ibid.
14. Suryanarayan, n. 1.
15. Census of Population, n. 2.
16. K. Sivathamby, "Some Aspects of the Social Composition of the Tamils of Sri Lanka," in *Ethnicity and Social Change in Sri Lanka* (Colombo, 1984), pp.121-45.
17. Ibid.
18. Walter Schwarz, *The Times of Sri Lanka*, Report No. 25, *Minority Rights Group* (London, 1975), p.12.
19. Census of Population, n. 2.
20. "Estate Labour," *Economic Review* (Colombo), Vol. 5, March 1980, pp. 3-18.
21. For an account of the problems of the stateless people refer Lalit Kumar, *India and Sri Lanka: Sirimavo-Shastri Pact* (New Delhi, 1977).
22. V. Suryanarayan, "The Rehabilitation of Sri Lankan Repatriates", in I.J. Bahadur Singh, ed., *Indians in South Asia* (New Delhi, 1984), pp.92-114.
23. Suryanarayan, n. 1.
24. For a collection of Thondaman's speeches during recent months refer Congress Workers Foundation, *Illankayil Tamizhar Prachnai—Illankai Tozhilalar Congress—Nokkum Seyalaum* (Tamil Publication) (Colombo, 1984).
25. Sri Lanka, Parliamentary Debates, Vol. 15, 24 July 1981, 1351-67.
26. Congress Workers Foundation, n. 24.
27. Quoted in Karthigesu Sivathamby, "Evolution of the Tamil Question," *Lanka Guardian*, 15 January 1984, p.12.
28. Census of Population, n. 2.
29. For good accounts of the Muslim community in Sri Lanka, refer 1) Urmila Phadnis, "Political Profile of the Muslim Minority in Sri Lanka," *International Studies* (New Delhi), Vol. 18, January-March 1979, pp. 27-48 and 2) K.M. de Silva, "The Muslim Minority in Democratic Policy: The Case of Sri Lanka—Reflections on a Theme" (Paper presented to the Seminar on Muslim Minorities in Sri Lanka, South and Southeast Asia, Colombo, January 5-9, 1984).
30. Phadnis, Ibid.
31. Census of Population, n. 2.
32. Violations of human rights in Sri Lanka are recorded in 1) Virginia A. Leary, *Ethnic Conflict and Violence in Sri Lanka* (Report of Mission to Sri Lanka in July-August 1981 on behalf of the International Commission of Jurists) (London, 1982); 2) Sieghart, n. 8; 3) *Report of the Amnesty International Mission to Sri Lanka*, 31 January-9 February 1982 (London, 1983); 4) Amnesty International, *Sri Lanka: Current Human Rights Concerns and Evidence of Extra-Judicial Killings by the Security Forces, July 1983-April 1984* (London, 1984) and 5) LAW ASIA, *The Communal Violence in Sri Lanka, July 1983* (Sydney, 1984).

33. S.V. Kodikara, "The Separatist Eelam Movement in Sri Lanka: An Overview", *India Quarterly* (New Delhi), Vol. 37, April–June 1981, pp. 194–212.
34. M.Y. Mohammad Siddique, "Land and Colonization Problems in Amparai District," *Cintanai* (Jaffna), Vol. 1, July 1983, pp.94–120. (in Tamil).
35. Committee for Rational Development, *Sri Lanka's Ethnic Conflict, Myths and Realities* (Colombo, 1983), pp.7–8.
36. Ibid., p.2.
37. "An open Letter to Premadasa from LTTE," *Towards Liberation* (Selected Political Documents of the Liberation Tigers of Tamil Eelam) (1984), p. 11.
38. K. Sivathamby, "Role of Sri Lankan Tamil Expatriates" *Lanka Guardian*, 1 March 1984, pp.12–13, 16.
39. *Murasoli* (Madras), 26 July, 1984.
40. Selected Speeches of Amirthalingam are included in Tamil United Liberation Front, *Amir Speaks* (Madras, 1984).

CHAPTER EIGHT

# Ethnic Conflicts in Pakistan
Sind as a Factor in Pakistani Politics

## Uma Singh

THE TERM ethnic group is most frequently applied to any group which differs in one or several aspects of its patterned, socially transmitted way of life from other groups, in the totality or that way of life or culture."[1] Following from this, ethnicity can be defined as the emergent expression of primordial feelings long suppressed but now re-awakened, or as a "strategic site" chosen by disadvantaged persons as a mode of seeking political redress in the society.[2] Ethnicity becomes a badge that one can wear more openly as a mode of self-assertion. In the process, the significance of group distinctiveness and identity and the new rights derived from this group character become more pronounced.

While some analysts have emphasized the familiar issues of economic development and political modernization to explain ethnic conflicts, they have failed to take into account the strong emotive force of ethnic identities in the social structure of some multi-ethnic societies. The recent upsurge in the ethnic conflicts within the more industrialized states of Europe and North America challenges the contention that modernization dissipates ethnic consciousness and indicates that multi-ethnic societies at all levels of modernization have been afflicted by it. Ethnic conflicts, thus, have posed a serious systemic challenge to a large number of states.

Walter Connor describes the "nation as a self-differentiating ethnic group" and the pre-requisite of nationhood is an awareness that one's own group is unique in a "most vital sense."[3] What is fundamentally involved in ethnic conflicts is that divergence of basic identity which manifests itself in the "Us" and "Them" syndrome. He has observed that "national identity may survive substantial alterations in language, religion, economic status or any other, tangible manifestations of its culture."[4] It has been very well argued by him that even social changes stimulated by modernization could not eliminate ethnic groups but have merely modernized it. This often triggered internal political crises threatening the very survival of the state.

Nowhere is such a crisis so clearly manifested as in a multi-ethnic state like Pakistan. The major threat to the regime has been from internal violence along regional-ethnic identities. The Punjabis, Bengalis (before 1971), Sindhis, Pashtuns and Baluchis constitute important elements in Pakistan's ethnic mosaic. Approximate populations of provinces in 1982 are: Punjab, 54 million, Sind, 19 million, NWFP, 14.6 million and Baluchistan, 3.35 million. For Pakistan, the task of nation-building was even more difficult than most newly independent countries. Each of these provinces represented a distinct ethnic group which had a fully or quasi-sovereign state of its own before the British conquest. Furthermore, they differed greatly in their size, population, resources, level of social development and proximity to power. Ever since Pakistan came into being, the country has been facing the dilemma of creating a viable national identity. The perennial problem in Pakistan has been the inability and lack of willingness of the rulers to accommodate the regional and political claims of the different ethnic groups within a flexible federal framework.

The problem was intertwined with historical, political, economic and socio-psychological factors, There was serious opposition to the creation of a separate independent state of Pakistan with the Baluchistan and the North-West Frontier Province exemplifying it. In the NWFP, the call for a Pakhtun entity predates the creation of Pakistan. One of the major components of Pakhtun consciousness was the development of Pakhtun language and literature on the part of intelligentsia and the students. Similarly, according to Feroz Ahmed, the crystallization of the Sindhi nationality had taken place as far back as 1200 years.[5] He contends that before the British conquered Sind in 1843, the latter had established itself as a fully sovereign state ruled by Talpur Mirs. All the resistance put forward by the Sindhis, before, during and after the conquest was in the name of the independence of Sind and no other entity. The British decreed Sind to be the official language; to be used in the schools, courts and revenue records. A standard Sindhi script for the Sindhi language was developed. In 1955, the civil-military oligarchy had to use coercive measures to impose the one-unit scheme on provinces like the NWFP and Sind. All the major ethnic groups have been harbouring the belief that their way of life and particularly their distinctive cultures are in jeopardy. The more the government makes efforts to eliminate separatist tendencies, the deeper the fissures grow in the Pakistani society.

This paper contends that (1) Islam has failed to nationally integrate such ethnic groups. Particularly, the creation of Bangladesh has proved that the integrative force of Islam has failed to overcome ethnic consciousness. (2) The ethnic domination by one ethnic group (the Punjabis) of others has increased ethnic conflicts in Pakistan. Pakistan's ethnic groups: the Sindhis, Baluchis, and Pashtuns resent the domination of the Punjabi elite. When Pakistan was created, it was hoped that the bond of religion will supersede other bonds, e.g. regional, linguistic and cultural among Pakistanis. But soon, it became clear that religion was not a very strong bond to create firm ties of nationalism among various ethnic groups in West Pakistan, let alone the two culturally diverse and geographically incongruous wings of East and West Pakistan.

When Bangladesh came into existence, it was felt that Pakistan had become more cohesive and an integrated state with the removal of the geographical incongruence. But contrary to general expectations, the basic dilemma facing Pakistan in the post-1971 period still remains the question of national identity, whether Pakistanis consider themselves as Pakistanis first and then Sindhis, Baluchis, Punjabis or Pathans or vice-versa. The country is passing through another difficult period of domestic turmoil and Pakistan is a house divided against itself. The Pakistani society is still polarized along ethnic lines—the ethnic groups are groaning under a sense of economic deprivation—a phenomenon which threatens the integrity of the state.

A perusal of ethnic consciousness of the Pathans, Baluchis and Sindhis will indicate that the feeling of relative deprivation has existed all along among all the three groups and the present upsurge in the ethnic conflict in Sind can mainly be attributed to this factor. It is pertinent to mention here that political violence results from an intolerable gap between what people want (expectations) and what they get (gratifications).[6] Relatived eprivation as conceptualized by

Ted Gurr in his book "Why Men Rebel", arises when an individual does not attain what he thinks is justifiably due to him. Relative deprivation, according to Gurr, "is the mechanism that produces frustration of sufficient intensity to motivate people to engage in political protest and violence."[7] He has argued the point quite forcefully:

> The basic relationship is as fundamental to understanding civil strife as the law of gravity is to atmospheric physics: relative deprivation is a necessary pre-condition for civil strife of any kind. The greater the deprivation an individual perceives, relative to his expectations, the greater his discontentment. The more widespread and intense is discontent among members of a society the more likely and severe is civil strife.[8]

The British also encouraged the growth of ethnic identities in pre-independent India. Those ethnic groups which identified themselves with their political strategy benefitted the most. Those who collaborated with them were exposed to modernization, while others were deliberately left at the peripheral level of development. The tribal Pathans of the NWFP were left on the periphery because of the volatile tribesmen: the Afridis, Orakzais, Utman Khels and Mohmands. The Pathans, therefore, remained outside the pale of modernization and maintained a strong ethnic identity.[9]

The British faced a similar problem in Baluchistan from the Marri and Bugti tribes. At least in Sind, partial urbanization took place due to the strategic and political importance of its seaport, Karachi. On the other hand, the Punjabis were patronized by the British from the very beginning as they had supported them. A new elite of landed aristocrats was created by the British through gifts of large tracts of land. This province became the principal arena for the recruitment of soldiers. The British Indian army was "Punjabized" as almost 50 per cent of the Muslims in it were Punjabis.

The role of the Punjabis in the politics of Pakistan makes it evident that Punjabi ethno-centricity failed to structurally assimilate or politically integrate other ethnic groups but instead sensitized them to ethnic boundaries. The enormous concentration of executive power in the hands of the civilian-bureaucracy which consisted largely of Punjabis and their ruling collaborators the

Muhajirs, refugees who occupied important positions in the country's bureaucracy, determined national policy at the higher levels. The dominant economic force was the capitalist class which again consisted of the Punjabis. Finally, it was the military which emerged as the dominant force consisting again mainly of the Punjabis.

Besides, the Pakistani rulers imposed a centralized unitary form of government and the domination of the powerful economic and political groups by perpetrating discriminatory policies. All legitimate grievances of the lesser privileged and lesser developed ethnic groups were dubbed as anti-national and subversive activities. These ethnic groups resented the imposition of Punjabi value-system on the rest of Pakistan. In the name of securing Pakistan's national unity, the very bases of unity were eroded. "Islam, integrity of Pakistan and the Urdu language became the code words for national domination."[10] These attempts at "Punjabization" of other ethnic communities meant a loss of their ethnic identity alienating them in the process, from the Punjabi dominated centre.

It is necessary to mention here that ethnic identities have great potential for group mobilization. The ethnic political elite who were denied political participation, fully exploited this sense of deprivation due to Punjabi colonialism, a rather sweeping generalization. This fear was based on certain structural factors also. The Punjabis constituted 57.58 per cent of the population compared with the Pakhtuns (12.94 per cent), Baluchis (3.71 per cent) and Sindhis (21.92 per cent). They perceived that in any election, such minority ethnic groups could never play a nationally important role. This led to "Us" and "Them" syndrome symptomatic of the ethnic cleavages and the ethnic groups in Pakistan began to press their legitimate claims for the protection of their way of life, for a redefinition of the relationship between their own peripheral society and the centre.[11]

The results of the insensitivity and ruthlessness of Pakistan's rulers culminated in the separation of East Pakistan from West Pakistan in 1971. Yet no lessons, were learnt from this experience and the Baluch people were subjected to armed suppression from 1973-77, resulting in complete alienation of Baluchistan from Pakistan. The struggle of the Baluchis, against what they call the "tyranny of the Punjabi elite" has been going on for the last three decades.[12] Their efforts resulted in the birth of Baluch People's Party in 1963. Its major aims were to struggle against dictatorship and national oppression, fight for the dismemberment of the one-unit, establishment of national provinces, restoration of democracy and the abolition of the Sardari System in Baluchistan. From 1973 onwards, the main focus of dissent in Pakistan had shifted to Baluchistan and the NWFP. Serious rifts had emerged between the Bhutto Government and the Baluch and Pakhtun leaders. The rising ethnic consciousness in these two provinces has had a great "potential for the emergence of a nativistic movement revolving round the feeling of relative deprivation has been greater in Baluchistan than in North West Frontier Provinces." Notwithstanding their call for greater regional autonomy over the decades. The desire for improvement of socio-economic conditions of the "Sons of the Soil" is stronger in Baluchistan.

Initially, Zia did make some efforts to defuse the situation in Baluchistan. He made some efforts to accelerate development projects, under federal government allocation. The total development programme for Baluchistan was an all time high of Rs.1,443 million in 1982-83, as disclosed in the evaluation report for the Sixth Five Year Plan. A special programme was prepared for Baluchistan incorporating a list of important development projects in the provinces. The share of the provinces and the special development programme of Baluchistan was 4.4 per cent of the total public sector development programme in 1982-83 as against 1.8 per cent in 1977-78. It has been claimed in the official figures that Baluchistan has claimed the highest share of industrial credit sanctioned by the Bankers Equity-led syndicate of Financial Institutions and banks in the past three years. Mahbubul Haq, Federal Minister for Planning and Development said at Quetta on 7 May 1983, that Baluchistan was the new frontier for development and would receive the lion's share of Rs.15 billion during the Sixth Five Year Plan to accelerate the tempo of economic uplift in this backward area. But it is doubtful whether this would convert the Baluchi frustrations and disenchantment into pro-Pakistani sentiments.

The people of NWFP have also been extremely conscious of their distinct ethnic and cultural identities. The demand for the creation of a separate state called "Pashtunistan" which includes all Pashtu-speaking areas in the NWFP, parts of Baluchistan and

Afghanistan emerged under the leadership of Khan Abdul Ghaffar Khan with the creation of Pakistan. According to 1972 Census, the population of the NWFP was 8.38 million of which approximately 76 per cent were Pushtu-speaking Pashtuns. Twenty eight per cent of the population of Baluchistan were also Pashtu speaking. The Pakhuns held important positions in the civil and military bureaucracy of Pakistan and in terms of influence and numbers were ahead of Sind and Baluchistan. Their share in the armed forces was also between 15 to 20 per cent though they constituted 13.5 per cent of Pakistan's population.

Like the Baluchis, the Pakhtuns were also alienated by the repressive policies of Bhutto who interpreted their regional discontent as an act of treason. Conflict between the growing Pakhtun aspirations and the Centre arose because the province had been kept in a state of underdevelopment and mainly because of the dominance of the central government by non-Pakhtuns and particularly by the Punjabis. In the National Assembly during 1972-77, Punjab had 82 seats as compared to 60 seats held by Sind (27), NWFP (18), Baluchistan (12) and women (3).[14] The National Awami Party of Wali Khan put forward the demand for provincial autonomy and he was later arrested by Bhutto on charge of treason. Under Zia, there seems to be a gradual polarization between the moderates and the extremists. The moderate Pakhtuns seek a political settlement based on greater autonomy within the existing Pakistani political structure. They have been appeased by the increasing economic links between Pakhtun areas and the rest of Pakistan, better representation in the Army, and the bureaucracy, and greater economic benefits.

The response to the MRD call for civil disobedience was low-keyed in the NWFP and Baluchistan being limited to protest marches, periodic boycott of courts by lawyers and the leaders of the movement offering themselves for arrest. The Sindhi leaders allege that some key NDP leaders have derived economic benefits from the Zia regime and have become the ruling partners of the Punjabis.

Pakistan has lately experienced (August–December 1983) sporadic political unrest in Sind. This is reminiscent of similar developments earlier (1971 being the most recent) in the country's short but turbulent history. The Movement for the Restoration of Democracy (MRD) (to press demands for the withdrawal of martial law and holding of early elections) has managed to initiate what is potentially the most serious threat to the regime in its seven years in power. Political violence consequent upon the rising ethnic consciousness has always proved to be the ultimate instrument of political change in Pakistan. Two of Pakistan's strong leaders, Ayub Khan and Z.A. Bhutto, lost power after prolonged unrest. Given the continued determination of the present military ruler, Gen. Zia-ul-Haq to rule by force, reluctance to hold elections and restore democratic institutions, insistence on its own form of Islamization and failure to resolve economic and social problems, the present regime has been progressively isolated.

We find all the ingredients which make the situation ethnically explosive in Sind. It brought to the surface the simmering discontent and alienation that permeates the Sindhi speaking populace of Sind. The major reason for the Sindhi resentment can be traced to the execution of Bhutto, the extremely poor representation of the Sindhi speaking population in the higher echelons of the army and the few prospects for an early change in Pakistan's existing power structure characterized by the Punjabi military dominance. It resulted in intense violence and manifested strong ethnic sentiments. Sind comprises 23 per cent of Pakistan's population but contains about 60 per cent of its industry, consumes 42 per cent of commercial energy and has a per capita income about 40 per cent higher than in Punjab. Since Bhutto's overthrow in 1977, the Sindhis have been one of the most active ethnic groups. After having Bhutto, a Sindhi, as their prime minister, there was a resurgence of hope among the Sindhis, who began to feel for the first time that they had a stake in Pakistan. Their ethnic politics involves not only conflict between the Sindhis and the Punjabis but also between the "Old Sindhis" and "new ones" (Muhajirs) who migrated from India. The bulk of the migration occurred in the four months between August and November 1947. It is estimated that in this period, some 6 million refugees moved into Pakistan. In Karachi, Hyderabad, Lyallpur and Sargodha, over 60 per cent of the population was made up of refugees.[15]

The exchange of population between India and Pakistan, made Punjab and the NWFP ethnically more homogeneous and did not affect Baluchistan; it affected Sind, where the number of Sindhis was reduced. Thus Karachi in the 1950s became a city dominated politically, economically and socially by the Urdu-speaking Muslims of Delhi and UP. In Karachi, in 1959, some 83 per cent of the population was of immigrants—refugees from India, accounting for 65 per cent and in-migrants, i.e., those born in other parts of Pakistan, accounting for 18 per cent of the city's population.[16] Sind is the most important province in Pakistan, as far as the processes of population, migration and urban growth rates are concerned.

These migrations, because of the numbers involved, have had the greatest effect on the ethnic politics of the country. Before independence, linguistically Sind was a relatively homogeneous province. For instance, according to the 1941 Census, only 32,000 persons claimed Urdu as their mother-tongue in Sind and Khairpur state in a population of 4,084,000 which was only .8 per cent of the total. But by 1951, Urdu speaking Muhajirs made up about 476,000 or 12 per cent of the total population of 4,608,514. It will be interesting to look, at the language composition for Karachi Districts in 1961. Of a total population of 2,044,044, as many as 1,101,776 or 53.9 per cent declared Urdu to be their mother-tongue. Even Punjabi speakers were found more frequently in Karachi (260,747 or 12.8 per cent) than Sindhi speakers who numbered only 174,823 or 8.6 per cent. In fact, if only the urban population was counted in Karachi district, then the third largest linguistic group becomes Gujratis with 152,471 or 7.5 per cent of the population and Sindhis would become the fourth because a substantial number of Sindhis lived in "gots" (Sindhi Villages) on the outskirts of Karachi city. Baluchis (5.3 per cent) and Pathans (5.2 per cent) were other important groups in Karachi.[17]

As a result of this infiltration, it is natural that it led to con-

hindrance in career advancem
is similar to the threat which the locals of Baluchistan and NWFP feel from Punjabis, who have continually migrated to Quetta, Peshawar and other cities. On the other hand, in Baluchistan and the NWFP there is hardly any prejudice against the Muhajirs, inspite of the fact, that the latter hold good positions in many respects. Since both locals and non-locals are competing for the same limited economic and job opportunities, the ethnic leaders have capitalized on these grievances and put more political demands of their ethnic groups. More than half of Pakistan's industry is located in Sind, but Sindhis

have practically no participation in it whether as owners or as workers. The commercial, transportation, construction and service sector which comprises 55 per cent of Pakistan's Gross Domestic Product is also located largely in Sind. In Government service, educational institutions and other white-collar jobs, the Sindhis are represented far below their population proportion, whether it is on an all-Pakistan basis or within Sind itself. A survey done by Sindhi students in 1969-70 showed that out of one million workers employed in private industries in Sind, not more than one thousand in the province were Sindhis. In the Central Government service, there was only one Sindhi per five thousand, while in the Sind government, Sindhis comprised less than 40 per cent. Most of the jobs held by Sindhis were low-ranking and low-paying. Under the Pakistan People Party's government, Sindhis got some jobs in the nationalized sector; but according to Feroz Ahmed, the present military ruler has purged tens of thousand of Sindhis from government service and public sector enterprises.[18] Even the land (nearly two million acres) left behind by the Hindus was awarded to Punjabi retired army personnel by the Ayub Khan regime, who went to the rural Sind as farmers. Over one million acres brought under cultivation by the construction of Kotri and Guddu barrages were awarded to non-Sindhi military and civil officers. As much as 40 per cent of Sindh's agricultural lands has passed into the hands of non-Sindhis while three-fourths of Sindhi peasants own no land at all. The Sindhi peasants have also suffered from the violation of the 1945 Punjab-Sind Agreement on the distribution of Indus Water. New irrigation works have begun without the consent of Sind which have resulted in decreasing the latter's share of irrigation water.[19] Recently, oil has been discovered in large quantities near Badin, and the Sindhis are apprehensive whether it would be utilized for the benefit of the local population or simply pumped out on the pattern of national gas in Baluchistan.

Indisputable disparities exist in the respective levels of developments of the four provinces. Inequality has increased and state policies to reverse the trend have yet to be framed. Comparisons at the district level are useful for commenting on the relative development of four provinces. The ranking of districts by provinces according to overall development criterion will show (Table 1) that Karachi, Lahore, Rawalpindi/Islamabad, Quetta, Peshawar and Hyderabad are the most developed districts and populations concentrated in large cities have benefitted most from development in all the four provinces.

Table 1. Development criterion in Pakistan.[20]

|  | Punjab | Sind | NWFP | Baluchistan |
|---|---|---|---|---|
| Most developed | 2 | 2 | 1 | 1 |
| Intermediate | 11 | 4 | 2 | — |
| Least developed | 6 | 5 | 3 | 9 |

Thus the highest concentration of population in developed districts is in Punjab and Sind (42 per cent), whereas it is less than 12 per cent of the total population. in NWFP and Baluchistan. Punjabis overwhelmingly lie at the intermediate stage of development while Sindhis, Baluchis and Pathans are disproportionately represented in Pakistan's population living in the least-developed districts. Most Pakistanis, however, live in rural areas. The urban conglomerates receive a disproportionate share of resources and do not represent the trends in the provinces where they are located. For instance, Karachi and Hyderabad districts are highly urbanized where more than half of the population consists of new-Sindhis.

The rural indicators of development reinforce the results of Table 1. Overwhelmingly, it is the Punjab districts that are the most developed, NWFP districts are either at the intermediate stage or are the least developed ones while most Sindhis and all Baluch rural areas are the least developed in the country (Table 2).

Table 2. Ranking of districts of provinces according to rural development criterion.[21]

|  | Punjab | Sind | NWFP | Baluchistan |
|---|---|---|---|---|
| Most developed | 12 | — | — | — |
| Intermediate | 9 | 1 | 5 | — |
| Least developed | — | 12 | 2 | 9 |

An important feature of Pakistan's economy since the 1970s has been the phenomenal growth in overseas migration particularly to the Middle East. It is estimated that nearly 2 million Pakistanis working in the Middle East remit over $3 billion. The remittances are a mixed blessing for the country as a whole because the dependents of overseas migrants are concentrated primarily in the Punjab province (nearly 70 per cent of the migrant dependents belong to Punjab, 14 per cent to Sind. 12 per cent to NWFP and only 4 per cent to Baluchistan).[22] Thus, it can be inferred that regional income disparities may have worsened sharply. Also the regional inequalities are obvious and are being articulated by Sindhis, who belong to the less-developed region. This explains why Sindhi Awami Tehrik has now emerged as a new potent factor in Sind politics. This sense of deprivation formed the core of a political movement when the situation became ripe last year in October-December 1983. This happened before in East Pakistan in 1960s, Baluchistan in the mid-70s and was recently experienced in Sind.

In context of recent developments in rural Sind, it can be argued, that the leaders were *waderas* who forced their tenants, bound to them through exploitative tenancy contracts to agitate against the state. Most anti-government violence has been, concentrated in rural Sind where the traditional leadership of *waderas* and Pirs holds sway. The incidence of tenancy is high in Sind. Quite a number of landlords (*waderas*) are members of the PPP who were given special privileges and high offices under Bhutto. Now, under Zia, these landlords have no say in the government. Unlike feudal families in Punjab and the NWFP, the Sindhis were not represented in the army and bureaucracy. Besides the PPP two small leftist organizations have taken in violent clashes with authorities. The pro-Soviet Sind Awami Committee and the Trotskyist Sindhi Awami Tehrik have limited but well organized group of supporters in various parts of Sind. Economic development of Sind, under the present social system, has been characterized by Feroz Ahmed as "de-Sindhization" of Sind.[22] The Sindhis have no participation in the military. It is, therefore, not a surprise that the Sindhis have reacted with great vengeance during the recent agitation in the province.

The Sindhis also accuse the government of perpetrating cultural suppression. Ever since Pakistan's creation, the Sindhis in Karachi behaved like strangers because very few people spoke their language and were forced to learn Urdu. No new Sindhi medium school has been opened in Karachi. Whereas the non-Sindhis were exempted from learning Sindhi, the Sindhi students in Karachi were supposed to learn Urdu. Censorship and suppression of the press and publications have been a common phenomenon in Sind. Sindhi writers are refused freedom of expression in their own country and any Sindhi writer or poet who wants to publish in India is declared a traitor to Pakistan. How the various oppressive and discriminatory practices have affected the cultural development of the Sindhi people can be seen from the figures on female literacy in the 1981 population census: 42.2 per cent for urban Sind (largely non-Sindhi); only 5.2 per cent for rural Sind (almost all Sindhi).

While concluding, we can say that the present ethnic conflict in Sind is reflective of the deep-rooted sense of deprivation among the Sindhis. The nature of the grievances of the Sindhis pertain to what is perceived by them as a denial of job opportunities, acquisition of their land by outsiders and almost total absence of representation in or access to corridors of power and the cultural oppression by the government. This perception of relative deprivation has resulted in ethnic conflict, and cleavages in the society and military governments' ruthlessness turned the animosity against the dominant group into a rationale for launching the struggle.

The disaffection among the Sindhis is not yet perceived as a desire for secession or Sindhu Desh. G.M. Syed (leader of the Jiya Sind Movement) is dubbed as an extremist. Barring him, no Sindhi leader has sought a role for himself outside Pakistan. Rather they seek an accommodation with the government. Abdul Hamid Jatoi, President of Pakistan National Party, Sind, has categorically stated: "Smaller provinces like Sind only want a fair deal not separation. They want access to jobs, they need safeguards for their own resources and then provincial autonomy." The insentivity and even ruthlessness of the rulers to redress the consequences of inequalities between the ethnic groups have contributed a great deal to the alienation of Sindhi people from the State of Pakistan. An ethnic group will not secede from the State if the living standards are improved both in real terms and relative to other segments of the state's population. What has happened in Pakistan has undoubtedly underlined a strong sentiment against the perpetuation of military rule. Equally, it can be described as an expression of resentment against the Punjabi domination of the entire political and economic structure of Pakistan. To that extent, the situation in Sind portends a danger of far more intensity in future.

The problem in Pakistan is basically structural. The military and civilian bureaucracy have concentrated enormous powers in their hands. The representation of the Punjabis is out of proportion to their population. The flow of military and economic assistance from the USA has affected the national integrative processes indirectly. It has increased the ruling elites capacity to adopt repressive policies towards the ethnic conflicts in Pakistan. This has also accentuated disaffection as more resources are used to favour one region. The Zia government has conveniently blamed the Indian government for instigating this movement in Sind and has maintained that it has not emerged from genuine ethnic cleavages but from instigation by an outside power. The response of the Zia regime to these challenges from within, has been to strengthen the country by securing military and economic aid from the US. But the question that arises is whether Zia will be able to cope with these political challenges?

The role of the external dimension cannot be ignored in the present ethnic conflicts in Pakistan. Notwithstanding repeated denials by Pakistan, it is no longer a secret that America has set up a naval base in Baluchistan's. The disclosure has been made by Attaullah Mengal, former chief minister of Baluchistan. Mehdi Ye-Koh has been cordoned off for military purposes by the Pakistani authorities. Construction work of a highly mysterious nature has been going on in this restricted area for over four years. A major highway has been constructed which goes right upto the summit of Mehdi-Ye-Koh and connects it with the town of Gwadar. The restricted area is under the tight control of Pakistani army. This unit is believed to be a part of the newly created Pakistani Rapid Development force which again has direct connections with the American Central Command. American naval vessels frequently visit the Gwadar port. But no government in Islamabad can retain its legitimacy by functioning as a tool of United States.

For the present, General Zia seems to have been able to ride the storm. It was in Sind alone that the MRD exploded into violence. This has enabled the government to concentrate its forces in one province only and adopted repressive measures. The main problem for the MRD and Pakistan's political opposition as a whole is, that they agree on nothing except the need for general elections. Their sharp rivalries are perhaps the best guarantee of the military regime staying in power indefinitely. Zia has proved to be shrewd enough by initiating a dialogue with several banned political parties—particularly those of the right and with an Islamic colouring. Also, the PPP has serious problems with internal disputes about leadership and strategy. A majority of the political parties still share with the military government the objective of excluding the PPP from power. They realize that the military has an advantage over civil society in that it possesses an organized might, legitimized in the name of the country's defence.

Notes

1. For the definition of ethnicity, see, *A Dictionary of the Social Science* edited by Julius Gould, and William L. Kolb, compiled under the auspices of UNESCO, (New York, 1964).
2. Daniel Bell, "Ethnicity and Social Change" in Nathan Glazer and Daniel Moynihan, eds., *Ethnicity: Theory and Experience*, Massachusetts, (1975), p. 169. Also see Urmila Phadnis, Ethnicity and Nation Building in South Asia, *South Asian Studies*, Vol. 14, Jan–Dec. 1979, pp.73-101.
3. Connor Walker, "National Building or Nation Destroying?" *World Politics*, Vol. 24, no. 3, 1971-72, p.341.
4. Ibid.
5. Feroz Ahmed, "Sind: A Question of Nationality Rights?" Paper presented at the seminar on India-Pakistan Relations held under the auspices of Indian Centre for Regional Affairs in New Delhi on 24-26 April 1984.
6. Ted Gurr, ed., *Handbook of Political Conflict: Theory and Research* (New York, 1980), p.167.
7. Ted Gurr, *Why Men Rebel* (Princeton, 1970), p. 23.
8. Ibid.
9. Asaf Hussain, "Ethnicity, National Identity and Praetorianism," *Asian Survey*, Vol. 16, no, 10, Oct. 1976, p. 918.
10. Mohammad Arif Chayur and Henny Kosson, "The Effects of Population and Urbanization Growth Rates on the Ethnic Tensions in Pakistan" in Ahmed Manzooruddin, ed., *Contemporary Pakistan: Politics, Economy and Society* (North Carolina, 1980), p. 204.
11. Asaf Hussain, n. 9, p. 910.
12. Urmila Phadnis, "Ethnic Movements in Pakistan", in Pandav Nayak, ed., *Pakistan Society and Politics*, (New Delhi, 1984).
13. A Baluchi leader, "Baluchistan—A factor in Pakistan's Politics," Paper presented on the Seminar at Indian Centre for Regional *Affairs*, 24-26 April 1984.
14. Khalid Bin Sayeed, *Politics in Pakistan: The Nature and Direction of Change* (New York, 1980), p. 122.
15. Shahid Javed Burki, "Migration, Urbanization and Politics in Pakistan"

in Howard Wriggins and James Guyot, eds., *Population and Politics of South Asia* (New York, 1983). pp.147–148.
16. Ibid.
17. Ibid.
18. Ahmed, n. 5, p. 259.
19. Ibid.
20. For details, see, POT Pakistan Series, April-July, 1983.
21. For details, see, POT Pakistan Series, no. 11, Sept-Dec. 1983.
22. Feroz Ahmed, n. 5, p. 19.

CHAPTER NINE

# Regionalism in Nepal

## Ramakant and B.C. Upreti

REGIONALISM has been a major force moulding the nature and texture of the politics in the developed as well as the developing countries. It is a political force generated and sustained by a variety of factors. Various dimensions of regionalism are concentrated on the concept of a 'region'.

A region can be defined as "a perceived segment of space differentiated from others on the basis of one or more defining characteristics."[1] These characteristics are geography, economy, social structure, political and administrative set up.[2] Thus a region is a cohesive geographic unit having certain economic and social-cultural characteristics which distinguish it from other areas.[3] Regional identity becomes more prominent when the natural factors coincide with cultural variables, i.e., religion, language and ethnicity.[4] It can be said that regionalism as a phenomenon emerges out of a combination of variables pertaining to socio-cultural, economic and politico-administrative factors. It may take the form of either a movement against excessive concentration of political and administrative powers in the hands of the central authorities of a country of which the region is a part, or a movement against economic disparities or imposition of a monolithic national unity, etc.

The present paper seeks to analyse some aspects of the problem of regionalism in Nepal where it assumes a peculiar shape. The country is split in many ethnic groups, with different traditions, cultures and languages, spread over a wide area, and separated from each other by mountains which are extremely difficult to cross. The population is spread over several small valleys between the mountain ranges. As a result, the feeling of nationhood is not so well developed. Paradoxically, while regional diversities and disparities in Nepal are clearly discernible in political, administrative, economic and socio-cultural spheres, regionalism as a viable movement has yet to capitalize. It would be, therefore, worthwhile to analyse why regionalism, though existing as some force, has not taken the form of a strong movement, or at least has not been converted into a viable political force.

II

NEPAL ENDOWED with tremendous geographical variety, has highly plural society. The difficult terrain, criss-crossed by mountain ranges, rivers and jungles, has isolated the villages, districts and regions from each other. Existence of a number of religions and social groups, with their own dialects, remains a special feature of the Nepalese society. The nature of the economies of the different regions has also been quite dissimilar. Historically, before the advent of Shah rulers, the country remained divided among many petty principalities—the four principalities in the Kathmandu valley, the *Chaubisi* and *Baisi* states, and a large numbers of small states both in the south and the north. Lack of adequate means of transport and communication kept the various regions isolated from the central authority.

THE ECOLOGICAL SETTING

AS ALREADY noted, geography plays an important role in creating regional diversities in Nepal.[5] It has indeed contributed to the strong sense of ethnicity in different regions. The country can be divided into two broad geographical units—the hill region and the tarai region.[6] The two regions not only bear distinctive topographical features, but also represent different economies and patterns of life.

The hill region is a sub-tropical belt ranging between the Mahabharata range in the south and the great Himalayan peaks towards the north. It is generally inaccessible and serves to reinforce the traditional sense of a separate identity among the various communities inhabiting this region. The northern partly covered by snow with big glaciers sliding downwards. The mountainous region offers marginal human settlements. The Kathmandu Valley, although forming a part of the hills, bears a separate identity because of its having been for long the centre of political power, as the concentration of development activities in modern times. The hilly terrain and the generally inclement weather, offers very little scope for agriculture in this area. Further, the lack of means of transport and other infrastructural facilities, seriously impede industrial development. Thus the hill region, offers very little economic opportunities, the only exception being the Kathmandu Valley. It may be noted that because of internal migration, the population of the hill region has increased only by 1 per cent annually, while in the Tarai, the rate of population increase has been quite high. In some of the Tarai districts, population has even grown by 5 per cent annually.

The tarai is a narrow strip forming Nepal's border with India and comprises a small area in comparison to the hills. Geographically, it is an extension of the Indo-Gangetic plains. Once a neglected area for habitation owing to dense forests, swamps and the fear of malaria, it has now become an important region. It is the richest agriculture belt of the country, and industrially the most developed region. Because of its relatively bright economic prospects, it has attracted a large number of people from the other regions. The importance of the Tarai has further increased because of its contiguity with India, with which Nepal has vast economic and socio-cultural contacts. It may be noted here that the majority of the population of the Tarai consists of the Indian settlers, most of whom still maintain socio-cultural links with the neighbouring Indian states of Bihar and Uttar Pradesh. Since the Tarai region is better linked with India by rail and road, the people of the Tarai prefer economic contacts with India instead of the hills.

### Socio-Cultural Milieu

NEPAL IS a multi-structured society characterized by diversities in ethnic composition, religion, language and the patterns of life in different regions.[7]

The main ethnic groups of the hills are: Brahmin, Chettri, Newar, Rai, Limbu, Gurung, Tamang, Magar, Sherpa, Thakali, Dolpa, etc. Most of these communities belong to the Austro-Mongoloid origin.[8] Brahmins, Chettris, and Newars have been dominating the power structure of the kingdom for centuries. The Newars are a traditional business community mainly inhabiting the Kathmandu Valley and other trade centres.[9] The main language of the hills is Nepali. The Newari is the language of Newars. Other languages and dialects spoken in the hills are Bhotia, Kirati, Magar, etc. These have originated from the Tibeto-Burmese linguistic family.

The main communities of the Tarai are the Brahmins, Rajputs, Rajbans, Sutras, Muslims, Tharus, Bhimals, Bodos, etc.[10] These communities belong to the Indo-Aryan racial stock.[11] Linguistic diversity is, greater in the tarai region. A large number of languages and dialects spoken in the neighbouring Indian regions such as the Maithili, Bhojpuri, Hindi, Urdu, Awadhi, Bengali, Marwari, Tharu, etc.[12] are also prevalent here.

Hinduism is the dominant religion of the Kingdom. In the hills, however, a few communities follow Buddhism and there is a small percentage of the Muslims in the Tarai.

The topographical conditions have also played an important role in shaping distinct patterns of life in the two regions. In the hills, particularly the Himalayan region, the social belief system and pattern of the life has been influenced by the neighbouring Tibetan region. In the Tarai, Indian cultural influence is clearly evident. However, inspite of different patterns of life, the caste system and social hierarchies are common to both the regions.[13]

It is quite clear from the foregoing that Nepal is a plural society with marked differences evident in the religion, language and the ways of life in the two main geographic regions.

### III. BASES OF REGIONALISM

ECONOMIC disparities between the Tarai and the hills form an important basis of regionalism in Nepal. These disparities can be observed in the spheres of land-man ratio, employment opportunities, agriculture and industrial development, etc.

The hill region contains more than 55 per cent of Nepal's population, but only a quarter of the land, out of the 74.2 per cent of the total land that it covers is cultivated.[14] As a result of this, there is a heavy pressure of population on land in the area.[15] The Tarai accounts for barely 29 per cent of the area but more than 64 per cent of it is cultivated land; it also accommodates nearly 43 per cent (which is steadily increasing) of the population. This has enhanced the agricultural importance of the Tarai.[16] It is also

Table 1. Population in different regions.

| Census | Hills | Tarai | Nepal |
|---|---|---|---|
| 1952/54 | 5,331,070 | 2,904,009 | 8,235,079 |
|  | (64.74) | (35.26) | (100.00) |
| 1961 | 6,343,493 | 3,069,503 | 9,412,996 |
|  | (67.39) | (32.61) | (100.00) |
| 1971 | 7,210,017 | 4,345,966 | 11,555,983 |
|  | (62.39) | (37.61) | (100.00) |
| 1981 | 8,460,926 | 6,559,525 | 15,020,651 |
|  | (56.33) | (43.67) | (100.00) |

SOURCE: Y. P. Pant, *Population Growth and Employment Opportunities in Nepal*, New Delhi, 1983:12

Table 2. Per capita and per family land and person per hectare of cultivated land in development regions 1976/1977.

| Geographical regions | Agriculture land | Eastern | Central | Western | Far western | Nepal average |
|---|---|---|---|---|---|---|
| Hills | Per Capita | 0.14 | 0.08 | 0.15 | 0.10 | 0.11 |
|  | Per family | 0.86 | 0.51 | 0.84 | 0.66 | 0.69 |
|  | Persons per hectare of cultivated land | 7.59 | 11.60 | 7.43 | 8.52 | 8.95 |
| Tarai | Per capita | 0.30 | 0.26 | 0.33 | 0.38 | 0.30 |
|  | Per family | 1.74 | 1.56 | 1.91 | 2.63 | 1.81 |
|  | Persons per hectare of cultivated land | 3.34 | 3.84 | 3.05 | 2.62 | 3.34 |
| Nepal Average | Per capita | 0.23 | 0.17 | 0.16 | 0.18 | 0.18 |
|  | Per family | 1.35 | 1.03 | 0.95 | 1.22 | 1.10 |
|  | Persons per hectare of cultivated land | 5.47 | 6.31 | 5.51 | 4.31 | 5.41 |

SOURCE: Y. P. Pant and S. C. Jain, *Regional Imbalance and Process of Regional Development in Nepal*, Berlin, 1980: 2.

important to note that while the Tarai is a food surplus region, the Hills suffer from chronic food deficit.[17] Interestingly, for a long-time the surplus food of the Tarai could not be supplied to the Hills; and had to be exported to Indian markets because of easily available transportation and market facilities. This situation is slowly, although not adequately, changing with the gradual improvement of transport facilities between the two regions.

Again, on an average, a hill family survives only on one acre of land.[18] Such heavy pressure on land has resulted in surplus agricultural labour in the hills, while many of the Tarai areas are short of it.[19]

In terms of development expenditures, also a disproportionately large part of the total investment has gone to the Tarai and the Kathmandu Valley.[20] Nearly 62.5 per cent of the large scale industries are located in the Tarai, and more than 75 per cent of the private industries are also in this region.[21] The Tarai is, thus, rightly termed as the economic backbone of Nepal.[22] On the other hand, there are no large scale industries in the hills, which has caused glaring disparities in employment opportunities and per capita income of the people of the two regions. Further, it has been noted that the gulf between the economies of the Tarai and the hills is widening and the "process of development is adding to the problem of economic heterogeneity."[23]

Nepal being a plural society, the heterogeneous nature of the society provides a social basis for regionalism in Nepal. The most important aspect of this phenomenon is the steady migration of the hill people to the Tarai. Migration is, however, not a new phenomenon in Nepal. During the early days, when the Tarai was not found suitable for human settlement, people from the hills used to migrate to Sikkim, Bhutan and India. Even after 1860, when the Nepalese government thought of developing the Tarai, the hill people could not be attracted in large number by the government incentives. Later, the Nepalese government encouraged migration of Indians to this region, who made it cultivable.[24] It was only after 1950, with the rapid development of the Tarai, that the hill people also began migrating on a large scale to the Tarai region.[25]

This large-scale migration has given rise to certain serious problems in the Tarai. Problems of adjustment by the hill people to the new environment have caused acute social tensions in this region.

Table 3. Regional disparities in development activities.

| S. No. | Variables | Hills | Tarai | Kathmandu | Nepal |
|---|---|---|---|---|---|
| 1. | Land area (percentage) | 73.8 | 23.8 | 0.4 | 100.00 |
| 2. | All weather road (percentage) | 45.4 | 34.4 | 20.2 | — |
| 3. | No. of airports (1969) | 1 | 12 | 2 | 15 |
| 4. | Large scale industries (percentage) | — | 62.5 | 37.5 | 100.00 |
| 5. | Education: high schools and colleges (1969) | 150+7 | 124+11 | 74+18 | 348+36 |
| 6. | Health centres and hospitals (1969) | 70+18 | 24+25 | 2+11 | 96+54 |
| 7. | Number of development projects (1950-70) | 14 | 29 | 34 | 22 'x' |
| 8. | No. of commercial banks (1978) | 74 | 118 | 39 | 231 |

'x' Nation wide projects.

This has given rise to a serious controversy here as to the definition of a Nepali as an outsider.[26] The migrants from the hills consider themselves as the main repository of the Nepali culture and the earlier immigrants as outsiders. The irony of the situation is that the economic development of the Tarai region is largely attributed to the Kathmandu based hill elite instead of the local Tarai elite. It is this that they now consider themselves as the main well-wishers of the region and the Tarai people as rank outsiders.

Migration from the hills has also led to a major involvement of the government in the planning and settlement schemes.[27] The Nepalese government has, indeed, encouraged migration of the hill people and facilitated their resettlement by providing them surplus land obtained through land reforms. In fact, there is a feeling among the ruling elite as well, that the people of the Tarai are more sympathetic to the neighbouring Indian people. Hence, it is believed that with the settlement of the hill people in this region, Tarai's loyality towards the rest of Nepal would be strengthened. However, such an approach has alienated the Tarai problem and also deprived them from their rights on land.

Table 4. The pattern of migration. 1971.

| Origin | Destination | | | | | |
|---|---|---|---|---|---|---|
| | Mountains | Hill | Kathmandu Valley | Tarai | Total out migration | Net migration |
| 1. Mountain | — | 11,905 | 3,762 | 33,990 | 49,657 | −39,959 |
| 2. Hill | 8,401 | — | 19,513 | 352,837 | 380,751 | −340,992 |
| 3. Kathmandu Valley | 857 | 27,390 | — | 23,237 | 45,484 | −19,044 |
| 4. Tarai | 440 | 6,534 | 3,165 | — | 10,139 | +399,925 |
| 5. Total migrants | 9,698 | 39,829 | 26,440 | 410,064 | 486,031 | — |

SOURCE: *Census Report*, 1971. Central Bureau of Statistics, HMG, Nepal, Kathmandu, 1971.

## POLITICO-ADMINISTRATIVE STRUCTURE

DISPARITIES between the two regions can also be observed in the representation of the people in the national power structure. Ever since the days of the Rana rule, three castes of the hills— Brahmins, Chettris and Newars—have dominated the political structure in the country.[28] Their domination is so overwhelming that even the opposition has by and large remained confined to these caste groups.[29] Representation of the hill people in the various representative bodies being more than 80 per cent, it is quite obvious that the Tarai people are not adequately represented in Nepal politics. Domination of the hill people has continued under the Panchayat system also.[30]

As in politics, the bureaucracy and the army have also been dominated by the hill people. The Brahmins, Chettris and Newars together occupy nearly 67 per cent of the senior positions in the army and administration.[31] Thus, the social and spatial structure of the political elite and the bureaucracy reflect the inequalities prevalent in the Nepalese society. Further, the hill people, because of their political and administrative domination, have also succeeded in controlling the economy of the Tarai. It may be pointed here that because of their political domination, hill Brahmins and Chettris also became absentee landlords in the Tarai, without even becoming part of the Tarai society.[32] The inequalities within the apparatus of state have given rise to discrimination against the people of the Tarai on major issues like national language, economic policies, etc.

Table 5. Regional/ethnic representation in 1959 Parliament and 1967 National Panchayat.

| Regional and ethnic groups | 1959 Parliament No of representatives | 1959 Parliament Percentage of the total | 1967 National Panchayat No. of representatives | 1967 National Panchayat Percentage of the total |
|---|---|---|---|---|
| Hill Brahmin | 31 | 28.4 | 30 | 24.0 |
| Chettri | 30 | 27.4 | 47 | 37.6 |
| Newar | 5 | 4.6 | 15 | 12.0 |
| Low caste hill people | 1 | 0.9 | 1 | 0.8 |
| Hill tribals | 22 | 20.2 | 19 | 15.2 |
| Hill people sub-total | (89) | (81.7) | (112) | (89.6) |
| Hindus & Muslims of plains | 13 | 11.9 | 11 | 8.8 |
| Plain tribals | 7 | 6.4 | 2 | 1.6 |
| Plain people Sub-total | (20) | (18.4) | (13) | (10.4) |
| Total | 109 | 100.0 | 12.5 | 100.0 |

SOURCE: Fredrick H. Gaize, *Regionalism and National Unity in Nepal*, Berkeley, 1975.

Table 6. Distribution of ethnic groups in government positions above the under-secretary level, 1969.

| S. No. | Group | No. of identified officials | Group percentage of total population |
|---|---|---|---|
| 1. | Brahmin | 97 | 5.05 |
| 2. | Chettri | 102 | 12.11 |
| 3. | Newar | 72 | 4.64 |
| 4. | Gurung | 3 | 1.97 |
| 5. | Magar | 1 | 3.23 |
| 6. | Rai | 1 | 2.86 |
| 7. | Limbu | 1 | 1.76 |
| 8. | Tamang | 1 | 5.99 |
| 9. | Tharu | 1 | 4.36 |
| 10. | Thakali | — | 0.04 |
| 11. | Muslim | 7 | 0.04 |
| 12. | Tarai People | 6 | 24.42 |
| 13. | Others | 3 | 32.12 |
| 14. | Marwari | 1 | 0.05 |
|  | Total | 290 | 100.00 |

SOURCE: A. Beenhakar, *A Keleidoscopic circumspection of Development Planning, with Special Reference to Nepal*, Rotterdam University Press, 1973.

Table 7. Caste wise breakdown of senior army officers, 1967.

| S. No. | Caste groups | Number | Percentage of total |
|---|---|---|---|
| 1. | Chettri | 137 | 74.0 |
| 2. | Hill Brahmin | 12 | 6.5 |
| 3. | Newar | 12 | 6.5 |
| 4. | Gurung | 12 | 6.5 |
| 5. | Sanyasi (Gin) | 2 | 1.1 |
| 6. | Rai | 2 | 1.1 |
| 7. | Tamang | 2 | 1.1 |
| 8. | Magar | 1 | 0.5 |
| 9. | Kayastha | 1 | 0.5 |
| 10. | Unknown | 4 | 2.2 |
|  | Total | 185 | 100.0 |

SOURCE: A. Beenhakar, op. cit.

After 1970 some thought seems to have been given to the solution of the problem of regional disparities by introducing regional development planning. Consequently, the country was divided into six administrative regions. However, there is enough evidence to show that such an attempt has not been helpful in solving the problem of regional disparities for two reasons. First, even among these regions disparities exist. The central and eastern regions are more developed in comparison to other regions. Most of the industrial and agricultural activities are concentrated here. Secondly, each of these regions contain parts of both the hills and the Tarai. The hill people dominate politics and economy of the constituent Tarai regions as well.[33]

## IV. Manifestation of Regionalism

It is evident that despite its weak manifestation, Nepal is faced with the problem of regional disparities and these have found expression in various forms, some of which will be discussed below.

### The Language Issue

Despite Nepal being a multi-lingual country, Nepali language has been accepted as the national language. A controversy about the use and status of Hindi in the Tarai arose soon after 1951 when the post-Rana leadership undertook the task of developing a national language. In 1951, a National Education Commission was constituted, which recommended 'Nepali' as the medium of instruction in schools and colleges.[34] These recommendations became the basis of Nepal's subsequent language policy, which was resented in the Tarai when Hindi was the medium of education with a large number of Indians teaching in the schools and colleges. The Tarai Congress put forth the demand of Hindi also being given the status of a state language.[35] The issue become rather serious after 1956, when the government of Nepal took sustained steps to develop Nepali as the national language. While *Nepali Pracharini Sabha* was formed to promote the use of Nepali, the supporters of Hindi launched *Save Hindi Movement* leading to violence at some places in the Tarai.[36] The constitution of 1959 eventually declared Nepali as the national language of Nepal.[37]

During the general elections of 1959, the Hindi issue became rather important in the Tarai. But nothing tangible could be achieved, since most of the political parties supported the cause of Nepali being the only national language.

After 1960, steps were taken to further strengthen the Nepali as national language as a symbol of nationalism. In 1961, the Second Education Commission was constituted which recommended Nepali as the sole medium of instruction in schools and colleges.[38] In 1964, Nepal Company Act was passed as a result of which Nepali was to be used for business purposes as well. The ten minute Hindi broadcast of the Nepal radio was abandoned. The movement of the Tarai people against the language policy of the government received a setback with the banning of organized political activities. It may, however, be observed that despite Nepali being the national language there is a large chunk of population in the Tarai which speaks Hindi. They have resisted, though ineffectively, the language policy of the government.

## Resentment against Economic Policies

The Tarai people have also raised their voice against the discriminatory economic policies of the government, particularly in the sphere of land reforms. Although the land reform programme of the Nepalese government is, by and large, a failure, yet its implementation has caused serious problems in the Tarai. The surplus land obtained by the implementation of land reforms has been redistributed to the hill migrants and not to the tenant farmers of the Tarai. In the mid-western Tarai, the Tharu tenants were replaced by the hill settlers which caused violence in the Naval parasi district in 1966. The abolition of Ukhada land tenure system also gave rise to serious disturbances in Navalparasi and Rupandehi districts. The Compulsory Deposit Scheme introduced in the Tarai in 1965 was also resented, leading to violent incidents in Kapilbastu district and had to be suspended in 1969.

Although, a Tarai Liberation Front was formed in 1964 to fight against the grievances of the Tarai people, it disappeared without achieving any results.

## Citizenship

THE CITIZENSHIP rules have also been discriminatory to the Tarai people. According to these rules, a person acquiring Nepali citizenship must know Nepali, which goes against a large number of people in the Tarai who speak Hindi. Similarly, people of Nepali origin require a two year stay while non-Nepali origin need 15 year stay in Nepal in order to acquire citizenship.

Resentment against the discriminatory policies of the government is not confined to Tarai. The hill people have also begun to organize themselves to fight for their grievances. Some ethnic groups of the hill region like, Magar, Limbu, Gurung, etc. have tried to organize themselves. Their main resentment has been against the concentration of the economic activities in the Tarai. These ethnic groups are becoming steadily conscious of their backward conditions. In fact, some of the Kathmandu based leaders belonging to these communities have taken a lead in organizing them and pointing out that the development policies of the government have not benefited these communities. These groups are also demanding due representation in politics and administration.

## V

DESPITE THE fact that the people of the Tarai, and more recently the hill people, have tried to raise their voice against discrimination, regionalism has yet to emerge as a viable force in the kingdom. Whatever may be the magnitude of anti-government activities, there are no separatist tendencies evident so far in Nepalese politics.

This situation can be attributed to number of factors. Regionalism is basically a political phenomenon, which begins to have defined contours when people are politically conscious, aware of the discrimination against them, and there is adequate leadership to organize them to fight for the solution of their problems. The closed nature of the political system in Nepal has not allowed such a leadership to take roots. During the fifties, when the political system was open and more democratic, certain movements took place in the Tarai. The panchayat system has, however, disallowed organized mass movements. Even the political parties are not allowed to function. Trade unions are banned. Therefore, the resentment of the people has remained suppressed.

The ruling elite of the country has developed economic interests in the Tarai, and have shown interest in its economic development softening the resentment of the people.

It may also be stated that both the hill region and the Tarai lack cohesiveness. The Indian settlers belong to different origin, speak diverse dialects, and even follow different religions (of course, a large majority of them are Hindus). They also maintain social relations with their Indian counterparts. The local people are also illiterate, poor and backward. The situation, thus, does not permit formation of strong regional organizations.

The situation in the hills is even more discouraging. The peoples of the hills not only belong to different ethnic, linguistic and religious stock, they are further divided between the ruling and non-ruling classes. The Brahmins, Chettris and Newars, who form the power elite, are hardly concerned about the problems of rest of the hill people, who are mostly illiterate, poor and backward. Socio-economic difficulties and compulsions of geographical conditions have not permitted them to organize themselves and fight their problems.

It may also be pointed out here that the past history has played an important role as a unifying force. Nepal has a fairly longer history as a nation in modern times than any other South Asian country. Consciousness of 'being Nepali' has existed for more than two hundred years in that area. Prithvinarayan Shah started the process of unifying the various principalities from the mid-eighteenth century and gave a sense of identity to the area presently known as Nepal. Two wars with the British reinforced a sense of identity, as also distinctiveness of Nepal from the rest of South Asia, which had steadily come under the British empire. This feeling was strengthened by the geo-strategic location of Nepal, situated as it was between India and China—indeed, it has fought wars against both.

Historically, the institution of monarchy has also been playing an important role in restraining the regional movements. It has been an important factor in welding the various heterogeneous groups and farflung areas into a nation.

Notwithstanding its declining role, monarchy continues to be the axis around which the political life of Nepal revolves. The King's role is much politicized today, responsible as he is for all the policies and programmes of the government. Yet he symbolizes tradition and thus plays a significant role in national unity.[39] For many Nepalese he still remains 'the ruler of the country' and thus the rallying point of their loyalty towards the country.

Regional consciousness has been further discouraged by the role that Hinduism and the Nepali language have played in unifying the country. Notwithstanding the existence of Buddhism and other religions, Hinduism is not merely a state religion, it has been responsible for bringing the various religious groups within the larger fold of the consciousness of being Nepali. The spread of Hinduism may be termed as process of increasing *Sanskritization,* wherein its norms have come to be widely accepted and shared even by the non-Hindi sections of the country.[40] The use of Nepali in the business and official matters in most areas of the country for the last two hundred years has made for an emotional bond for the various socio-cultural groups from far-flung areas. Notwithstanding the existence of a large number of languages and dialects, Nepali has been accepted as the lingua franca of the country.

The role that caste system has played in bringing about a feeling of social cohesion in the Nepalese society, may also be mentioned here. Despite the existence of different ethnic groups, caste consciousness has penetrated even among those groups which do not follow Hinduism. Caste, indeed, overlays the variegated social order of the kingdom, and to no mean extent discourages regionalism.

It may also be stated here that regionalism has often emerged out of the process of "modernization." In Nepal this process has been painfully slow and the political system (except during the brief interlude of the parliamentary system) has discouraged the ventilation of regional sentiments. The Panchayat system and even its modified variant, encourages centripetal rather than the centrifugal pulls.

Last, but not the least, many social groups which occupy distinct regions are too small in terms of population, and too loosely organized, to give vent to their regional feelings in any significant manner.

On balance, it would seem that notwithstanding serious regional diversities and disparities, regionalism as a major force has yet to emerge in Nepal, partly because pulls of cohesion and unity act as a counter-balancing force, and partly because regionalism itself has not yet acquired the necessary thrust and momentum.

## Notes

1. Joseph Schwartzberg, "Prodegemone to the Study of South Asian Regions and Regionalism," in Robert I Crane (ed.) *Region and Regionalism in South Asian Studies*, Duke University, 1967.
2. Myron Weiner, "Political Integration and Political Development," *Annals of the American Academy of Political and Social Sciences*, Vol. 358, 1965: 52.
3. *Encyclopedia of Social Sciences*, Vol. XIII, 1968: 378.
4. James R. Modonald, *A Geography of Regions*, W.M.C. Brown Company, 1972: 50.
5. For a study of Nepal's geography, see P.P. Karan, *Nepal: A Cultural and Physical Geography*, Lexington, 1960; N.B. Thapa and Y.B. Thapa, *Geography of Nepal, Physical, Economic, Cultural and Regional*, Calcutta, 1969.
6. According to a classification Nepal is divided into nine geographic regions: (i) Western hills, (ii) Kathmandu Valley, (iii) Western Tarai, (iv) Eastern hills, (v) Central Tarai, (vi) Eastern Tarai, (vii) Western Inner Tarai, (viii) Eastern Inner Tarai and (ix) far Western Tarai, C.B. Shrestha, "Problems of Regionalism in Nepal," *The Himalayan Review*, Vol. II-III, 1969-78: 14.
7. Christoph von Furer-Heimendorf, "The Interactions of Castes and Ethnic Groups in Nepal," *Bulletin of the School of Oriental and African Studies*, Vol. XX, 1957: 244.
8. See Bor Bahadur Bisht, *People of Nepal*, Kathmandu, 1970.
9. For a study of Newars, see Gopal Singh Nepali, *Newars: An Ethno-Sociological Study of a Himalayan Community*, United Asia Publishers, 1965.
10. See for details, Bor Bahadur Bisht, n. 8.
11. Ibid.
12. Stanley Maron et al., *Survey of Nepal Society*, Human Relations Area File, South Asia Project, Berkeley, University of California, 1956.
13. Christoph von-Furrer Heimendrof, n. 7.
14. Y.P. Pant, *Population, Growth and Employment Opportunities in Nepal*, New Delhi, 1983: 12.
15. Piers Blaikie et al., *Nepal in Crisis, Growth and Stagnation at the Periphery*, New Delhi, 1980: 18.
16. *Nepal Rastra Bank*, Annual Report of the Board of Directors, HMG, Nepal, 1965.
17. See Ratna S. Rana and Tulsi R. Joshi, "Nepal's Food Grain Surplus of Deficit Regions," *The National Geographical Journal of India*, June-September, 1968.
18. Leo E. Rosa and John T. Scholz, *Nepal, Profile of a Himalayan Kingdom*, Select Book Service Syndicate, 1980: 94.
19. B.P. Shrestha, "Regional Planning in Nepal," *Vasudha*, Vol. XI, No. 9 August-September, 1968: 2.
20. See B.P. Shrestha and S.C. Jain, *Regional Development in Nepal. An Exercise in Reality*, Development Publishers, 1978: 74.

21. B.P. Shrestha, *The Economy of Nepal*, Bombay, 1967.
22. Fredrick H. Gaige, "The Role of Tarai in Nepal's Economic Development," *Vasudha*, Vol. XI, 1968.
23. K.P. Malla and Pashupati Shumsher JBR, "Introduction," in Malla and Rana (eds.), *Nepal in Perspective*, CEDA, Kathmandu, 1973: 20.
24. See, Ramakant and B.C. Upreti, "Indian Community in Nepal: A Study of the Indian Migrants" in I.J. Bahadur Singh (ed.), *Indians in South Asia*, New Delhi, 1984.
25. See Mohan N. Shrestha, "International Migration of People in Nepal," *Eastern Anthropologist*, Vol. 32, No. 3 July-September 1979.
26. Rishikesh Shah, *Nepali Politics, Retrospect and Prospect*, New Delhi, 1978: 23.
27. Piers Blaikie et al., n. 15: 67.
28. Pashupati Shamsher, "Towards an Integrated Policy of National Integration," *Aspects of Development Administration*, CEDA, Kathmandu, Occasional Paper no. 2, 1971: 42.
29. Bhuwan Lal Joshi and Leo E. Rose, *Democratic Innovations in Nepal*. University of California Press, 1966: 41.
30. See, Pashupati S. JBR, and Mohammad Mohsin, *The Pattern of Emerging Leadership in Panchayats*, HMG, Kathmandu, 1967.
31. Fredrick H. Gaige, *Regionalism and National Unity in Nepal*, University of California Press, 1975.
32. Leo E. Rose, n. 18: 74.
33. See, Pashupati Shamsher JBR and Mohammad Mohsin, n. 30.
34. *Report on Education in Nepal*, National Education Planning Commission, HMG, Kathmandu, 1953.
35. *The Hindustan Times* (New Delhi), 4 May 1953.
36. *The Commoner* (Kathmandu), 1 November 1957.
37. See article 70 of *The Constitution of Nepal*, Ministry of Law and Justice, HMG, Kathmandu, 1959.
38. *Report of the National Education Commission*, HMG, Kathmandu, 1962.
39. Bengt Erik Borgstrom, *The Patran and the Pancea*, New Delhi, 1980: 17.
40. Rishikesh Shah, *Nepali Politics, Retrospect and Prospect*, Oxford University Press (Delhi), 1975: 9.

CHAPTER TEN

# Monarchical System of Bhutan
Challenges of Modernization

## Kapileshwar Labh

THE DOMESTIC milieu of Bhutan is somewhat different from that of other South Asian countries. Unlike other countries of the region, Bhutan of late has not witnessed ethnic and communal riots or political agitations against the Wangchuk regime for establishing a popular political system. However, the country has not been free from political dissension. In 1964, Jigmie Palden Dorji, the then Prime Minister of Bhutan, was assassinated. Such a domestic situation as obtains in Bhutan today raises some questions. What is the nature of the monarchical polity of Bhutan? Is it a traditional ruling monarchy or modern constitutional monarchy? What factors led to the political tensions which resulted in the assassination of the Bhutanese Prime Minister? Was it a factional struggle for power or the challenge of modernization that caused the political crisis in 1964? What are the challenges of modernization that the monarchy of Bhutan has been facing? What is the prospect of monarchical system in Bhutan? These are some of the questions to which this paper seeks to address itself.

There is a traditional ruling monarchy in Bhutan. Unlike a modern constitutional monarch who reigns but does not rule, the Bhutanese monarch reigns as well as rules. He plays an active political role in governing the country. The source of legitimacy lies not in the Bhutanese people but in him.[1] Although both the Himalayan Kingdoms of Nepal and Bhutan have ruling monarchies,[2] they do not have identical political systems. The difference between the two monarchies is discernible in more than one way. While Nepal has the only surviving Hindu monarchy, in Bhutan there is the only existing Mahayana Buddhist monarchy. Moreover, Nepal has a long tradition of monarchical form of government which Bhutan lacks. It was in 1907 that a hereditary monarchy was established in Bhutan. Prior to the establishment of monarchy in Bhutan, the country had a political system which was called "The Shabdung political system" in which the concept of dual authority, one supreme in religious affairs and the other in temporal matters, prevailed. While the Dharma Raja exercised authority over religious matters, the Deb Raja looked after secular affairs; the former was chosen through the reincarnation process, the latter was elected by a council of lamas. This division of authority did not, however, prevent the rise of civil strife in the country. The Deb Raja who was initially elected by a council of lamas became merely a nominee of the most powerful of Ponlops (governors) in the nineteenth century. There were a number of civil wars during this period. The country was virtually divided among semi-independent chiefs. The monarchy was established in 1907 "out of sheer necessity to save the country from disintegration."[3] Besides, the monarchies of Nepal and Bhutan differed in the method of their origin and operation. While Prithvinarayan Shah made himself the monarch of Nepal in 1769 by force of arms, Ugyen Wangchuk had a unique distinction of being elected by a "unanimous vote of the Bhutan chiefs and principal Lamas as hereditary Maharaja of Bhutan."[4] The manner in which the monarchy was established in Bhutan had its impact on the style of its functioning. The Bhutanese monarch maintained a small palace guard, and unlike his counterpart in Nepal, had no army until the mid-1950's. Unlike other monarchs, he did not establish a highly centralized and autocratic rule. In Nepal the Ranas pushed the monarch into background and held themselves effectively in power for about a century (1846-1949). They had no counterparts in Bhutan. Ugyen Dorji, Bhutanese Agent in India, became a powerful official in Bhutan and acted as prime minister of the country. Like the Ranas of Nepal, Dorjis of Bhutan made this office hereditary, but unlike the Ranas, the Dorjis did not overshadow the monarch of Bhutan and assumed no absolute power in administering the country. They acted as advisors to Bhutanese Kings.

## II

THE MONARCHY in Bhutan became the first national institution which commanded loyalty of all Bhutanese people. The installation of Ugyen Wangchuk, the then Tongsa Ponlop, as the hereditary monarch ushered in a new era in the history of Bhutan. It marked the beginning of modernization process in Bhutan. "Modernization refers to the process of directed change through which a nation achieves economic growth, political development and autonomy, and social reconstruction based on the principles of equality, fraternity, enhancement of freedoms, and satisfaction of basic needs."[5] The first two Bhutanese monarchs, Ugyen Wangchuk (1906-26) and Jigme Wangchuk (1926-52), did not introduce such a comprehensive programme of innovations in the country. They made no attempt to create national institutions of politics, law and voluntary associations which could penetrate into regions and localities. However, they introduced rudiments of modernization. They endeavoured to eliminate or weaken local or regional forces and to strengthen the authority of the state. By 1918 when Dawa Paljor, the then former Paro Ponlop, died, Ugyen Wangchuk extended his sway over the western province of Bhutan which was more or less beyond the control of the central authorities of the country. Jigme Wangchuk, the second monarch, consolidated his authority over the entire country. During his reign the authority of the Ponlop was assumed by the monarch himself and the office of Ponlop remained but an honorary title.[6]

Ugyen Wangchuk also introduced in the country modern education which is a most potent instrument of modernization. During his visits to Calcutta (1905) and Delhi (1911), he saw the progress that India had achieved in educational field and became convinced of the need to introduce modern education in Bhutan. He set up a school at Ha, in Western Bhutan, in 1914. He also established another school at Bumthang in Central Bhutan. He sent about 15 Bhutanese students who passed Matriculation Examination for training in different technical institutions in India during 1924-29. Ugyen Wangchuk also attempted to develop the economy of his country. In 1914 he appointed J.C. White, ex-political officer in Sikkim, as his agent empowering him to enter into agreement with capitalists desirous of making investment in Bhutan. White drew up schemes for the exploitation of mineral and timber resources of the country. However, the scheme for development, of the natural resources of Bhutan came to nothing, for the appointment of White as Bhutan's agent was cancelled following differences over the payment of White's remuneration which he estimated at Rs. 45,000 a year.[7] The lack of capital was a big stumbling block in the way of introducing programmes of modernization. Bhutan lacked economic resources and no foreign aid was available in those days. Hence the pace of modernization was extremely slow. However, the modernization process was not stopped completely. Jigme Wangchuk continued modernization efforts initiated by his father. He also opened new schools and sent Bhutanese students to different cities in India for technical training. He sent about 15 Bhutanese youngmen to India for military training in 1933. However, there was no change in the political, economic and social spheres in the country. By the 1950's certain developments took place in and around Bhutan which impelled its ruling elite to introduce changes in the country. The "modernizational ideals" which became the "official creed" were sweeping the nations of South Asia.[8] Thus Bhutan could not remain insulated. The countries around her were moving ahead in the development of communications and social services. On her northern border, Tibet was undergoing a radical change under communist China. On her southern and eastern border, India had initiated development programmes. On her western border Sikkim had launched a plan for economic development in 1952.

There was also a significant change in the domestic affairs of Bhutan. The second monarch, Jigme Wangchuk, died in 1952 and was succeeded by his son, Jigme Dorji Wangchuk. The third monarch was the product of a different political socialization process from that of his predecessors. He considered that it was necessary to reform the existing system of government if the monarchy in Bhutan was to survive in a fast-changing world. In 1953 he established a National Assembly (the Tshogdu) which was aimed at involving different sections of the people in the decision-making process of the country. There were at first about 130 members—10 from the government officials, 10 from the monastic bodies and 110 were the representatives of the people. In the 1960's the membership was increased to 150 with the addition of 20 members from the government service. The members of the National Assembly have been guaranteed complete freedom of speech. They can discuss and pass resolutions on any subject. The decisions of the National Assembly require a two-thirds majority under the 1953 royal order and have to be approved by the monarch before becoming law. Thus under the 1953 royal order Jigme Dorji Wangchuk remained as the sole sovereign authority in the country with a veto power on all legislative measures.[9] Apart from establishing the National Assembly no other step was taken towards introducing reforms in the country in the 1950's. Socio-economic conditions in Bhutan remained unchanged. However, in 1958-59, two events took place which prompted the Bhutanese authorities to modernize their country. First, the late Prime Minister of India Jawaharlal Nehru visited Bhutan in September 1958 and promised all the financial and technical assistance that Bhutan needed for her economic development. He also made it clear that Bhutan would remain independent and would choose her own direction and progress. Secondly, the ruthless repression of the Tibetan revolt by China, the flight of the Dalai Lama and the assemblage of Chinese troops near Bhutan's northern border made a strong impact on the Bhutanese authorities. Hence they decided to develop their country on modern lines and embarked on development plans with India's financial and technical assistance.[10]

### III

THE INTRODUCTION of major changes in Bhutan in the beginning of the 1960's had its impact on the Bhutanese society. Prior to the formulation of development programmes the country was by and large free from conflict and tension. Bhutan was more or less a harmonious society with a conspicuous absence of different competing groups. Towards mid-sixties Bhutan became one of the participants in the "Asian Drama" which was marked by conflicts of diverse sorts. As a result of modernizing efforts in Bhutan, the monarchy began to face challenges on social, economic and political fronts. With the initiation of reforms in the country, there arose different competing groups such as traditionalists and modernists, haves and have-nots, and the army and the civil authorities. The prospect of their mutual conflict and struggle for power increased. The attempt by the monarch to maintain a balance between these groups constituted a great challenge for him. The traditionalists and the modernists were at loggerheads. The traditionalists were disinclined to change the old order whereas the modernists led by Jigmie Palden Dorji, the then Prime Minister, were determined to initiate major changes in the country. The antagonism between the two groups resulted in the assassination of Jigmie Dorji in April 1964.

There are differences of opinion among scholars of Bhutanese affairs over the issue of assassination of the Bhutanese Prime Minister. While Nari Rustomji and Ram Rahul hold that the traditionalists were responsible for the assassination of Jigmie Dorji, Leo E. Rose does not think that a traditionalist/modernist framework is applicable to the political system of Bhutan. According to Nari Rustomji, the development programmes envisaged by Jigmie Dorji alarmed the traditional group, particularly Buddhist lamas. He wrote: "Apart from the threat to religion, the lamas apprehended that their own influence and hold over the people would be undermined by changes they saw looming ahead."[11] Jigmie Dorji also offended the lamas by deriding them and their institution. Therefore "they felt gravely disturbed". Besides the lamas, there were other sections of the traditional group, particularly the old-timers in the Bhutanese civil service and army who were apprehensive that their vested interests would be endangered by Jigmie Dorji's development programmes and were "hostile" to Jigmie Dorji.[12] According to Ram Rahul, "the reforms and innovations did not go down well with old guard of Bhutan...The old guard, therefore, decided to act by assassinating the man most closely identified with new order—Jigmie Palden Dorji of Ha."[13] However, Leo E. Rose considers the 1964 crisis more of a struggle for power within the political elite than an ideological conflict over modernization policy. According to him, "political factionalism plays a major role in Bhutan political system. But these factions have generally lacked ideological class interest...and in most instances would almost seem to be incidental alignment of individuals on a specific issue or more commonly on an event-by-event basis."[14]

Politics of most of the Third World countries may be characterized as factional. There is no reason why tradition/modernity concept should be applicable to them and not to Bhutan. Leo E. Rose holds that there is no such strong traditional class in Bhutan that could resist reform programmes. He feels that big landowners, not the lamas, would oppose reform programmes. By holding this view Rose minimizes the influence of *religion and religious groups in* traditional societies. In a deeply religious society, religious groups influence almost all sections of society, including the landowning class, the army and bureaucracy. Bhutan has been a basically traditional society, and the influence of religion on the people may be gauged from the fact that prior to the establishment of monarchy in 1907 the country had a theocratic political system.[15] Even after the emergence of monarchy in the country, the influence of religion remained predominant in the society. The monasteries have been practically independent of the monarch's control. The lamas remain a priviledged class and command much respect from the people. It is probable that they perceived threats to their privileged position in Jigmie Dorji's reform programmes. Interestingly, Rose seems to have admitted it when he wrote; "the Lonchen's (Prime Minister's) political socialization had taken place largely in India, and he may have been somewhat insensitive in certain respects to some aspects of Bhutan's political culture, a deficiency for what he paid the ultimate price in 1964—assassination."[16]

## IV

THE ASSASSINATION of the Bhutanese Prime Minister posed a threat to the Wangchuk regime. Jigmie Dorji was not only the leader of the modernizing group, he was also the chief spokesman of the regime, and the army, which was regarded as the main support base of the regime had been involved in the assassination of the Bhutanese Prime Minister. Moreover, on 16th December 1964, a group of dissident officials led by Ugyen Tangbi attempted a *coup d'etat* but their attempt was foiled.[17] Jigme Dorji Wangchuk sensed the peril to his regime. In the post-1964 period, he endeavoured to overcome the peril by taking some measures towards transforming the traditional ruling monarchy of Bhutan into a constitutional monarchy in which authority was to be vested in the Bhutanese people. He created some new political institutions and took steps to invest the National Assembly with sovereign authority. In 1965, he established the Royal Advisory Council (Lodoi Tsokde) to advise him on the implementation of development programmes and on other matters of national importance. The Royal Advisory had eight members—five representatives of the people, two representatives of monastic order and one nominee of the King. In 1968 he appointed three ministers and constituted what may be regarded as the first council of Ministers in Bhutan. In 1968, he surrendered his veto power on the decisions of the National Assembly. The decisions of the National Assembly were thenceforth to be treated as "final" without the approval of the King. Jigme Dorji Wangchuk, however, retained power to address the Assembly, and refer back to it any resolution about which he had "serious misgivings." He also recommended to the National Assembly that all appointment of ministers "be decided by the National Assembly." But even more radical, indeed unprecedented in monarchical polities, was the King's recommendation to the National Assembly in 1968 that all government officials including the King be obliged to resign from office if they receive a no-confidence vote in the Assembly.[18]

Scholars have described Jigme Dorji Wangchuk as the great "innovator" but have not analysed factors behind his innovations in the post-1964 period. Indeed the King was apprehensive of "rebellion" and "chaos" in the country during this period. His fear of revolt and his concern about stability of his regime was explicitly expressed in his statement to the Assembly on 13 November 1968. He said:

> During the last spring session of the National Assembly, I had expressed my desire to form a government combining the monarchical and democratic systems in order to ensure the stability and solidarity of the country... We have a hereditary monarchy, but the public must also realize their duties and responsibilities. Even if you feel that the system of hereditary monarchy should be abolished, this should be achieved by proper means, the procedure of which is to be decided. Rebellion will only bring disaster and disgrace to the country accompanied by loss of lives and chaos which will be exploited by outsiders to the detriment of the country. In case of misunderstanding between the King and the people or if the King resorts to repression, the people, instead of rebelling, should convene the National Assembly.[19]

V

Never before did the monarchy of Bhutan face such a challenge. As a matter of fact the reforms that had been introduced in the country since the 1950's produced diverse challenges before the monarchy. The development of a modern army in Bhutan posed such a challenge to the monarchy. Prior to the mid-1950's, there was no regular military force in Bhutan. The Royalty maintained a small palace guard but this was not a trained force. In every district, the Dzongpon (district officer) maintained a small militia which served more in a police capacity than a military force. In 1955, the king of Bhutan undertook the task of organizing the Bhutanese army as a regular military force. By 1964, the size of the Bhutanese army grew to about 9000-strong. While the Wangchuk regime attempted to strengthen itself through the organization of the army, the latter turned out to be a challenge to the regime itself. "Some army officers were involved in the 1964-65 conspiracies and counter-conspiracies that seemed to threaten at one point the very existence of the regime."[20] With the growing modernization of the army, the army's potential for political involvement in Bhutan is likely to increase.

Similarly, the modernization process in Bhutan threw up ethnic challenges for the monarchy. The ethnic groups which had been dormant until the mid-1950's are getting politicized with the spread of modern education and are growing assertive as distinct linguistic and cultural groups.[21] Like other South Asian societies, Bhutan is a multi-ethnic society. The ruling elites of the country have been the people of Tibetan origin. They are by and large concentrated in western Bhutan. They speak Dzongkha, a dialect of the Tibetan, which has developed a distinct characteristics of its own over the past few centuries. They constitute about 28 per cent of the population. The people of north-eastern Bhutan constitute a separate ethnic group. They belong to the Indo-Mongoloid group and are akin to those of the state of Arunachal Pradesh in India. They are about 57 per cent of the population. They speak about eleven different dialects of non-Tibetan origin. They have some distinctive dress and food habits as well as local traditions and festivals. Besides, they are Nepali Bhutanese who reside in southwestern Bhutan. They are comparatively recent immigrants. They are a distinct linguistic and cultural group. The size of this group is a subject of controversy. While the Nepalese claim that they constitute 25 to 30 per cent of the total population, the Bhutanese official estimates are that they do not constitute more than 15 to 20 per cent of the population. The Nepali Bhutanese constitute a serious challenge for the ruling elite of Bhutan. Until the 1950's, the Bhutanese government made no attempt to integrate them into the political system of the country. They were treated virtually as aliens and the Bhutanese policy was to isolate them by confining them to southern Bhutan. After Jigme Dorji Wangchuk ascended the throne in 1952, there has been a change in the policy towards the Nepali Bhutanese. The Bhutanese government has been making efforts to integrate them into the political system of the country. They were given representation in the National Assembly when it was established in 1953. Now they are recruited in the army and civil service on the same basis as other Bhutanese nationals and are posted in the Bhutanese capital and other cities. The Bhutanese government has been encouraging inter-marriages between the Nepali Bhutanese and the people belonging to other ethnic groups of Bhutan. It has also introduced liberal policy with regard to land ownership and taxation in southern Bhutan, changing the discriminatory policy that had led the Nepali Bhutanese to regard themselves as second class citizens.[22]

Jigme Singye Wangchuk who succeeded his father as the fourth monarch of Bhutan on 24 July 1972, is also keen to integrate the Nepali Bhutanese into Bhutanese national life. In December 1973 he undertook a tour of southern Bhutan and exhorted the Nepali Bhutanese that they should not regard themselves as "aliens" and they "must remain united as one people, one nation and forge ahead together."[23] The integration of the Nepali Bhutanese is likely to increase competition for limited jobs in the army and civil services, and in the economic field. Some people belonging to the ruling elite may be averse to sharing power with the Nepalese. Thus the modernization process in Bhutan presents the prospect of conflicts not only between the ruling elite and the ethnic groups but also within the ruling elite over the extent of sharing power with the ethnic groups. The efforts at reconciling such conflicts constitute serious challenge for the Wangchuk regime.

The difficult challenges that the monarchy faces are economic. The modernization of economy requires a lot of capital resources. Bhutan lacks adequate resources. The country is almost entirely mountainous except for a few river valleys in western and central Bhutan and a thin flat southern belt contiguous to India. Thus, only about 9 per cent of Bhutan's land is under cultivation. Bhutan is the poorest nation in terms of the per capita GNP which is about $80. Tourism is her principal foreign exchange earner which is estimated at US $1 million a year, followed by philateclic sale at about US $250,000 a year. Bhutan is heavily dependent on external aid, espectially Indian aid, for her economic development. Between 1961 and 1981 she implemented four five-year plans, largely with India's financial and technical assistance.[24] Ever since she became a member of the Colombo Plan in 1962, she has also been receiving some assistance from members of the Colombo Plan. The total Colombo Plan assistance to Bhutan upto 1980 is Rs.16 million in which the largest contribution has come from Australia, which is about Rs.12 million, followed by UK and Japan, contributing a little more than Rs.1.3 million each. Bhutan's fifth Five-year Plan (1982-87) envisages an aggregate investment of Rs.3.8-4.2 billion, of this Rs.1.34 billion will come from India as non-project aid. The United Nations and other external sources are expected to provide about 30 percent of the plan outlay.[25] Nevertheless there will be a sizeable deficit because Bhutan's own resource mobilization is only a fraction of the plan outlay, Jigme Singye Wangchuk is concerned over his country's dependence on external aid. At the National Day celebration on 17 December 1983, he said:

> Planned development programmes were introduced in Bhutan since the beginning of 1961 and until now, the government has concentrated all its thought, and efforts in carrying out developmental activities for the benefit and welfare of the people. As a result, we have managed to achieve substantial progress but we have not yet been able to obtain economic self-sustenance. We are still not in a position to stand on our feet in economic terms. This is indeed a matter of great urgency and concern to us, and it will continue to be so until we make our country self-sustaining if not self-sufficient.[26]

In fact, Thimphu's efforts to reduce dependence on external aid for its economic development constitute one of its major challenges.

## VI

However, Thimphu's dependence on external aid, is likely to grow, instead of being reduced, in view of its development programmes. Recently, the King said: "We do not want our people to be poor, illiterate and diseased. We want roads and electricity, the best without haphazard development."[27] There may be strong pressures by the modernizing group on the Bhutanese authorities to develop the country and to widen the source of foreign aid. Some elements belonging to this group would like to seek economic aid from China and other countries. Indeed, the problem of meeting the growing aspirations of the modernizing group constitutes one of the severest challenges faced by ruling monarchies. It is one of the reasons why Samuel P. Huntington projects a bleak future for modernizing monarchies which, according to him, not only lose the support of the traditional group but also create more enemies than friends among the modernist group as a result of their policies. Huntington wrote:

> These (monarchical) political systems were involved in a fundamental dilemma. On the one hand, centralization of power in the monarchy was necessary to promote social, cultural and economic reforms. On the other hand, this centralization made difficult or impossible the expansion of the power of the traditional polity and the assimilation of the new groups produced by modernization. The participation of these groups in politics seemingly could come only at the price of monarchy.[28]

The monarchy in Bhutan is, however, not faced with such a dilemma, for the two adverse factors, i.e. the "centralization of power" and the problem of participation of "new groups" in politics, envisaged by Huntington as the two horns of the dilemma, have not developed in Bhutan. There are indications that the Wangchuk regime has not been centralizing all powers in its hands. It shares powers with such representative institutions as the National Assembly and the Royal Advisory Council. All cabinet decisions are approved by the National Assembly and the King who takes part in its debates seldom uses his royal veto. In 1982, the status of the Royal Advisory Council has been raised to that of the country's supreme watchdog body. It can now report against the King to the Cabinet and the National Assembly if the King persists in ignoring its advices.[29] Moreover, Royal Civil Service Commission, which was established in June 1982, now attends to almost all appointments and promotions, which were previously the prerogatives of the King. Thus, the emerging trends in Bhutan are towards decentralization rather than centralization of power. This is also discernible from the fact that district plans under the Fifth Plan were prepared after district-level discussion. According to Huntington: "Centralization in monarchy was necessary to promote social, cultural and economic reforms." This is not the case with the monarchy in Bhutan. Jigme Singye Wangchuk has been endeavouring to modernize his country without centralizing powers in his hand. Furthermore, there are no large "new groups produced by modernization" in Bhutan whose participation in Bhutanese polities would be ruinous for the monarchy. The Wangchuk regime has not sought to intervene in societal change in such a way as "to shatter it to bits" and to "recreate from it something totally new." It has adopted "the gradualist approach" to modernization in which the emphasis is on institution-building and the effective use of man's acquired knowledge, and in which the society would be transformed in such a way that the people would be freed from hunger, misery, and the other vicissitudes of nature.[30] Thus the modernization process in Bhutan has not produced too large a modernizing group to be assimilated in the Bhutanese politics. Literacy among the Bhutanese people is still very low. The people of Bhutan are not as politicized as their neighbours in other South Asian countries. That is why there are no political agitations against the regime for establishing a multi-party political system. With the expansion of education and growth of unemployment and frustration among the Bhutanese youths, the monarchy may face problems in the future. For the present, Jigme Singye Wangchuk enjoys loyalty and confidence of all sections of the people of Bhutan. He is in the saddle and bids fair to continue the modernization process initiated by his predecessors.

### NOTES

1. For the differences between traditional ruling monarchies and modern constitutional monarchies, see Samuel P. Huntington, *Political Order in Changing Societies* (New Haven, 1970, Fourth Printing), pp.177-78.
2. The Sovereignty of Nepal is vested in the king of Nepal and all powers executive, legislative and judicial emanate from him. See P. Saran, *Government and Politics of Nepal* (New Delhi, 1983), p.45.
3. Nagendra Singh, *Bhutan: A Kingdom in the Himalayas* (New Delhi, 1972), p.92.
4. Ibid., p.50.
5. Baidya Nath Varma, *The Sociology and Politics of Development: A*

*Theoretical Study* (London, 1980), p.15.
6. Leo E. Rose, *The Politics of Bhutan* (Ithaca, 1977), p. 37.
7. Kapileshwar Labh, *India and Bhutan* (New Delhi, 1974), p.191.
8. Gunnar Myrdal, *Asian Drama: An Inquiry into the Poverty of Nations* (Middlesex, 1968), Vol. 1, p.54.
9. Rose, n. 6, pp.151-53.
10. Labh, n.7, p. 216.
11. Nari Rustomji, *Bhutan: The Dragon Kingdom in Crisis* (Oxford, 1978), p.12.
12. Ibid., p.93.
13. Ram Rahul, *Royal Bhutan* (New Delhi, 1983), p.41.
14. Rose, n.6, p.115.
15. In theocracies political and religious associations are one and the same. See David E. Apter, *Some Conceptual Approaches to the Study of Modernization* (New Jersey, 1968), p.204.
16. Rose, n.6, p.151.
17. Rahul, n.13, p.41.
18. Ibid., pp.42-43. See also Rose, n.6, p.153.
19. Cited in Rose, n.6, p.154.
20. Ibid., p.204.
21. An ethnic group is broadly defined as a social collectivity which possesses and is aware of its distinctiveness by virtue of certain shared historical experiences as well as certain objective attributes such as race, descent tribes, language, religion, dress, diet, etc." See Urmila Phadnis "Ethnicity and Nation-building in South Asia, A Case Study of Sri Lanka," *India Quarterly*, Vol. 35, No.3 July-September 1979, p.329.
22. Rose, n.6, pp.44-47.
23. *Kuensel*, Vol. 9, Nos. 1-2, 6-13 January 1974, p.2.
24. India solely financed the first two five-year plans. Indian aid for the First Five Year Plan (1961-66) was Rs.103 million and for the Second Five Year Plan (1966-71) was Rs.200 million. See *Kuensel*, No. 32. April 2, 1972. India also contributed major part of the outlays of the third and fourth plans. Third Plan (1971-75) had an outlay of Rs.475 million and Fourth Plan (1976-80) Rs.1106 million. India provided Rs.425 million and Rs.850 million for the third and the fourth plan respectively. Besides, she also provided aid for non-plan projects. According to R.N. Anil, during the first four five-year plans Indian assistance had been to the tune of Rs.1,981.6 million. See R.N. Anil "India and Bhutan: Partners in Progress," *Hindustan Times*, 24 July 1984.
25. *Asia Year Book* (For Eastern Economic Review) 1983, p.118.
26. *Kuensel*, Vol. 18, No. 52, 25 December 1983, p.2.
27. Sunanda K. Datta Ray "Flight of the Dragon-II: Challenge of Settlement with China," *The Statesman*, 28 April 1984.
28. Samuel P. Huntington, n.1, p.177.
29. Sunanda K. Datta Ray, n. 27.
30. For the gradualist approach to modernization, see Baidya Nath Varma, n.5, p.83.

# Index

Agricultural labourers, wages of, 6
Ahluwalia, Montek, 4, 5, 8, 11, 12, 13, 20, 36
Ahmed, Feroz, 150, 158, 160
Alamgir, Mohiuddin, 3, 5, 6, 10, 11, 16, 17, 19
Alavi, Hamza, 67, 69, 71, 72
Amrithalingam, A., 134
Anil, R.N., 192
Apter, David E., 188
Arasaratnam, S., 126
Ayub Khan, 64, 66, 69, 71, 156, 158

Balasuriya, Tissa, 43, 51, 53
Baluchi struggle, 153f.
Bandaranaike, Sirimavo, 130, 131, 132, 137, 138
Bangladesh
 agricultural wages, 22
Banks (Nationalization) Act (Pakistan), 67
Bardhan, P.K., 8, 19, 36
Bastian, Sunil, 52
Beckerman, W., 11
Beckford, George L., 41
Beenhakar, A., 174
Bell, Daniel, 149
Bhatia, B.M., 61
Bhutan
 army's role, 189
 cabinet system, 90
 cultural diversity, 84
 debt problem, 96
 demographic structure, 84, 86
 economic development, 82f.
 ethnic diversity, 84, 190
 expenditure on education, 95
 external, influences, 85, 89
 five year plans, 89f.
 foreign aid, 90
 Indian aid, 85
 isolation, 82
 modernization challenges, 182f.
 modernization process, 85
 monarchy, 83
 monarchical system, 182f.
 national consciousness, 82, 97
 political system, 191
 power structure, 193
 role in South Asia, 92, 94f.
 role of King, 96f.
 social changes, 82f.
 task of national integration, 97f.
 trade policies, 92
Bhutto, Zulfikar Ali, 69, 76, 77, 154, 155, 156, 160
Bisht, Bor Bahadur, 167, 168
Bizenjo, Mir Ghous Bakash, 78
Blaikie, Piers, 168, 171
Borgstrom, Bengt Erik, 179
Brass, Paul R., 104, 108
Bromkey, Yulian, 107
Burki, S.J., 71, 72, 156, 157

Casanova, Gonzalez, 106
Ceylon workers congress, 131, 132
Chayur, Mohammad Arif, 153
Choudhury, M. Ghaffar, 69
Concentration ratio, 3
Concentration ratio asset holdings, 4
Currie, Jean, 52

Dandekar, V.M., 5, 17, 19, 36
Das, B.S., 82
Das, Nirmala, 83
Datta Ray, Sunanda K., 193
De Silva, C.R., 126
De Silva, K.M., 135
Deb Raja (Bhutan), 183
Despress, Leo, 105
Development, levels of, 1f.
Development Decade (Pakistan), 64
Dharma Raja (Bhutan), 183
Domestic conflicts
  conditions for, 1
  economic causes, 26
  potential for 1f
Dorji, Jigmie Palden, 182, 187, 188
Dutta, Bhaskar, 5, 9, 20

ECAFE, 4, 6, 10, 17
Economic disparities, 61f.
Economic growth, 1f.
Economic growth in South Asia, 1f.
Education Commission (Nepal), 176
Ethnic
  approaches, 103
  configurations in South Asia, 109
  definition, 101
Ethnic conflicts
  causes, 149
  cultural pluralist approach, 104, 105
  developmental approach, 104
  geographical factors, 109
  modernization process, 107
  primordialist approach, 103f.
  role of power structure, 110
  Sri Lanka, 121f.
Ethnic group

definition, 149

Free Trade Zones (Sri Lanka), 43, 44, 50, 51f., 53
Furer-Heimendorf, Christoph von, 167, 168

Gadgil, D.R., 27
Gaige, Fredrick H., 170, 172, 173
Gandhi, Indira, 131
Ganguli, B.N., 27
Garrison state, 115
GDP, 2
Ghaffar Khan, Khan Abdul, 155
Gini concentration ratios
  income and consumption, 16
  landholdings, 17
Gini coefficient, 3, 11, 16, 17
Gould, Julius, 149
Griffin, Keith, 13, 64, 74, 75
Gunatilleke, Godfrey, 14
Gupta, S.P., 4, 13, 16
Gumaste, V., 30
Gurr, Ted Robert, 108, 151, 152

Hameed, A.C.S., 136
Haq, Mahbubul, 63, 65, 154
Hechter, Michael, 106
Helbock, R.W., 8
Herring, Ronald, 69
Hicks, N.L., 9
Horowitz, Donald, 105
Huntington, Samuel P., 182, 193, 194
Hussain, Asaf, 152, 153

Ibrahim, A.R., 64
Income disparities, 30
Income distribution (Pakistan), 75
Income inequalities, 3
Income inequality measure, 5
India
  agricultural performance, 12
  consumer expenditure, 38
  employment, 32

## INDEX

estimates of poverty, 28, 36
ethnic conflicts, 102, 116
income disparities, 30, 37
money and real wages, 21
persons below poverty line, 29
poverty incidence, 26f.
private consumption expenditure, 30
regional disparities, 7
relations with neighbours, 101
share of income, 38
trend of poverty, 21f.
Indian Tamils (Sri Lanka), 129
population, 129
Integrationist approach, 115
Irfan, M., 77
Isajiw, Wsevolod W., 101

Jain, S.C., 169, 170
Jatoi, Abdul Hamid, 161
Jayawardena, Kumari, 42, 124, 125
Jayawardene, J.R., 121, 132, 133, 134, 138
Joshi, Tulsi R., 170

Kailasapathy, K., 126
Kamal, A.R., 77
Karachi
demographic structure, 156
linguistic structure, 157
problems of Sindhis, 160
Karan, P.P., 166
Karunanidhi, K., 144
Karuntillake, H.N.S., 42
Katzenstein, Mary, 101
Khaleel, M.C.H., 136
Khan, A.R., 5, 6, 10, 19, 22, 64, 74, 76
Kodikara, S.V., 139
Kolb, William L., 149
Kosson, Henny, 153
Krishna, Raj, 30
Kuiten Brouwer, Joost B.W., 69
Kuznets, Simon, 11

Labh, Kapileshwar, 182f., 185, 186
Labour, cultural division, 106
Lamaism (Bhutan), 82
Land distribution, 4
Land Reform Commission (Pakistan), 69
Leary, Virginia A., 139
Lee, B.L.H., 7, 17, 22
Lerner, Daniel, 107
Lewondowski, Susan, 101
Lokanathan, P.S., 27
Lorentz concentration ratio (India), 31, 37

Mahmood, Zafar, 3, 14, 16
Malays and Burgers of Sri Lanka, 137
Malla, K.P., 170
Maron, Stanley, 168
Masani, M.R., 27
Mas'hur Rahman, A.R.M., 42
Mathew, Cyril, 138
Mathur, O.P., 7
Mehta, Asoka, 27
Mengal, Attaullah, 162
Minhas, B.S., 5, 8, 19, 36
Minocha, A.C., 4, 8
Mohammad Siddique, M.Y. 140
MRD, 155, 162
Mukherji, I.N., 1
Muslims of Sri Lanka, 135
Myrdal, Gunnar, 185

Naqvi, Nawab Haider, 67
Narayan, Sriman, 27
Naseem, S.M., 5, 8, 10, 17, 20
Nation, state model of, 114
National Assembly (Bhutan), 85, 86
National Sample Survey (India), 28
Nawang Namgyal, 82
NCAER, 31, 37
Nehru, Jawaharlal, 1, 30, 186
Nepal
army composition, 174
border with India, 167
citizenship, 177

## INDEX

development expenditure, 170
dominant religion, 168
ecological setting, 166
economic composition, 169
economic policies, 176
ethnic diversities, 111f.
ethnic groups, 167
ethnic group in government, 174
geography, 166
Indian settlers, 167
King's role, 178f.
language of, 168
language issue, 175
medium of instruction, 175
migration pattern, 172
national language, 176
National Panchayat, 173
Parliament of., 173
politico-administrative structure, 172f.
population, 169
power structure, 110f.
regional disparities, 8, 171
regionalism, 165f., 168, 175, 177
social groupings, 166
socio-cultural milieu, 167f.
spread of Hinduism, 179
Nepal Education Commission, 175
Nepal, Gopal Singh, 168
Nepali Bhutanese, policy towards, 191

Obeysekera, Gananath, 123, 124
Obidinski, Eugene, 101
Ojha, P.D., 36

Pakistan
Baluchistan policy, 153f.
bifurcation of, 153
capitalist class, 61
civil-military bureaucracy, 61
concentration of economic power, 61
demand for autonomy, 155
development criterion, 159
dismemberment, 72

economic disparities, 61f.
economic policies, 62
effect of US aid, 162
ethnic conflicts, 115, 149f.
foreign aid, 63, 78
income distribution, 75
income inequalities, 10
industrial growth, 74
industrial policy, 62
land distribution, 70
landholdings, 68f.
land reform, 69
national identity, 151
population structure, 150
poverty incidence, 74
Punjabi dominance, 156
Punjabization, 153
regional disparities, 8, 72
role of Islam, 151
role of Punjabis, 153
rural inequalities, 68
threat to political stability, 77
US military bases, 162
Pakistan Economic Survey, 74
Pakistan Industrial Development Corporation, 62
Pakistan People's Party, 159, 160, 163
Pandey, S.M., 6, 21
Pant, Girijesh, 41
Pant, Pitambar, 27
Pant, Y.P., 168, 169
Parthasarathy, G., 134
Pashupati, Shamsher, 170, 172, 175
Paljor, Dawa, 184
Pennambalam, S., 9, 42
Phadnis, Urmila, 100, 101, 108, 135, 136, 149, 154
Planning Commission (India), 28
Pluralist approach, 115
Politicized ethnicity, 102
Ponnambalam, G.G., 132
Ponnambalam, Kumar, 132
Poverty, concept of, 26f.
trend of, 27f.
Poverty line, population below, 5, 19, 29
Poverty, trend of, 27f.

Prasad, Kamta, 26, 35

Rahul, Ram, 187, 189
Raj, K.N., 12
Ramachandran, M.G., 133
Ramakant, 165, 170
Ramanathan, Poonambalam, 128
Ranadive, K.R., 36
Rana, Ratna S., 170
Rao, V.K.R.V., 27
Rath, N., 5, 17, 19, 36
Region, concept of, 165
Regional disparities in South Asia, 7
Regional disparities (Pakistan), 72f.
 reduction of, 73
Regionalism, 165
Relative deprivation, 107
Robinson, Francis, 104
Rose, Leo E., 170, 173, 184, 186, 187, 188, 189, 190
Rothschild, Joseph, 102
Roy Choudhury, Uma Datta, 31, 32
Royal Advisory Council (Bhutan), 188, 193
Rubin, Vera, 105
Rustomji, Nari, 187

Sahak, Baluch, 78
Sahastrabudhe, Anna Saheb, 27
Samaraweera, Vijaya, 57
Saran, P., 182
SARC, 92, 94, 95
Sarma, I.R.K., 31, 38
Sarmad, Khwaja, 67
Sastri, S.A.R., 37
Sayeed, Khalid Bin, 155
Schermerhorn, R.A., 101
Scholz, John T., 170
Schwartzberg, Joseph, 165
Schwarz, Walter, 128
Senanayake, D.S., 121
Shabdung political system, the, 183
Shah, Prithvinarayan, 183
Shah, Rishikesh, 171, 179
Shanmugaratnam, N., 54, 55

Sharwani, Khalid, 66
Shastri, Lal Bahadur, 130
Shoaib, M., 64
Shrestha, B.P., 170
Shrestha, C.B., 166
Sieghart, Paul, 125, 139
Sind
 ethnic crisis, 156
 political unrest, 155
Sind in Pakistan politics, 149f.
Sindhi Awami Tehrik, 160
Singh, Nagendra, 183
Singh, Uma, 149
Sinhalese chauvinism, 57
Sinhalese-Tamil conflict, 122
Sirimavo-Shastri Pact, 129, 131
Sivathamby, K., 57, 128, 135, 143
SLFP, 121
Smith, M.G., 105
Social conflicts, 100f.
 ethnic factors, 100
Social justice in South Asia, 1f.
South Asia
 agricultural wages, 6
 determinants of inequalities, 11
 distribution of assets, 4
 economic growth, 1f.
 ethnic conflicts, 100f.
 GDP growth, 2
 Gini concentration ratios, 16, 17
 income inequalities, 3, 9
 non-agricultural sector, 13
 per capita income, 15
 population below poverty line, 5, 9, 19
 population growth, 2
 poverty ratios, 5, 9
 regional disparities, 7
 separatist movements, 101
 social justice, 1f.
Sri Lanka
 agricultural growth, 48, 49
 budget deficit, 56
 Buddhist revivalism, 124
 communal riots, 121, 131
 debt burden, 46
 demographic structure, 122
 early settlements, 123

economic aid, 44
economic crisis, 41f.
economic discrimination, 141
economic policy, 41f.
ethnic conflicts, 116, 121f.
export-led policy, 42f.
food subsidy scheme, 43, 47
foreign investment, 50, 55f.
GDP, 44, 45
growth rate, 44
import policies, 41
Indian Tamils, 129
labours cost, 52
merchant class, 42
Muslims of, 135
plantation wages, 54
plantation workers, 130
political parties, 132
problem of Tamils, 121
problem of repatriates, 131
regional disparities, 7
relations with Arab countries, 137
rise of extremism, 142f.
role of Malays and Burgeres, 137f.
socio-economic tensions, 45
status of Indian Tamils, 129f.
tourism, 58
Sri Lanka Tamils, 128
Srimavo-Shastri Pact, 55
Sundaram, K., 30
Suryanarayan, V., 121, 127, 131
Syeed, G.M., 161

Tamil militants (Sri Lanka), 137
Tamils in Sri Lanka, 126
economic neglect, 141f.
problem of insecurity, 138

rise of extremism, 142
traditional homeland, 139
Tendulkar, S.D., 30
Thimphu, 192
Thondaman, Savmayamoorthy, 132, 133, 134, 135
Tiwari, Padma Nath, 6, 8, 20
Tiwari, R.T., 7
TULF, 121, 129

UNP, 121, 128
UNP Government of Sri Lanka, 137f.
Upreti, B.C., 165, 170

Vaidyanathan, A., 37
Varma, Baidya Nath, 184, 194
Vyas, V.S., 37

Walker, Connor, 149, 150
Wangchuk, King Jigme Dorji, 85, 185, 186, 189, 191
Wangchuk, Ugyen, 183, 184
Weiner, Myron, 101, 165
White, J.C., 184
White, Lawrence, 65
World Bank, the, 1
Wriggins, W.H., 56

Yahya Khan, 76
Young, Crawford, 105, 107, 108

Zia-ul-Huq, 154, 155, 156, 160, 162